The Legendary Jackrabbit Johannsen

The Legendary Jackrabbit Johannsen

ALICE E. JOHANNSEN

McGill-Queen's University Press
Montreal & Kingston • London • Buffalo

© McGill-Queens University Press 1993
ISBN 0-7735-1123-7 (cloth)
ISBN 0-7735-1151-2 (paper)
Legal deposit fourth quarter 1993
Bibliothèque nationale du Québec

Printed in Canada on acid-free paper

Publication of this book has been supported by the Canada Council
through its block grant program.

Canadian Cataloguing in Publication Data

Johannsen, Alice E. (Alice Elisabeth), 1911-1992
The legendary Jackrabbit Johannsen
ISBN 0-7735-1123-7 (bound) – ISBN 0-7735-1151-2 (pbk.)
1. Johannsen, Jackrabbit, 1875–1987.
2. Skiers – Canada – Biography. I. Title.
GV854.2.J32J315 1993   796.93'2'092   C93-090456-7

This book was typeset in Weiss 11.5/13

This book is dedicated to
the Jackrabbit himself,
and to the thousands of skiers,
young and old,
who follow in his tracks.

Contents

A Legend is Born

This story is too good to keep to oneself. Over the years many of these events have been reworked and embellished by well-meaning friends or enterprising journalists until, sometimes, it is difficult to separate fact from fiction. But there are many more stories as yet untold: heartwarming, serious, hilarious stories. I want to record them here for the enjoyment of the thousands whose paths crossed my father's, but not for them only. The story will, I hope, give pleasure to countless others who have heard of Jackrabbit Johannsen, and wish they had known him. He was a man of extraordinary qualities, with a unique strength and an outlook on life that nourished him in his own times of need, and survived the catastrophes and triumphs of many years.

He was a man, vibrant and active to the end, whose life spanned more than eleven decades. The tale throws sidelights on fascinating times, which saw the invention of the telephone, the automobile, the airplane, television, computers, nuclear fission, and even space travel. These immense changes in themselves are remarkable, but for most of us they are only history, and not essentially related to our own lives. For Herman Johannsen, however, they were the background against which his own real life drama was played. It began in times when success in many fields depended more on personal initiative and perseverance than on mechanical inventions or advanced technology.

Others have lived as long, or even longer. But how many are there who at his age were active, alert, forceful and intensely involved with living and sharing life, who overflowed, as he did with kindly wisdom and joyous good humour? Two documentary films were produced on the man known to so many as "Jackrabbit" during his one-hundredth year. In different ways, both are remarkably successful in conveying his enthusiasm for the out-of-doors, his concern for our endangered environment, and his happy interaction with people of all ages – not to mention his puckish sense of humour, distrust of gadgetry, and almost fanatical spirit of independence. He will live on in these films as a very real and lively presence for generations yet to come.

This book, however, serves another purpose and will do so long after the light has flickered from the motion picture screen. I hope it will allow readers to glimpse the inner man, as he was seen by those who lived close to him over the years: a loving and devoted husband, a warm and lighthearted father, and a memorable and steadfast friend.

CHAPTER ONE

The Family Looks Back

"What a lot we have to be thankful for."

Herman Smith Johannsen, the old Jackrabbit, sat in his ancient wing chair, pulling thoughtfully at his pipe, as the fire crackled comfortably in the well-banked hearth, sending shadows dancing up the pine-panelled walls and over the rafters of the low ceiling. Outside, the wind roared relentlessly, driving blurred streaks of snow against the window panes.

It was one of those rare occasions when Herman had managed to gather his three grown children together for a few hours, under his own roof, at Piedmont, Quebec. Peggy had come from Mont Tremblant, an hour's drive to the north, Bob was visiting from Norway, to which he had retired in 1970, and I had made the two-hour trip from Mont-St-Hilaire.

"The only one missing is Mother," said Herman quietly, "and I almost feel as though she is here, too."

The warmth and cosiness, in contrast with the storm outside, drew the four of us more closely together. This snug little room held the cherished memories of a century of winters in the life of the man who now sat musing by the fire. From this room he had set out in the early morning on many a long trek, and to this room he had returned when the day's work was done, to find Mother, a hot supper waiting, and a bright blaze in the hearth.

The walls were hung with treasures. A worn and battered ski, a gift from the Norwegian Ski Museum, hung above the door. It was of a type similar to the skis he had worn in the 1880s, with a channel under the foot through which a tow-and-heel strap of twisted willow withe (now long since gone) had passed. On the wall hung his 1899 diploma in mechanical engineering from the Königliche Technische Hochschule in Berlin, side by side with framed photographs from later fondly remembered canoe and camping trips in Canada. There was an original marker from the Maple Leaf Trail, and pictures of the Laurentian Ski Train of the 1930s. Medals from the Sno Birds of Lake Placid and from the Canadian Ski Marathon hung in a mobile by the window. There was the 1972 Order of Canada, of which Governor General Roland Michener had named him a member, and the Order of St Olav, presented by Norway's King Olav in 1975. And there was the magnificent feather headdress given him by the Ojibway of Wisconsin during trials for the 1980 Winter Olympics.

These were visible reminders of a life lived out of doors by a man whose prowess on skis was legendary, a man who is credited with having made skiing a household word in North America. Over the years "the Jackrabbit" had marked and cleared, almost single-handed, hundreds of miles of cross-country ski trails, spanning the wilderness and linking isolated communities. His trails now serve as the basis of scores of profitable ski resorts in Canada and the United States, resorts that proudly claim a connection with the legendary Jackrabbit.

We three children had been born to skiing as a family tradition. It was something one did naturally, at minimum expense. It was a way of life, a means of transportation, a key to health and enjoyment, and a wonderful way of exploring the world in winter. In our early days a single pair of skis served all the needs of cross-country, slalom, and downhill. A good pair of boots could be used for hiking in summer, then adapted to our ski harness when snow fell in November. Clothing in those days was simple and practical, and a small knapsack on our backs contained all we needed for lunch, when we stopped beside the trail to build a fire and brew our noontime pot of tea.

Now, however, times had changed. We each had our own lives to lead. I was established in Mont St-Hilaire, where I had recently retired as director of the Nature Conservation Centre, but where I continued to work fulltime. Bob lived in Norway, where he continued to work as an inventor and researcher in physical chemistry. Peggy, the youngest, was herself the mother of five children, and lived with her family in Mont Tremblant.

Now Peggy sat mending in the little Windsor rocker we remembered from our childhood. Just so our own mother used to sit, knitting needles clicking, as she rocked contentedly back and forth. Bob had been discussing with Peggy the next move in production of Jack Rabbit Ski Wax, a product he had developed as a student at McGill, and had named for Father, claiming (with justification) that "with Jackrabbit you are always one jump ahead." Recently, Peggy and her husband had set up a manufacturing company, which had established the product firmly on the North American market.

I, the oldest, was catching my breath between the waves of visitors, both expected and unexpected, who came year in and year out to reminisce with the Jackrabbit, or simply to "see with their own eyes what the Old Man really looks like."

"What a phenomenon!" they would say, shaking their heads in wonder. "To have lived for over a century, and still to be so full of life and the joy of living." Then, turning to me, they would add, "Take *good* care of him. You realize, of course, that he is one of Canada's national treasures!"

The wind roared in the chimney; the windows rattled. Bob tossed another log on the fire.

"Bon feu et bonne mine," mused Jackrabbit, quoting from one of his much-loved French-Canadian authors, "c'est la moitié de la vie." "A warm hearth and good health, that's half of a good life." He smiled. "The other half is companionship. I'm lucky. I've had full measure."

We sensed he was in a reminiscing mood, and the three of us settled back to listen.

CHAPTER TWO

Childhood: 1875–1885

The town of Horten lay basking in the sun on a hot summer morning in 1880. Herman, a lively five-year-old, hopped up the springy gangplank of the little paddlewheeled steamer waiting at the wharf. With him was Far (Father in Norwegian) Johannsen, an officer at Karljohansvaern, the Royal Norwegian fortress and naval station at Horten. Herman waved back excitedly to Mor (Mother), who stood on the sunny dock with Johannes, his three-year-old brother, and his baby sister, Agnes, in her carriage. Mor smiled across to them amidst the bustle of last-minute passengers and the loading of freight.

"Be a good boy, now," she called to him. "And don't forget to say *'Takk for maten'* after every meal." This was part of the Norwegian mealtime ritual. As everyone rose from the table, each would nod ceremoniously and say, "Takk for maten!" thanking God, and at the same time the host, for the food. Boys were expected to shake hands solemnly with the host and hostess, and little girls would curtsey. It was an unthinkable reflection on one's upbringing if one forgot.

Hastily, Herman promised he would not forget. At that moment, more pressing matters claimed his attention, and hand in hand with Far, he turned eagerly to investigate the big paddle wheels poised on either side of the ship, ready to churn their way over the water. Father and son peered into the engine room from the door in the companionway. They could see the great boiler and

The entire family on Herman's mother's side on the steps
outside the dining room at Ekeli in Horten in 1885. Herman sits
on the railing to the left. The four Smith sisters pose
with their fourteen children and Bestefar and Bestemor Smith.
Mor is seated at bottom right.

its gleaming pipes, and could smell the mingled odours of motor
oil and live steam. The powerful engine, hidden away in the heart
of the ship, was out of sight of the captain up on the bridge, but
he gave his instructions to the crew through a speaking tube, and
they responded at once to his slightest wish.

The engine, though, was the power behind it all, and it needed
a special person to run it, an "engineer." Herman imagined himself
down there in the hold with a long-spouted oil can, tending the
engine, twisting the valves, and reading the gauges. He longed
very much to understand how it all worked, and some day, he told
himself, he would.

When they came out on deck again, they could see the home
of Herman's Bestefar (Grandfather) Smith on the hill above the
town. Clearly visible were the stable and the gardens where he

and his cousins played, shaded by the stately oaks that gave the house its name, Ekeli ("Sheltering Oaks"). Bestefar's family name, Smith, was by no means a common one in Norway. It was an echo of certain ancestors, who for generations had been smiths: iron workers. "Smed," or "Smid," had finally become "Smit," and indeed his grandfather's grandfather, back in the 1780s, had owned and operated one of the largest iron mines in Norway.

Bestefar Smith had four daughters, all of whom had married officers in the Navy; in a way one might say that the navy had become the "family business." Two of the girls had married men with distinctive Norwegian names – Proet and Platou – but the third and fourth had married a Nielsen and a Johannsen, and thus had acquired family names shared with many others in Norway. In the navy, some of these Johannsens even had the same initials, which often led to great confusion. Fritz Johannsen had neatly solved this identity problem, however, by giving his children his wife's maiden name, Smith, as a second given name. They thus became the *Smith Johannsens*, as distinguished from all others. Herman, their first born, never added a hyphen between the two names, though some of the other children did, later on.

Now things were beginning to happen on deck. It was exciting to watch the captain as he stood commandingly on the bridge, giving orders to cast off. First, the ropes were loosened. Then a cloud of steam enveloped everyone on the pier. The captain grasped the signal cord, gave two sharp toots on the whistle – and the ship moved off. From the smokestack a long black cloud drifted over the foamy wake at the vessel's stern. At last they were on their way. "Goodbye," they shouted as the ship steamed slowly past the other vessels anchored in the harbour, and they watched Horten recede slowly in the distance.

Horten and Karljohansvern occupied a strategic location on Christianiafjord, just where the waters narrowed leading up to Christiania (now Oslo), the capital. Both the city and the fjord were named in 1624 after King Christian IV of Denmark and Norway, when the city was rebuilt after a disastrous fire. The fortress was named for a later king, Karl Johan, who, as Jean-Baptiste Bernadotte, came from France to become King of Sweden and Norway under the Treaty of Kiel in 1814.

Herman and his father were on their way to visit Bestefar and Bestemor Johannsen, who lived in Laurvig (the spelling has since been changed to *Larvik*), a small town half a day's journey down the coast. With a freshening breeze, the ship moved south past Tönsberg, where high on the hill they could see the ruins of the castle that marked the oldest town in Norway. Soon, as they rounded some sheltering islands, they encountered a strong current and a heavy sea. The ship rolled and pitched in the waves, and Herman began to have trouble keeping his feet.

Off to port they could see the lighthouse that marked the outermost limits of Christianiafjord. Straight ahead lay the open sea, with white caps gleaming, and to starboard, at the place called Verden's Ende (the "End of the World," a promontory where people loved to picnic and enjoy the view far out to sea) they could just make out the great iron basket hanging from a pole above a square tower. It was in this container that the lighthouse keeper – so they were told – used to keep a huge bonfire burning to warn passing ships away from the dangerous reefs.

The sea became rougher and rougher, and somehow Herman lost interest in anything but hanging on. Just off the high precipice marking the entrance to Tönsbergfjord, where the sea is always choppy and the scudding breeze sends huge breakers against the cliff, he found himself clinging frantically to his father's trouser legs. The world suddenly turned topsy-turvy ... without warning he was terribly seasick, and in one awful moment he lost his entire breakfast all over his father's beautiful shiny new shoes!

It was an event that he vividly remembered. Looking back on it in later years, he was sure it had a strong influence on his decision, despite family tradition, *not* to become a sailor. After all, it seemed so much more sensible for him to stay on dry land, where everything was solid and dependable. He consoled himself with the fact that there would always be plenty of engines on land, too, and that they would surely need engineers to tend them. In fact, he had heard it said that within a few years the railway would actually reach as far as Horten, and after that continue all the way to Laurvig and even beyond. When that time came, he realized happily, he could visit Bestefar and Bestemor Johannsen by train.

From here on the sea became calmer, and by the time they reached Laurvig's sheltering harbour Herman's queasiness had vanished. He followed Far and the baggage onto the pier to find Bestefar and Bestemor Johannsen and Tante (Aunt) Anna as a welcoming committee.

After a happy reunion, they walked together up into the town, along the crooked, unpaved street, with its many cart tracks and its cobbled gutters. They exchanged greetings with people they met along the way, for Bestefar Johannsen was a respected merchant and seemed to know everyone. Almost every dwelling they passed contained a small shop of some kind. There were the carpenter, the harnessmaker, the wheelwright, the watchmaker, the tailor and the shoemaker, the baker and the butcher; and each of these had an appropriate sign over his door, announcing his trade. Finally they emerged on the marketplace. There, across the square, they could see Bestemor's little white house with its lace-curtained windows, and the giant walnut tree standing guard, exactly as Herman remembered it from his last visit.

The Christiansen boys, friends of his from the previous summer, were playing beside their father's brewery, and the big wagon with its powerful horses and load of barrels was turning into their courtyard. Herman was overjoyed to see the horses again, and to recognize the friendly driver who last year had let him sit up beside him on the wagonbox and "help." How wonderful those horses smelled. And how good it was to be back in Laurvig!

Across from the brewery, just below Bestefar's house, was one of the two pumps from which they and all the neighbours carried water. This pump also served as a fire hydrant, and beside it stood a tall paraffin streetlamp. It was never lit in summer because then it was daylight almost all the time, but he could easily imagine the welcome glow it would cast on the snowy drifts during the long dark nights of winter.

From Bestefar's house they could look out over the little harbour with its rocky shores, and hear the red-beaked shorebirds, the oyster-catchers, screaming as they swooped back and forth along the strand. Beside the house, hidden from public gaze by a tall board fence, was a lovely big garden and the famous walnut tree. Here the family would sit in summer, the women with their knitting, Bestefar with his pipe, and Herman playing in the garden – taking great care, as he had been told, not to trample the flowers and the vegetables.

In the year when Johannes was five and Herman seven, the railroad was finally completed all the way to Laurvig. That year they make their first trip by train – alone! It was a glorious adventure. At Horten, before they left, they carefully examined the burly locomotive with its short, squat smokestack and its plume of white steam. They scrutinized the fat round boiler, the windowed cab for the engineer, and the open car for the cordwood that was burned as fuel. There was a closed-in baggage car, followed by two passenger carriages, and in one of these Mor installed them safely with their bags. They knew they would be met in Laurvig, but for the time being they were going to be on their own.

Mor issued a special warning before saying goodbye. "Remember, boys," she said with a meaningful look, "No fighting." They promised. Herman handed the conductor their tickets. He punched them. And the boys felt very grown-up indeed.

As the train puffed out of the station, they sat with faces pressed to the window. They felt the train gather speed as it rolled through the fields. This was the life. No bouncing waves, no motion sickness, just the click of the rails as the kilometres sped by. What a thrill when they went through a dark tunnel! Then out again into the sunshine, past fields of hay, and pastures of placid cows, and occasional horses who snorted and ran, frightened by their belching locomotive. Then, all too soon, the journey was over, and Bestefar Johannsen, Bestemor, and Tante Anna welcomed them back to Laurvig with open arms.

In Laurvig there was much more activity than in Horten, for this was really a larger town, with much to see. One special attraction was the beautiful park Bökeskogen ("beech forest"), spreading over the hill above the town where they used to go for picnics among the trees. And they looked forward to hearing the gay music in the little bandstand in the woods, and seeing the many families who walked there on Sunday afternoons.

Another favourite summer excursion was to the neighbouring town of Stavern to see the famous old fort of Frederiksvaern, built in 1750 by King Frederik V. Prior to removal of the naval high command to the more strategic port of Horten in 1820, Frederiksvaern had reigned as naval headquarters, but after that it dwindled in importance until the town was little more than a shipyard. But the old fort was still there, and its bastions and earthworks were enormously exciting for the boys to investigate. Most impressive for Herman and Johannes was the big munitions storehouse, for which, so they were told, Tippoldefar (Great-great-grandfather) had provided cannon balls from his iron foundry near Arendal. This, of course, made the fort seem almost as though it belonged to the family.

Every summer, they visited Herr Hansen, the local photographer, for a picture to record how much they had changed since the previous year. Dressed in their best sailor suits and escorted by Tante Anna they made their way sedately down to the studio. They especially liked to see the "props" Herr Hansen used to liven up these portraits. He had a painted garden scene, in front of which a group could pose, pretending they were out-of-doors, and in a corner of the room there was a special table at which a lady could sit for her portrait, with her skirts arranged just so, and her husband beside her, leaning against a high-backed chair so that he could be motionless during the picture-taking. At her feet was a little tasselled stool, on which a boy could sit with his ankles crossed, and he too could hold himself perfectly still.

But most exciting of all was the camera mounted on its tripod. There, behind those impressive bellows, Herr Hansen would crouch with a black cloth draped over the camera and himself, while he said in muffled tones, "Take a deep breath now ... and hold *very* still." Then he would squeeze a red bulb to explode the flashlight powder and make the exposure. The boys would shout for joy, hoping he would take a second shot, and sometimes he did.

The two of them usually got on very well with each other, but occasionally they had their disagreements. That must have been in Mor's mind when she had warned them, "No fighting, boys." They could not remember just what the argument was that day (it probably had something to do with the strain of being on their best behaviour) but just before they entered the studio they had taken a few pokes at each other. Tante Anna had grasped each of them firmly by the hand, and sternly marched them in, but they were not in a very cooperative mood when Herr Hansen, in an effort to suggest brotherly love, insisted that they hold hands for their portrait. They did, but the result was not altogether con- vincing. Years later, whenever they saw that picture, they laughed uproariously, although at the time neither of them had felt it to be a laughing matter.

Four young Johannsens in 1885:
Herman, 10, Agnes, 7, Johannes, 8, and Fred, 3.

Shortly before the trip to Laurvig the following year (1881), the family was saddened by the death of Bestefar Johannsen. It was hard to think of Laurvig without him, but Bestemor and Tante Anna insisted that the boys should continue their summer visits, as these gave them all something to look forward to.

As the two grew older, they graduated to playing games with the bigger boys: hide-and-seek, cops and robbers, sometimes even Frenchmen and Germans, a game inspired by the recent Franco-Prussian War. But their all-time favourite was Indians and white men. This was based on stories brought home by sailors who had been to America and had come back with vivid tales of "scalpings" and all the tribulations of the western settlers. The boys would retire to one of the fields above the town, and some would lie in ambush, to emerge whooping and hollering as the "settlers" rode by; or they would lead mock assaults on whoever happened that day to be the "enemy." These activities, needless to say, were not applauded by the nearest neighbours. However, they taught the boys resourcefulness and the art of being nimble on their feet.

Laurvig continued to grow from year to year, and every time they came back there was a new attraction. One year it was the new bath house at the sulphur spring, located at the base of a rocky hill on the waterfront, in the garden of a private home. Passersby had always complained of the sulphur smell – like "rotten eggs," but the town wagon drivers had a habit of stopping there to water their horses as they returned from delivering a load to the nearby docks. Sometimes they even took a nip themselves. Analysis of the water revealed some health-giving properties, and with the encouragement of the local doctor the owner decided to open a small pavilion in her garden where, for a fee, visitors could drink from the pump and bathe in a special pool.

Later, when an enterprising new doctor bought the property, he built a fine new log building in the old Norwegian style, incorporating the spring and straddling the stream. Here there was a pleasant "salong" (salon) where one could drink the water, and also sit and chat with other partakers. The doctor had his own office in the building, and there were numerous dressing rooms with access to the treatment areas.

But it was the mudbaths that the boys found most fascinating. Clay was brought by boat from the head of a neighbouring fjord and delivered by horse and wagon to the bathhouse. There it was mixed with clear salt water pumped from the depths of the fjord, or with fresh water from the surrounding hills. People with rheumatism or arthritis would come from far and near to soak in a mudbath, and hope for a cure. The arrival of the railroad contributed greatly to the success of the baths at Laurvig, bringing visitors from all over the country. The boys were filled with curiosity, and listened avidly to talk about the fine folk who came to "take the waters" and enjoy the social life that grew up around this new industry.

As time went on they became more and more adventurous. One day the Christiansen boys lined up in formation on their side of the market square, while the Smith-Johannsens and some other boys ably defended the opposite side. Then they unleashed the firehose. It was great sport to feel the hose come to life in their hands as the water coursed through it, pumped by one of them by hand from the town well. They aimed at each other and splashed and romped about, and the water ran down the cobbled gutter; they had a simply hilarious time, until the sudden appearance of the town policeman, who, being quite unexpected, came in for a full dose of cold water.

"Boys! Boys!" he shouted. "Stop! This will never do! Hoses are meant to fight fires with, not people. Think if we had another disaster like that one when twenty-three houses in the town burned down! That was a terrible day. We were helpless. It just burned and burned. Think of that now, and stop this nonsense. You should be ashamed!" Shocked out of their hilarity, they *were* ashamed. They had not meant to be bad, but the temptation of the waterhose had been irresistible.

Bestemor and Tante Anna were very upset when the boys came home all wet and muddy. Herman and Johannes were given dry clothes, and a serious lecture on how not to behave, but aside from that, there were no repercussions. "Boys will be boys," said the two ladies, and shook their heads. They only hoped it would not happen again.

Back in Horten, the boys returned to school. Summer seemed a long way behind them, and winter gripped the land. Then, tragedy struck: on a cold and blustery January night, fire somehow broke out in Laurvig in a building not far from Bestemor's house. Whipped by strong winds from the harbour, the flames swept ravenously through house after house. Many of them, including the little white house under the walnut tree, were utterly destroyed.

For Herman and Johannes this was the end of an era. Many of their favourite playing places were gone, and Bestemor and Tante Anna had to move into smaller quarters where there was no room for grandchildren. The houses were gradually rebuilt, but the whole character of Laurvig changed abruptly. It could never be the same again. The boys, however, clung to their many happy memories: they had grown up in a prudent and encouraging environment; their pleasures were simple, their pastimes uncomplicated; they had

had good companions, and a devoted family. And that was the Laurvig they continued to cherish as they looked back over the years.

Meanwhile in Horten, there were plenty of other interesting activities, especially in winter. When deep snow lay everywhere, a whole new world opened up. All their energy was channelled into conquering this new element, and the children took to skiing quite as naturally as they had learned to walk.

Far had put Herman on skis for the first time when he was two and a half. He began on the level, without poles, teaching him first to slide and to swing his shoulders rhythmically to help propel himself along. Falling was part of the process. He just had to scramble up and keep on trying, but before he knew it, he was sliding downhill with the older children, and eagerly climbing back up again. The youngsters would spend hours practising on the hill above Ekeli, learning to control their skis on varying degrees of slope.

Down in their part of town, close to open salt water, the snow was often damp and sticky, but up above Ekeli, the temperature was lower, and the snow conditions usually better. This became for them a welcome playground, and they would ski there until they nearly dropped.

Once in a while, after coming home from a strenuous Sunday afternoon, Herman would have mysterious cramps, sometimes in one leg, sometimes in the other, sometimes even in both. But Mor had a splendid remedy for this. She would sympathetically massage his legs to improve the circulation and loosen up the muscles. This helped a great deal. In fact, he found it was almost worth having the cramps in order to get this special attention.

"I remember one time," he recalled years later, "when I was in the first grade in school. I suddenly had terrible cramps in both legs. I could hardly stand, right there in the classroom! The teacher, concerned about this strange malady, lost no time in sending me home.

"However, once I was out in the sunny fresh air, the cramps began to fade, and by the time I reached my house they seemed to have vanished altogether. There was no point in going back to school, for I had already been sent away. Mor had gone up to market with the younger children, and there was no one else at home, so I could think of nothing better to do than to take my skis and go back up to the hill above Ekeli, and there I had a wonderful time in the strong sunshine all by myself.

"But when I returned home, it was difficult to explain just how it had happened that I had gone skiing when I should have been in school. This time there was no sympathetic leg-rubbing. I had played hooky for the first time – and the last time – and that was *that*!"

Herman had another favourite story of his childhood. "Our house on Bekkegaten," he said, "lay midway between the grammar school at one end of the street and the churchyard at the other. To me as a small boy that cemetery was a spooky place and I usually gave it a wide berth. I remember, though, how some of the older boys, whom I secretly admired, vanished one long spring evening and reappeared in the cemetery, draped in long white sheets. Pretending they were ghosts, they "haunted" the graveyard, flitting in and out among the headstones in a highly spectacular manner. This caused consternation among certain elderly ladies returning late one afternoon from a church meeting in the upper part of town. Their reaction was very gratifying to the "ghosts." We younger children, too, thought it a marvellous idea, and were all prepared to join in the fun. Our elders, however, took a strangely different view of the proceedings, and the practice had to be abandoned."

But of all those special childhood events, the most outstanding were the frequent Sunday dinners at Ekeli with Bestefar and Bestemor Smith. Bestefar was by that time a Kommandör (commodore) in the navy, very much looked up to by everyone. He was a jovial old man, with a great white beard and a wide gait, who walked as though he were still on the deck of a ship on the rolling sea. On these Sundays, the entire family would assemble – the four daughters with their marine-officer husbands and all their children, to say nothing of assorted older relatives who appeared from time to time. There were sometimes as many as thirty, young and old, who sat down around the dinner table. It almost looked like Christmas.

"There was always something specially good to eat," Herman recalled, "and we children would try to be on our best behaviour. After those dinners you may be sure we all remembered to shake Bestemor and Bestefar by the hand, the small boys bowing stiffly from the waist and the little girls curtseying politely as we each solemnly said 'Takk for maten.' Then we would scamper off to play in the children's garden, while the grown-ups sat endlessly around the table chatting over the latest community gossip and comparing notes on child rearing."

There was one particular Sunday, in the year that Herman was ten, when the whole family sat for a portrait on the steps outside the dining room. As the oldest of the grandchildren, Herman stationed himself in a commanding position on a corner of the railing. The four Smith sisters, including his mother, sat surrounded by all fourteen of their children, with Bestefar and Bestemor Smith in their midst, holding the youngest on their laps.

Bestefar had that day been telling them the story of how, as a child, he had visited *his* grandfather's house at the big iron foundry, from which had come those huge cannon balls the boys had seen at the old fort of Frederiksvaern. The house at Froland was a beautiful mansion, with a big garden in front where there were fruit trees and little paths among which Bestefar and his brothers and sisters used to play. While he was at Froland he had first seen the full-rigged cadet training ship when it visited nearby Arendal in 1824. Bestefar was only twelve years old at the time, but he had made up his mind then and there to become a naval officer.

It was a big decision, but his father had agreed, and they went up to Frederiksvaern some weeks later to enrol him in the Cadet Institute. "That was my first real adventure," Bestefar recounted, savouring the memory. "Strong head winds delayed us for eight whole days, and we had to tack back and forth and back and forth for what seemed like forever, before we finally reached Frederiks-vaern." He had continued his schooling for eight years, studying on land in winter and going to sea with the cadet ship each summer, until he graduated as a second lieutenant in the navy at the age of twenty.

"Those were really hard times in Norway," he told the children. "The economy was poor and jobs were scarce. Besides, the family iron business was failing, and I knew I would soon have to help my father with finances at home.

"It was the custom then in the navy to give young officers a chance to seek temporary employment on commercial ships in the merchant marine, where they could gain useful experience at no further expense to the Crown, and my first job was as an ordinary seaman on a full-rigged French freighter plying between Le Havre and New York. This was very hard work, for in order to make the voyage profitable, the ship had to be driven hard, with all the sail she could muster in all kinds of weather, carrying freight and passengers and post.

"A sailor's job is often dangerous, and on this trip I had the misfortune to be struck in the chest with a swinging boom which put me out of commission for some time." The boys looked him over sympathetically, shivering at the thought of that swinging spar. "But after I had recovered from this accident," Bestefar continued, "I took command of a commercial vessel, replacing my uncle, the captain, who had to retire unexpectedly because of ill health. This was good experience, and I graduated from it through a series of alternate jobs with the navy and with the merchant marine, until at last there came the big chance I had been waiting for, to be skipper of the sailing ship *Washington*, a brand new brig built especially for the emigrant trade."

The boys, enthralled, listened quietly. "Times were very difficult then in the rural districts here in Norway, where it was always the custom for the oldest child to inherit the farm. Younger sons could stay on and help, or they could go off and learn to be a doctor, a lawyer, or a minister, but if they wanted their own farm they had to seek new land. New farmland was scarce, and many of them found no land on which they could make a living. Often their eyes turned across the Atlantic to the New World, where the promise of almost unlimited space offered hope and incentive to any who were willing to break with family ties and set out for themselves. So I found myself for five years carrying settlers and their families from Norway to America. That was the beginning of a great wave of emigration, which lured thousands of Norwegian families over to Minnesota, Dakota, and the western prairies.

"On the first of these trips, in 1842, I had 250 tons of iron and sixty *Telemarkings* – men, women, and children from the Valley of Telemark – who were seeking a new life in the New World. Living conditions were desperately cramped, but I did my best to make them comfortable. Each family had brought with them their personal possessions, clothing, tools, and household goods, together with provisions for a six-week voyage. Sanitation and diet were constant problems on every emigrant ship, and many passengers suffered great hardship on the crossing. Not infrequently one or more of them died."

Bestefar warmed to his tale. "On my first voyage, however, things went fairly well until we reached the Grand Banks off Newfoundland. There, suddenly, almost half of the passengers became seriously ill. Scurvy and cholera were diseases we were always afraid of on long voyages, but we took every precaution of which we knew. The crew washed everything carefully down with chlorine and vinegar. We enforced as strict a diet as possible, and we used such household remedies as we possessed. To our vast relief, the sickness gradually faded, and fortunately everyone was more or less recovered by the time we finally dropped anchor at the quarantine station outside New York.

"The quarantine officer and the toll collector came on board to inspect. It was important that they check every passenger and all of the crew, and this took considerable time. But finally they finished their work, and the ship was given a clean bill of health.

"It had been arranged that on our final night on board we would celebrate our arrival in America, and we would have, as well, the wedding of two of our young people. For this we pressed into service these two officials to participate in the ceremony.

"Among the passengers was a clergyman, who read the service in Norwegian, while I translated for our guests. To the right of the groom stood the toll collector, and on the bride's left the quarantine officer. The crew and many of the passengers wore their *bunader*, the distinctive regional costume of Telemark, their home district. These costumes, with their colourful embroidery and special silver jewellery, had lain carefully packed in their baggage during that long voyage, but now came out in all their beauty, and the ship looked really festive. The ceremony was carried out with great solemnity as the minister read from the prayer book, summarized the rules of good health, and wished them true happiness and a long life. Then, putting up full sail, we cruised into the harbour of New York. That evening every one danced on board until midnight!"

But on the next day, when it came time to leave the ship, the passengers wept like children. The actual sailing from their homeland had not been as hard for them as was this final parting from friends with whom they had lived through so much in such a short time. They blessed Bestefar for every day they had been at sea, and one of the women, who several weeks before had been near death from the fever, took a traditional silver brooch, which she cherished as part of her bunad, and pressed it into Bestefar's hand. "This," she said through her grateful tears, "is a thank offering for all the good care you have given us on this voyage."

Several years later, Bestefar in turn gave the silver brooch to Bestemor when they were married. She wore it proudly for many years in memory of that eventful trip.

There were many other Sunday stories told, of trips to America, to Argentina, and finally to Madagascar, India, and Ceylon, where Bestefar lost a finger from the bite of a poisonous insect. But finally he retired from the merchant marine and resumed his commission with the navy. It was then that he and Bestemor moved to Horten, and here in 1853 he began to build his beloved Ekeli. Here all four of his daughters had grown up, and here also they were married.

In time, Bestefar became Kommandör of the new training ship *Ellida*, and cruised up and down the coast of Norway with a whole new generation of young cadets. His next appointment was the command of the beautiful newly built three-masted warship *Nornen*, which carried twenty cannon and a complement of 216 men: this marked the culmination of his career. During the American Civil War, he sailed to the United States with *Nornen* to protect Norwegian shipping in those waters, and as commodore of a neutral warship, was received at the White House by President Lincoln. Bestefar was very impressed by the monitor, a new, highly mobile combat ship that had just been developed in America. This peculiar craft had been nicknamed, in the Southern States, "the cheesebox on a raft," but, however insignificant it may have appeared to the opposition, it had already proved itself more than a match for the clumsy big iron-clad warships then coming into use. Bestefar made arrangements through the Norwegian foreign minister to have the plans of the monitor sent to His Majesty King Oscar in Norway. The Norwegian navy was properly impressed, and it ordered four replicas for its own fleet.

The special day that in later years Herman remembered above all others was one of those Sundays when the whole family sat together on the veranda at Ekeli, after dinner. Bestefar had just told them again the story of his trip to the White House. They all looked out together over the busy inner harbour of Horten to the great stone bastion and twin turrets of Karljohansvaern, whose cannon commanded both fjord and harbour. There was always a steady procession of tall-masted naval vessels in this well-guarded basin. Those under repair were either in drydock on land, or moored at dockside, and the harbour rang with continual hammering and the shouts of men as the work progressed. When the repairs were finished the masts would be temporarily unslung, the decks roofed over to protect them from the weather, and the ships anchored to await further orders. There they would float, like sleeping giants, resting, but ready for the call to action.

Bestefar surveyed the scene with great satisfaction. There, riding proudly at anchor, was his own stalwart old warship, *Nornen*, its three tall masts in sharp contrast to the four raft-like structures moored nearby. These were the four monitors that had been constructed according to the American plans sent back after Bestefar's visit, more than twenty years before. They were no longer the last word in naval design, but what they lacked in impressive appearance they more than made up for in mobility, and they were still very valuable to the Norwegian navy.

All good things must come to an end, and that year, life changed dramatically for Herman and Johannes. Far was posted to a brand-new job in Christiania, and his growing young family moved with him. They would revisit Horten many times in later years, but those happy family times at Ekeli with their grandparents and all their brothers and sisters and cousins were at an end. From now on their lives would centre around new friends and new experiences in the big city.

CHAPTER THREE

Nordmarka and Independence: 1885–1891

The move to Christiania meant a new job for Far, new neighbours for Mor, and a new school for the children. Herman was ten years old now, and Johannes was eight. After them came Agnes, who was seven, then Margarethe, Fred, and Helga, who were five, four, and two. The flock was expanding and it needed room to grow. Far was determined to find a house near the outskirts of town, where the children could have fields to play in, but where the walk to school or work would not be too long. Herman and Johannes were overjoyed when he decided to take them with him to the city for a first look around and a glimpse of the place they would henceforth call home.

The trip to Christiania was an adventure for these two country bumpkins. They stayed overnight in a real hotel right near the Stortorvet (the Marketplace), where the great red brick cathedral loomed high over everything else, its green copper-tipped steeple visible from all directions.

Far had plenty to do next day, and was glad to let the boys go out exploring by themselves. "Just stay together," he cautioned, "and remember, as long as you keep the Domkirken (cathedral) steeple in sight, you can always find your way back to the hotel." This was a good lesson in orienteering, and one they never forgot: "Find a good landmark on the far horizon, then steer for it."

The boys were fascinated by everything they saw: the vendors of fruit and fish and vegetables, other folk in from the country, carts, horses, dogs, and all the bustle of a marketplace that was so much larger than anything they had ever seen. They marvelled at the horse-drawn streetcars, which ran in real tracks laid in among the stone paving blocks that lined the street. But they were even more interested in going down to the waterfront to see the docks, and the great, ancient fortress of Akershus, which had guarded the harbour since the end of the thirteenth century. It had been the king's residence, and it had its own church, a dungeon, and lots of other buildings inside its walls. It was like a walled town. And it was still in use!

They stopped, entranced, to watch a group of young soldiers drilling on horseback in a field outside the fort. Every boy in Norway was required to perform one year of compulsory military service in either the army or the navy after leaving school, and as Herman had already made up his mind to take officers' training, he was excited to see real soldiers in action. Johannes, on the other hand, was leaning towards the navy, for he had always been interested in ships and a life at sea. There was certainly plenty here in Christiania to stir the imagination.

When they finally made their way back to the hotel, full of enthusiasm for all they had seen, they found Far with his own story to tell. He had succeeded in finding a suitable house for the family, and was eager to show it off. So the three of them set out up Karl Johans Gate (Karl Johan Street – *gate* is Norwegian for street), the main thoroughfare, which ran from the market square all the way up to the Royal Palace. They went through the park beside the palace, up past the newly built church on the hilltop behind it, and there, several streets beyond, was Eilert Sundts Gate, *their* street. It was really out in the country, with open fields on all sides and a fine view up toward the mountain that rose behind the city. Not many houses had been built in this area at that time, and those already there were made of notched logs in the old Norwegian style. One of them was to be their very own.

In later years, Herman remembered that house very well. One came in from the street to a hall between the living-room on one side and the dining-room on the other. The kitchen lay beyond. Upstairs were the bedrooms: one for Far and Mor; the girls' room for Agnes, Margarethe, and Helga; and the boys' room for Herman, Johannes, and Fred. Everything was snug and cosy.

In due course they moved in, and Herman lost no time in getting to know the neighbours. One family lived in a big house on a real old-time *gaard* (farm), where their parents and grandparents had lived before them. The city was creeping in on them from all sides now, but the farm remained more or less as it had always been. There was a big archway that opened from the road into a *tun* (courtyard), beyond which were various farm buildings, including a storehouse for grain, a barn, and a stable with several horses. This was of particular interest to Herman, and he soon made friends with the owners. After all, he was to be a mounted officer when he grew up, and it was good to know that near his new home were some real horses he could befriend.

Gjertsen School lay down the hill nearer the heart of town. Herman remembered in particular one teacher who taught them geography, all about faraway countries like the places Bestefar Smith used to tell stories about, down in Horten. The geography teacher had taken his training in the navy, and had been to sea for several years. He had marvellous tales of his adventures in the Caribbean and the East Indies, and of the people who lived there. He made all the world seem fascinating, and geography became Herman's favourite subject. In fact, it was the encouragement of this teacher that first stirred in him the wanderlust that came to be such an important part of his life.

Herman had started to study English back in Horten in the fourth grade, and now German was added. He was glad, because languages seemed to come easily to him and he enjoyed learning useful phrases like "Thank you," "How much does it cost?" and "Where is the railway station?" Very few foreigners bothered to learn Norwegian, and anyone from Norway who wanted to travel, to understand, and more important still to be understood, *had* to learn to speak at least three other languages. It was a real key to future success.

Two of his best friends at school were Asbjörn Nilssen and Victor Thorn. They were all the same age, and all eager for adventure; they loved to explore the forest that spread its evergreen mantle up over the mountaintop behind the city and into the country beyond. This territory also appealed to Far, who enjoyed taking the boys on outings. Each Sunday they would set off on a *tur* (expedition), each carrying his own *pakke* (travel pack) of reserve rations. They went a little farther every time, until at last they penetrated into Nordmarka itself.

Nordmarka was a large timbered plateau rising 250 metres above the fjord and covering about a thousand square kilometres. It was dotted here and there with lakes and streams, and here the snow lay long and deep from mid-November until well into May. To the boys it was a kind of "promised land."

At that time there were only three narrow, winding wood roads running through Nordmarka, connecting the small isolated farms that lay hidden in the hills. Some of these farms had been occupied by the same families for two hundred years or more, and the ensuing generations had come to know the mountains around them like the inside of their own pockets. They were woodcutters, timber floaters, charcoal burners, hunters, fishermen, and farmers, each with his own family, a horse, a cow, a few sheep, a pig or two, and several goats. They lived a simple, extremely independent life close to the land, with few diversions but many satisfactions. Their houses lay five to ten kilometres apart, but in times of need the men would band together in a work gang to improve a small bridge or complete any other job requiring more hands than one farm could muster. They looked after the forest, safeguarding the woodland and at the same time carrying on restricted lumber operations for the overall owner, Baron Lövenskiold. In winter their chief means of travel and communication was on skis from farm to farm, and their houses had become welcome stopping places for the energetic city skiers who by that time were venturing farther and farther into the hills, on a growing network of ski trails. Slagtern, Fyllingen, and Katnosa were homesteads that the boys and Far came to know very well. There the families greeted them as returning friends who brought with them news from town, and tales of their own exploits, and many were the nights when they would unroll their sleeping bags to share the cosy warmth of these small homes.

In fact, some of the more enthusiastic city skiers were beginning to attach themselves more permanently to one or another of these farms. As a group, they would rent a room for the winter, and every Saturday evening some of them would ski in, roll up in their sleeping bags and be ready for a long tour the next day. The Christiania Ski Club, the first officially organized ski club in

Norway, had been founded in 1877. Fridtjof Nansen, the famous zoologist and Arctic explorer, had joined the club as a twenty-year-old university student in 1881. By 1884 the club members had built their own *hytte* (cabin or hut) at Frönsvollen on the mountain overlooking the city, and they began to specialize in long, strenuous ski tours. This was, in fact, the beginning of cross-country ski touring as we know it today.

❦

One winter's day just before the Christmas holidays in 1887, when Herman was twelve and a half, he overheard some older boys at school planning a long ski trip on the weekend, and he longed to join them. In December the days are short and darkness falls in Christiania about three in the afternoon. When he came home and begged to go with the boys next day, Mor said, "All right, Herman, but remember you are expected home by three o'clock, so get an early start. I'll make you some *smörbröd* (bread and butter) to take along. Good luck, and have a safe trip." So off he went. It was nine in the morning, clear and cold, and the day was just dawning.

Up at Holmenkolmen he met his three friends. "Where are you going today?" he asked.

"We're going to cross Nordmarka!" they said enthusiastically. "Can you come?"

Herman thought hard. It was flattering to know that they had no qualms about his skiing ability in relation to their own. It would be a long day's trip, no doubt about that, but the weather was good, the snow was right, and he had plenty of energy. So, giving little thought (if any at all) to the length of time such a trip would take, he threw all caution to the winds. "Sure thing! I'll go!"

They set off at a strong pace and he was glad to find he had no trouble keeping up with them. They climbed up over the first hill, then down over some small lakes, on over one hill and down another. As the afternoon shadows grew longer and longer, he forgot completely that he was to be home by three o'clock. They were having a wonderful time.

It was long after sunset when they stopped for a short rest on a hill from which they could see a reassuring light in a farmhouse in the valley below. This, they decided, would be a good place to wait for the moon to rise, and to eat some of their provisions.

About eight o'clock the moon finally came up. It was round and full, and sent strong shadows across the snow, transforming the world into a veritable fairyland. They had been lucky early in the day in following already broken ski tracks, but now it was necessary for them to take turns breaking trail, and progress was much slower. They carried on, taking turns in the lead, until one of the boys began to have trouble with his toe strap. This was a disaster. They had nothing to repair it with, and could only do a makeshift job.

Disappointed, the leader decided it would be best to turn around. And so they plodded homeward, more slowly because of the damaged harness, but now they at least had their own broken trail to follow. It grew later and later as they pushed on up hill and down dale. At last even the moon went down, but they kept on going. The leader had some matches, so they lit some dry pine knots which served as torches to help them see better – but how good it was to look down at last and see the lights of Christiania glimmering far below them. It was a long downhill run from there, and when he finally reached home it was three o'clock – but in the morning, not the afternoon!

He came in to find Far and Mor holding an anxious vigil. They were *very* upset. What on earth had happened? Of course, there were no telephones in those days, no radios, no means of instant communication; he had simply vanished, they knew not where. And here he was, wandering in, twelve hours overdue. It was absolutely unthinkable.

Herman found the situation just as difficult to explain as the time in the first grade back in Horten when he had gone skiing during school hours. He recounted the whole adventure, telling them just where they had gone, what they had seen, and how they had come back safely, despite the broken harness. He made no excuse. He had simply misjudged the time it would take, and he had no idea that they would be so worried. After all, as he saw it, nothing had happened to him, so there was nothing for them to worry about.

As it turned out, both Far and Mor were so glad to have him home again, sound in body and unharmed, that they more or less forgave this escapade, setting it down to "experience." They did not, however, forgive his poor judgment, although they agreed that from that day forward he had earned the right to go on long trips, but with the proviso that he would never go alone, he would always report where he was going, he would carry provisions and emergency repair equipment, and he would make a reasonable estimate as to the approximate time of his return.

For Herman, this was a real turning point. He had proved beyond a doubt that he was a capable skier who knew his way around in Nordmarka, and this new freedom opened many new opportunities for him.

Asbjörn, Victor, Herman, and a number of other teenagers had by this time banded together and established their own headquarters at Slagtern, one of the small farms in Nordmarka. After his recent Nordmarka adventure Herman was allowed to pack his rucksack with all the necessities every Saturday afternoon, and then take off with the boys. They would congregate at Slagtern where they arranged to sleep in the farmhouse with good old Kristjan Slagtern, Mor Slagtern, and their children, all of whom kept an eye on their safety. The presence of these city boys certainly livened up the family, and brought in a little extra revenue for them, although it was hardly a paying proposition, at one *krone* (twenty cents) per person per night for the bed, and ten *öre* (two cents) for a cup of coffee.

But what fun they had there, sitting by the *peis* (corner fireplace), drying out after a long wet ski trip, and recounting their adventures for the family's entertainment while they tucked hungrily into the food. They would tell how they had seen an elk near Björnsjöen, or chased a hare up over Appelsinhaugen, or had followed the tracks of a *gaupe* (wolverine). And many were the tales old Kristjan told them in the candlelight – of his early days, when an occasional elk would be found grazing among his cows, and of local folk, such as Hans Paulsen from Fyllingen, who one autumn day twenty years before had been chased in a narrow pass by a she-bear and two cubs. The cubs had scrambled up a tree, and he had escaped by taking refuge on a huge boulder, while the she-bear sniffed and snorted around him, and he swung at her with the big timber pike he had been carrying.

By 1889 some of the older boys had formed the Odd Ski Club, with headquarters in a little one-roomed cabin on the Slagtern farm. Here the youngsters could be more independent, cooking their own soup and stew, and the family could once more have its privacy. In this cabin there was an iron stove, firewood, four double-decker beds, and a single cot. All the beds had hay mattresses, and any extra enthusiasts could always find space to unroll their sleeping bags on the floor. After supper the boys would set out from the cabin on a rollicking torchlit ski tour through the surrounding forest. They would come back then to the cabin for a frosty snow-bath and a singsong before turning in for the night.

Meanwhile, interest in cross-country ski competition was increasing on every side. Many of the farm boys in Nordmarka were really good skiers who expertly roamed their own hills, and some of them began to do very well in the annual jumping competitions in Christiania.

All of the boys knew the story of how, back in 1866, an almost unknown farmer from Telemark named Sondre Nordheim had come to Christiania to enter this competition. To everyone's complete astonishment, Sondre had won that event hands down, not only out-jumping the other competitors, but running away from all of them in the four-kilometre cross-country race that followed the jump. And he had done this with the help of a new type of harness he had devised himself, which attached his skis securely to his boots with home-made bindings of willow-root. This was a surprise to everyone, especially those of the older generation who were convinced that such "fixed" bindings were extremely dangerous. But by the end of that competition Sondre had demonstrated that his new bindings were far superior to anything anyone else had, and that besides being able to turn with ease to right or left, he could use them with assurance over uneven terrain.

Telemark was a rugged area several days' travel west of Christiania. It was steep-sided country and the boys who lived there were hardy and in excellent condition. They were farm boys, and to them skis were a means of transport, in a section of Norway where there were few roads and little other winter communication. It was here that "slalom" was invented. The word is derived from *sla*, to beat around, and *lom*, a track. To "beat around a track" is to make controlled turns in deep snow, as opposed to *hopplom*, which means "to jump." Slalom is the sport of skiing downhill around natural obstacles against time, and Telemark has since become known as the "cradle of the ski sport." The Telemark boys made their own skis out of pine, ash, or hickory, and had used them from time immemorial for hunting and for travelling long distances (there are Norwegian rock carvings of skiers that have been dated to 2000 B.C.), and by the late 1800s there was already a fine tradition of ski-jumping competitions in Telemark. As early as 1850 sport skiing had been practised by country folk both for fun and as a proof of skill. In Christiania, on the other hand, the general run of competitors, apart from the boys from Nordmarka, were "city folk" for whom skiing had always been a sport, never a necessity.

Sondre returned to Christiania over the next few winters, and led some of the more enthusiastic skiers on short trips into Nordmarka, showing them how to handle themselves under changing conditions. It was not long before both younger boys and older men, and even women, were adding a strap around their heels. But most important of all, Sondre brought with him other skiers from Telemark. By 1881 they had actually started a ski school in Christiania, where for a few years they gave instruction to both men and women in slalom and cross-country techniques.

Each year, the men from Telemark skied most of the distance from their homes to Christiania in order to enter the race. This in itself was a strenuous two-day accomplishment, which meant breaking trail for the rugged 160-kilometre route from Telemark to the railhead at Kongsberg. There they boarded the train for the remaining 40 kilometres to Christiania. And when the race was over they reversed the process, making the return journey on skis, but this time over their own well-broken trail.

There was plenty of life and excitement on the hills when these country boys came to the big city to show off their prowess. In fact, in 1879, with King Oscar in attendance, it was claimed that there had been as many as 10,000 spectators crowded at the jumping hill at Huseby. As each Telemark boy landed after his jump, he sped down the hill with his hat in one hand and sprig of juniper in the other, to end with a flourish in a spectacular swooping deep-kneed Telemark turn, giving out as he did so a loud Indian war-whoop! This, of course, made all the young boys wild with enthusiasm.

In 1888 it had been decided to hold a separate cross-country race of fifty kilometres. This would be a real feat of endurance, as well as a test of equipment and skill. However, certain of the older people felt that a fifty-kilometre course was really asking for trouble – it was far too strenuous.

A number of doctors disagreed. A skier who was in good condition, they said, and paced himself, should not find it impossible to go the whole distance. Finally, out of respect for the opposition, it was decided to run the race in two laps over the same twenty-five-kilometre course, beginning and ending at the same point. In this way, anyone who felt he could not complete the whole distance could drop out at the end of the first lap.

At last the day came. Asbjörn, Victor, and Herman were going out to cheer their favourites and to learn as much as they could about long-distance racing. Herman dressed warmly, pocketed some smörbröd for lunch and went out to his waiting skis. He was wearing, as usual, his ordinary shoes. He slipped them into his *finnsko*, furry Lapp overshoes insulated with hay. They had turned-up toes that kept the toestrap of the ski from slipping off. His shoes fitted snugly into the finnsko as he slid the curly toe under the loop of his toestrap and pulled the rear willow root over the heel of his boot. He was proud of these new bindings. They held well. He slapped his skis several times on the new snow to feel that everything was in readiness. And then he set off.

The starting point for the seventeen contestants was at Major-stuen where there was also a food station. Here competitors could "refuel" if they wished, on milk, coffee, or beer (!) and smörbröd before starting the second lap. Everywhere people were gathering along the course, to see the racers as they sped by. The excitement was electric. This was to be a stiff competition. There were entries from all over the Christiania area, as well as from Telemark, Hadeland, Hedmark, and even Trondheim.

Asbjörn, Victor, and Herman decided to go well out along the trail to a spot where they could see the racers as they sped down one long steep hill, then climbed up over the next. They wanted especially to see just how the men would handle themselves at this point. They each found a convenient tree overlooking the trail and clambered up to get an extra good view. And there they sat when the first Telemark man, Torjus Hemmestveit, rocketed into view – down the steep hill, around a curve, up the next rise, and out of sight. He was not far ahead of the next man, and then came the rest of them, the men from Christiania and Telemark, from Hadeland, Hedmark, and Trondheim, one after the other, with long easy strides.

When all had passed, the boys dropped from their perches and bolted across the course to find another place where they could again intercept the racers as they circled back to Majorstuen. They had a long wait, but eventually there they came, Torjus still in the lead, and Peder Eliassen from Hedmark close behind. But this time the temptation was too much for the youngsters. Despite warnings, they jumped onto the course behind the racers and began to follow as fast as they could, up the long slope, over the next hill, down the next dip. It was exciting to feel that they were skiing in the very tracks of their heroes!

But the men soon disappeared into the distance. The boys had to hop out of the way to let other racers go by, for they were certainly not of competitive calibre – yet. But the experience was something they never forgot. It seemed to lend wings to their feet.

And to the astonishment of everyone, only five of the competitors stopped at the end of that first lap. Twelve finished the full fifty kilometres, and the first six of these were within fifteen minutes of each other. Torjus won four hundred gold crowns, Peder Eliassen a gold watch, and the third man a silver watch; for the rest of the entrants the feeling of having taken part in an epoch-making event was a prize in itself. This was a race that would indeed set a mark for many a year to come.

As the years passed, Herman was fully occupied each winter with school and weekly expeditions into Nordmarka. During these trips he and his friends criss-crossed the country many times and made close friends with a number of the farm families. Herman remembered particularly Hans Bonna, the farmer with whom they occasionally stayed on the lake at Björnsjöen. Hans had a number of children, among them a pretty little girl, Valborg, who in later years became famous far and wide when a poem was written about her, in which she was hailed as "the Rose of Nordmarka."

And there were old Magnus and Gunhild Katnosa who took the boys in, once in a while, at their farm at the upper end of Lake Katnosa. It was here, in fact, that Fridtjof Nansen had spent some time training, for he always kept in excellent physical condition, and Katnosa was far enough from town that the trip there would really stretch his legs.

Nansen was fourteen years older than Herman, and very much looked up to by all the boys. They often thought of him as they had seen him down beside the fjord in the early winter, when the new sea ice was beginning to form in the little bays. Nansen and some friends of his used to experiment with what they called "rubber ice." They would run down the bank on one side, slide out fast across the shiny sheet, then dart up the bank on the other side, testing the new surface to see how well it would stand their weight. Herman and his young friends found that they could lie on their stomachs on the ice near shore, and as the older boys sped past they could feel the delicious ripple of the new ice as it yielded to their passing. There was always the risk, of course, that it would break, but fortunately there were no accidents.

Nansen was now twenty-seven years old, and had become curator of the Zoological Museum in Bergen. For several years he had been thinking of an expedition across Greenland on skis, something which had never been undertaken before. This year, 1888, he and a party of five other men, including Otto Sverdrup (who was later to accompany him on his Arctic expedition), were ready to go. Nansen had planned long and well, but had permitted very little advance publicity, as he thought it better to talk about something after it was done, rather than before. When his plans became known, many people were strongly opposed to the idea, which they declared was absolutely foolhardy. To abandon their boat on the ice-bound east coast of Greenland and try to ski across the unknown wastes all the way to the west coast, a distance of at least four hundred kilometres, hoping to reach the tiny settlement of Godhaab, was to them a mad scheme, without rhyme or reason. Herman and his chums, however, were fired with excitement, and took to pretending that they were skiing over the unknown wastes of Greenland with Nansen's men.

Nansen and his group were gone for more than a year, and when they finally returned to Christiania, there was a huge celebration. Not only had they crossed Greenland on skis, drawing after them heavy sleds without the aid of dogs, but they had also reached the settlement on the west coast too late in the season to catch the last ship back to Norway and had had to overwinter there. The trip was a truly tremendous accomplishment. It received worldwide acclaim, and opened the eyes of everyone to the true possibilities of skis as a means of winter transport. From then on, Nansen and Sverdrup were Herman's all-time heroes.

Herman's young life was not all winter in Nordmarka. There were also the lively family summers back on Christianiafjord. The first summer after the move to Christiania was spent again in Horten with all the cousins. Only this time their little sister, Margarethe, was no longer with them; she had died of scarlet fever that spring. In those days many children died young, for not much was known about the control of childhood diseases. Far and Mor found their loss very hard to bear, but they were truly thankful that the other children stayed sturdy and healthy and full of life. The parents faced their sorrow as something inevitable, praying for little Margarethe every night, almost as though she were still with them.

As soon as the family arrived at Ekeli that summer, Herman and Johannes dashed out to the stable to renew their acquaintance with Bestefar's two wonderful horses, Odin and Sleipner; and with Martin the stableboy, who took such good care of them. The horses had been named from the ancient sagas. Odin was the Norse god who ruled over all the other gods, and Sleipner was his famous horse. The Sleipner of the sagas could gallop so fast that he was always shown in the old picture books as having eight legs, although of course Bestefar's Sleipner had only four. Still, he was a fabulous animal, and he was as much a part of Ekeli as the ducks, the orchards, and the venerable oaks that spread their sheltering boughs above the driveway.

That was the family's last summer at Horten. In 1887 Far and Mor decided to take the family to Stolingen, a farm near Asker, much closer to Christiania. This opened up many new possibilities. The old farmer made a special trip to Eilert Sunds Gate with his big farm wagon, which the Johannsens loaded with beds and other furniture they would need for the season. Then he drove the wagon back the ten miles to Stolingen, while the family followed by train. That was the summer they had a new baby sister, Elisabeth, so Mor had plenty to do, and the boys kept busy "helping" the farmer.

The most exciting event for Herman that year was his friendship with a young foal. This colt was a real character, and they would romp and play together like two children. The only trouble was that the foal grew faster than the boy and was soon galloping in the lead with Herman puffing determinedly in the rear. But before long the tables were turned. When it became obvious that running would always be an unequal contest, Herman resorted to strategy. He would march along with some lumps of sugar in his pocket, and then it was the foal who followed. For the rest of the season, the colt trotted after Herman wherever he went.

It was a great day when the farmer harnessed one of his work-horses to an old cart heaped high with manure, and asked Herman to drive it out and dump it in the field. Herman was delighted to have the chance to do this all by himself. On his way back he stood proudly in the empty wagon, his legs widely spaced, his head held high, riding that jolting manure cart as though he were a real Roman soldier driving a speeding chariot. And the foal came galloping after! The farmer, however, was unimpressed, and decided that in future it would be better if Herman stuck to the colt, and left the horse and the wagon to him.

The next two summers were passed on yet another farm, where there were more horses to befriend, this time in company with a playmate, Harald Hals. One day Harald and Herman were driving the cart down a winding road on their way back from the field when things got out of control. The cart rode up on the side of a curve and suddenly toppled over, trapping Harald beneath the wagon box! Herman leapt free in the nick of time, but he had an awful struggle to raise the box and let Harald scramble out, fortunately unharmed. The boys then had to calm the frightened horse, and put everything to rights again. That was the end of their chariot racing, but it had been great fun – while it lasted.

Herman's two young sisters, Agnes and Helga, then ten and five years old, had considerable artistic skill. That summer, they spent a long time building a model farm, complete with stables, barns, horses, and cows, all carefully made of pine cones. It was an impressive display, and they were justly proud of it. Herman, however, ever the realist, felt there was something missing. What was a farm without manure? So, when the girls weren't looking, he saw to it that there was a liberal supply of manure in their farmyard. His sisters never forgave him. After that, he was their impossible big brother who couldn't appreciate the finer things of life and who had ruined their lovely farm. This was a heresy that came back to haunt him in later years, though at the time he dismissed it without so much as a second thought.

That was the summer, too, when they had a terrible experience which taught them not only that tragedy can strike at any time, but that one must always be prepared to avoid it. Herman, Johannes, Harald, and Harald's young brother, Ole, used to go swimming in the fjord where the water was extremely cold, and the rocks slippery. On this particular day there happened to be no one along to supervise. Somehow – they never knew how – young Ole got out into deeper water, and before they realized what had happened, Ole had sunk beneath the surface. They brought him back to the shore, but they knew nothing about life-saving, and could only scream for help. Someone on shore gave the alarm up at the farm and Mor and Fru Hals ran down to the beach as fast as they could. They tried to revive Ole, but in vain – it was too late. There was nothing any of them could do but stand helplessly by, realizing how unprepared they had been, and that no amount of preparedness in future would ever bring Ole back to life. In one brief moment, he was gone forever.

Still another shadow fell on the family that year, when their new baby brother, Hugo, died of a fever as a tiny infant. It was hard for the children to cope with these deaths, but they learned through them that life is fragile indeed. It can so easily and permanently be snuffed out. For the first time they sensed the importance of making the most of life, as long as it was theirs. But they also came to know that in the end they would have to accept the inevitable, whenever and however it might occur.

The family spent the summer of 1891 on yet another farm, this time in Ringerike on the northwest side of Nordmarka in a won-derfully fertile area with big, fruitful fields. Herman was by then fifteen and capable of doing useful work, so he pitched hay and generally contributed his share to the farm chores. Furthermore, there were really nice girls up there! He was growing, and had discovered that life was becoming more interesting in many ways. High school was nearing an end. Then would come military training. After that, who knew which way the wind might blow?

Those were on the whole happy, carefree days. There were no automobiles, no radios, no outside attractions. They had to create their own fun and, although they now and then got into mischief, they were on the whole not really "bad."

It was a great satisfaction many years later for the boys to go back to these same farms, to visit with their old friends, and to recall with them some of their childhood adventures. Those farm summers had taught them much about self-reliance and independence, and the boys would be forever grateful to Far and Mor for having made these experiences possible. It was an important part of their preparation for the business of living.

CHAPTER FOUR

The Challenge of Jotunheimen: 1892

The train from Christiania rattled its way up through the gentle hills of Romerike. The three boys were in high spirits, ensconced in their third-class carriage. Beside them sat their bulky knapsacks, crammed with everything they needed for two weeks of tramping in the high mountains from Rondane to Jotunheimen: heavy sweaters, wind jackets, rain gear, a change of clothing, extra socks, a small cooking apparatus, a barometer, and maps. There were bouillon cubes and dried pea soup. But for daily food and sleeping gear they knew they could count on whatever the small farms might offer as they picked their way from one *saeter* (small farm above the timberline where cattle are pastured in summer) to another, across the moors. They also had a copy of Yngvar Nielsen's 1888 *Reisehandbog over Norge*. This was a useful volume, which had supplied them with much information about the mountain country they would be hiking through. They had already pored over nearly every word and they almost felt as though Yngvar himself were travelling with them. In their pockets were forty kroner apiece, which had to cover board and lodging for fourteen days, plus train and boat fare and extra cash for any other emergencies that might arise.

This was the beginning of an adventure the boys would treasure to the end of their days. It was the first time any of them had been away from home on his own, and each was determined to make the most of it.

Herman, at seventeen, was leader of the expedition. Karl Johanssen, a school chum but no kin, was eighteen. He had relatives in the area and so was a natural liaison officer. Fifteen-year-old Johannes was the official recorder. He had with him a little note-book, on the first page of which he had carefully inscribed:

Johannes Johannsen
Dagbok
1892

and this *dagbok* (journal) has come down to us filled with obser-vations on what they saw, what they ate, and how they slept. Through Johannes's words we can trace that eventful journey through country that has remained almost unchanged in the ensuing hundred years.

The boys detrained at Eidsvold, to board the little paddle-wheeled steamer *Kong Oscar*, which daily plied the 100-kilometre length of Lake Mjösen. This lake lies 120 metres above sea level in a broad cultivated valley lined with rich, rolling farmland that climbs from the lakeshore far up the hills on either side. It was early July, and haying was in progress. Many long *hesjer* (temporary wire fences) were strung across the fields, looking like monstrous green caterpillars creeping across the land. The new-cut hay would be hung on them to dry in the wind for a week or more before being gathered and stored in ample barns for the winter.

From the boat there were sweeping views of well-settled farm-land, which had been in cultivation since the Middle Ages. Most of these farms had passed down from father to son to grandson for generations. The big red barns, white dwelling houses, and clustered log out-buildings were visible evidence of the farms' prosperity.

Higher up, the valley walls gradually became steeper, and the earth, seamed with rocky ledges, was less productive. Here the farms were smaller and more primitive. And over all, the evergreen forest came close, spreading its fingers down into the valley and merging upward in a dark, irregular band that stood out sharply against the azure sky.

In the summer, since the lower fields were needed for growing hay and vegetables, it was the custom for farmers to send the girls of the family to tend the cattle on their small summer farm or *saeter* in the high country just above timberline. Here the horses, cows, sheep, and goats would be free to graze in the verdant pastureland spread so abundantly around them. The girls worked as *budeier* (dairy maids) and would spend the entire summer making the winter's supply of butter and cheese, and picking great quantities of wild berries, which they made into jam. It was an isolated life for these young people, and they found any transient wanderer a welcome sight. The three boys knew they could depend on the hospitality of the young women whenever they might need it on their journey.

At Lillehammer, a thriving community of 1,500 souls in a great valley at the northern end of the lake, they stopped to call on Presten Vold, the local minister and an old family friend, who offered them cake and smörbröd, which they accepted with pleasure, as a good omen for their tour. It was already early evening when, after this visit, they shouldered their knapsacks and set off on the first lap of their journey.

It was good to be walking at last. The road was lined with frosty-white flowers, whose strong aroma filled the air. Here and there a cuckoo sang its plaintive notes, and many small birds darted back and forth over their heads in search of insects in the evening breeze.

It was the 11th of July. The long summer twilight would hold far into the night; darkness was still hours away. When they reached the place where the valley forked, they turned up the eastern valley, and followed the river Laagen as it swerved back and forth between the confining walls of Gudbrandsdalen. The late evening sun shone warmly on them, and they were glad at last to reach the thundering waterfall at Hunderfoss. They found a place to sleep at Fossegaarden, the carriage station, and turned in with the roar of the river echoing in their dreams.

They woke next morning to a cloudless sky. The sun was already scorching, and in gathering heat they continued along the valley bottom to Öyer. Occasionally a small horse-drawn farm cart would pass them, stirring up clouds of dust, and it was a great relief to leave the travelled route and turn their steps along the shady winding sideroad, which soon led abruptly up the eastern wall.

The road grew steeper and steeper. It twisted and turned as it mounted past sloping fields of grain and fresh-scented new-mown hay. At last they came to the farm of Skaaden, where some of Karl's relatives lived. The family offered them milk and cakes, which they accepted gratefully, and as they rested and ate they looked out over Gudbrandsdalen. Far below, on the other side of winding Laagen, they could see the new railway construction. Tracks were being laid and men were swarming like ants over the fresh ballast. The railway itself would not be in operation for another two years, but it signalled the beginning of far-reaching changes. Up here, however, high above it all, life continued in its even way. Those whose homes were situated on this brink were content with what they had. Here the air was clear, and one could see for miles. Change was something they did not really want.

At length, refreshed and invigorated, the wanderers said their "Takk for maten" and set out again on the upward-winding saeter road through a cool evergreen forest, which thinned gradually as they mounted. Little by little the trees were diminishing in height and spreading farther and farther apart, until at last the path broke out into the open altogether and the boys suddenly found themselves taller than the surrounding shrubby vegetation. This was the *vidda*, or high tundra.

Looking to the east they saw the vidda spread gently before them, but when they looked back towards the west they could see how it also continued on the other side of deep Gudbrandsdalen, and into the far distance, where they could clearly make out the jagged, snowy peaks of Jotunheimen, Home of the Giants, rising majestically against the sky. Had they not just spent several hours toiling up out of the yawning chasm of Gudbrandsdalen, they would never have suspected the existence of that great canyon, which now lay between them and those distant mountains.

It was through the great expanse of vidda that, millions of years before, the ancient River Laagen had slowly cut its channel, digging deeper and deeper into the rocky crust; at the same time the land was gradually rising. Eventually, a cooling climate caused masses of snow and ice to accumulate over thousands of years, filling the valleys and spreading in a great white mantle over the entire land. This ice mass crept slowly, spreading outward by the force of its own weight, much as molasses might spread on a gently sloping surface, and as the ice moved it cleared before it all signs of vegetation, as well as any loose rocks and other material lying in its path. Finally, as the climate warmed again, the ice slowly melted, vegetation gradually recolonized the hills, and the land began to look somewhat as it does today. The ancient plateau, into which the Laagen has carved its forceful way, remains a venerable presence, still admirably able to withstand the ravages of time.

The boys turned at last and continued over the rolling tundra until they came to Steinsaeter. This was really a whole community of summer farms, where they found pleasant shelter with more of Karl's relatives. As befitted visitors from far away, they were plied once more with milk and cakes, which they hungrily accepted. This was soon followed by coffee, fresh-baked waffles, and shortly afterwards by the midday meal of cream soup, dried salt meat, and bread and butter. After this, totally replete, they lay down on the warm turf for a *middagslur* (after-dinner sleep) from which they awoke to a further round of cakes and coffee.

By this time all three felt the need to work off some of what they had eaten, so they went for a stroll up a nearby hill, from which to the north they could see the slightly hazy Rondane Mountains, whose summits would be their first objective. Far to the west loomed the peaks of Jotunheimen towards which their path would eventually lead, and there the glaciers shone gloriously in the late afternoon sun.

When they returned contentedly to Steinsaeter, they found an evening snack of *flatbröd* (flatbread, a kind of crisp wafer), cheese, and other delicacies waiting for them. Meanwhile, the temperature had dropped to five degrees centigrade. They turned in and slept soundly, all three in one bed. Home, they agreed, was never like this!

Next morning, after hearty farewells, they set out over the marshy moor to the tune of baa-ing lambs and resounding sheep bells. The road wound on among tiny saeters where the pungent odour of woodsmoke hung constantly in the air. The budeier who tended these little farms usually worked in pairs, and they would often see no other living soul for weeks on end as they went about their chores from early morning until late at night. First there were the cows to milk, then cream to separate, the cows to be turned out to pasture, and the stable to be cleaned. There was the fire to be set for the day's cheesemaking, the churning of butter, the constant stirring of the cheese as it slowly steamed, and the endless replenishment of firewood. In the evening there were cows to be called in, more milking and separating to be done, and in between, the preparation and eating of their own meals. The life of a budeie was hard and strenuous, but the girls enjoyed their three-month interlude from valley routine and were happy to be up here on the vidda in the summer sun. It was no wonder, however, that when visitors came by, they were glad of the excuse to pause and to catch up on news from far and near.

That day, when the boys stopped at a small saeter for the midday meal, an unexpected problem arose. The smiling budeier were delighted to serve them sweet milk with crumbled flatbröd, followed by more flatbröd with butter and cheese, and then by finger-thick slabs of incredibly tough meat, which defied all chewing. The boys tried valiantly to down the meat, but to no avail. It absolutely refused to disintegrate. They were at a loss, not wanting to hurt the poor girls' feelings, but finally they had to give up. Herman, however, saved the day, for when the girls were not looking he slipped several slices of meat into his pocket so that it would appear that they had eaten well. They then went gaily on their way.

Next day, after scrambling through several deep gullies in scorching sun, Herman accidentally left their precious barometer hanging on a tree where they had paused to rest. When this loss was discovered there was no alternative but to go back to retrieve it. This Herman did, alone, and in haste. But the experience taught him a lasting lesson. Never again when he rose from a resting place did he forget to check thoroughly to see that absolutely nothing was left behind. He finally rejoined the others, and they went on together in the rising heat.

Gunstadsaeter, the next stop, provided a distinct diversion, for its walls were hung with reindeer antlers, a mounted falcon was flying from the rafters, and a hare and a young fox guarded the door. Here was proof of the good marksmanship of the owner, as well as evidence of careful hours of painstaking taxidermy. The boys lingered long that evening beside the cosy peis before turning in for the night.

The following day they came down into Atnadal, the valley which bounds the Rondane on the east, and here for a change of pace they rowed the seven-kilometre length of Atnasjöen (Lake Atna) under threatening skies. From the lake they could see the mountain range as a whole, with all its marshalled peaks along the skyline. The slowly moving continental ice, millennia ago, had smoothed and rounded the outer contours of these massive hills, and after the main ice mass had melted away the persisting local glaciers had continued their work, enlarging cracks in these now rounded summits, and carving into them great cup-shaped valleys with precipitous side walls, some of which were hundreds of metres deep.

It was a dramatic view, and one that hinted at fascinating possibilities for adventure, but the rapidly changing weather soon closed in, and the mountains disappeared mysteriously in a shroud of fog. By the time the boys had climbed from the lake to Musvoldsaeter it had begun to sprinkle, and there they were fortunate to find good lodging for the night. It was pleasant, then, to stand in the cosy warmth, and to stare out the window into a formless world as they listened in comforting security to the now pelting rain.

The rain continued aggressively in the morning, but as they had by then walked steadily for a week, they were glad enough to rest. The decision to linger in these comfortable quarters was made all the easier, Johannes recorded, by the fact that they had found here the pleasant company of several congenial girls from Trondheim and Christiania. So the time was not altogether lost!

Monday dawned moist and wet, but as soon as it showed faint signs of clearing they set off through stony, slippery Langglupdalen, where thick cloud hung solidly around them, completely obscuring the view. After six long, wet hours they reached Döraalsaeter. Here a good meal of pea soup and meatballs revived them, and they were happy to discover that Ingvar Nielsen, in his guidebook, had reckoned a full nine and a quarter hours for the trip that they had just completed in six. But after all, on this dismal day, they had wasted scant time in admiring the view!

The mountains were still obscure in the morning. It drizzled at first, then became a veritable downpour as they made their way along the trail and were surprised to overtake a young girl and a gnarled old companion plodding home to Dovre with a laden packhorse. They walked along sociably with them for a long time, then turned off in fog and continuing rain up through a still snow-filled valley, and at last descended, wet to the skin, through interminable bogs to Laurgaardsaeter at Hövringen. Here they searched their packs for dry clothing, and were glad to sit down to a meal of sweet soup and fresh trout, and to recount their adventures to their hosts. In nine days they had hiked from Lake Mjösen up onto the vidda and across it, around the cloud-covered Rondane mountains, then back through and over the Rondane; they now found themselves once more on the brink of Gudbrands-dalen. So far the trip had been a splendid preparation for the challenging high peaks of Jotunheimen. Their muscles were hard, their hearts were light, and they had a growing sense of achieve-ment.

On July 20th they left Hövringen in early morning mist, and as the fog cleared slowly they made their way down the steep twisting road to reach the valley bottom and their old friend, the River Laagen, foaming through its narrow gorge. They crossed the river on the carriage bridge, then climbed resolutely up among the tumbled boulders in the next valley, leaving behind them the rain-washed Rondane shining in the morning sun.

From the head of this valley they swung their way down steep switchbacks to the shores of Vaagaavatn where they found them-selves back amid farmland that bore the unmistakable imprint of centuries of care. The lake here lay like a turquoise gem in its rich valley, and the 800-year-old timber church at Vaagaa stood with soaring gables poised against the clouds. They crossed the bridge and followed the well-travelled road to Garmo, a full fifty-two kilometres from their morning start at Hövringen. Not a bad day's march!

Next day on the flat valley bottom they treated themselves to a fourteen-kilometre *skyss-tur* (a ride in an open buggy), along the lake. What a delightful sensation to sit for a brief change, bouncing in the little springless cart and letting the horse do all the work. But at the town of Lom they were glad enough to leave the jolting cart and take once more to their own feet as they began the long hike up wild Böverdalen. Here at last they were on the threshold of the Home of the Giants, and new adventures beckoned.

They ate their smörbröd at Roisheim, then continued onwards and upwards. At last they reached a saeter, where they stopped for milk and an absolutely breath-taking view of Glittertind, Norway's second-highest mountain, shimmering white on the other side of the valley. The path continued higher and higher, as more and more peaks sprang up on the horizon, until at last there stood Galdhöpiggen, highest of them all, confidently rearing his head against the sky. At his feet lay the little lake of Gjuvannet, still completely covered in ice in mid-July.

At Gjuvasshytte, where Knut Vole and his family kept the saeter, Herman and Johannes were remembered from their visit with their father the previous summer, and were welcomed as old friends. There each boy was delighted to have a bed to himself in which to settle comfortably for the night, and all three slept soundly and well, dreaming of their next day's climb.

They could scarcely believe their good fortune in the morning to find the weather absolutely ideal. On Galdhöpiggen the age-old glaciers were still at work, tearing away at the encircling slopes. Each year, during the spring and summer melting, the main ice mass would slip slowly downward, bearing with it as on a huge conveyer belt the many rocks that had tumbled from the heights. Each winter new snow drifted into cracks and crannies at the head of the glacier, freezing into ice and thus constantly replenishing the glacier from above. Rocks embedded in the mass moved slowly downward with the ice, being used as "tools" with which the glacier scoured any surface over which it passed, many of the rocks being ground to powder in the process.

This was the explanation of those huge moraines the boys had seen in the rain at Döralsaeter, the loose abandoned debris of thousands of years of glacial action left to block whole valleys, temporarily damming up the melt-water. This water, when finally released to flow again, carved new terraces in the moraine, carrying away the ground-up gravel, sand, and silt to spread them further in the lower valleys as layered deposits. It was fine silt from such deposits that, suspended in the water, gave Vaagaavatn its turquoise tinge.

The boys set out exuberantly at six-thirty that morning, with Knut Vole as guide, bearing borrowed skis on their shoulders. The hard snow offered good walking over the first glacier, but they finally had to take to their skis to avoid possible crevasses. They clambered over one moraine in their boots, then took again to their skis, and at last, where the steepest climb began, they stacked their skis and roped themselves together for the remainder of the way on foot. The temperature was one half degree centigrade above freezing. There was no wind. They broke out at last on the summit to find themselves on the roof-ridge of Norway, 2,469 metres above sea level, with scarcely a cloud in the sky.

Near at hand lay snow-covered Glittertind, 2,452 metres high. Farther south reared countless other sharp and dizzy heights. To the west and north the crests continued. Far to the northeast rose Snöhetta in the Dovre Mountains, and to the east the Rondane, whence they had come. It was an altogether unforgettable view.

They absorbed the scenery to their hearts' content before refreshing themselves with coffee in the tiny hut, which had been built several years before by Vole. Then they once more roped up and set off downhill at a terrific gallop. At one point they slid at full speed on the seat of their pants. Arriving at their skis, they removed their climbing rope, mounted the skis once more and whisked down the glacier as fast as anyone could desire. Then, briefly removing their skis to pick their way across the stony moraine, they remounted them for the glorious downhill run back to Gjuvasshytta. It had taken nearly two hours to struggle up, but it took only forty exhilarating minutes to come down. They ate their lunch in great spirits, and finally, with a hearty farewell to Knut, made their way on to Spiterstulen for the night. They were thoroughly enchanted with their adventure.

Next day, again in perfect weather, they went up through Visdalen, past a number of impressive heights, wading the icy river several times in wild and rugged scenery. They continued down through spectacular Storaadalen and finally reached Gjendebu, the fine new hostel that the Norwegian Tourist Association had recently opened. Here they were delighted to have a room in the new building.

The next morning, in wonderful sunshine, they climbed over the famous Bukkelegeret "the goat trail," with Ole Kvitten as guide. Ole led them up the steep and precipitous path, through moss and small bushes where it would have been very dangerous to go on their own, and there, in the most difficult spot of all, Karl was suddenly stricken with a terrible case of mountain sickness! He had a ghastly, dizzy sensation. He could move neither forward nor back. And there lay Gjendin, 400 metres below him, pale and green, while the heady heights of Svartsdalspiggen and Knuthol-stinden rose beyond on the other side of the lake.

Karl clung frantically to the rock as though frozen to it. Little by little, Ole coaxed him gently on, and he edged his way ever so slowly across the final stretch, to sink exhausted in the heather as he tried to calm his heaving stomach. Gradually, the scenery readjusted itself, and things returned to normal. When the worst was over, Ole turned back again to Gjendebu for more possible customers, and the boys continued safely by themselves.

From the summit they had another fantastic view, this time across to knife-edged Besseggen, over which the legendary folk-hero, Per Gynt, was supposed to have ridden on a reindeer buck, a feat they had no intention of trying to duplicate. And down beneath them lay tranquil, turquoise-green Gjendin.

It was remarkable how Karl's appetite revived as they descended the steep trail to Memurubu. There they ate their fill, and recounted this most recent adventure for the benefit of other travellers gathered there. And it was with a jolt that they suddenly realized that they were now almost at the end of their journey. The day after tomorrow they would be back again among familiar scenes at home. Today, however, as they rowed the long way down the lake to Gjendesheim, each of them quietly savoured the glo-rious view, reliving all the memorable events of the past two weeks.

It had been a spectacular trip, filled with difficulties, excitement, and new experiences, all of which would stay with the boys essen-tial landmarks of their growing up. Years later, they would recall the tour for the benefit of their children and grandchildren, and some of these exploits would grow with time; others would be almost forgotten. But through the whole story would run the comradeship of three teen-aged youngsters who had set out to pit themselves against the elements. In doing so, they had found perseverance, strength, courage, and a wonderful spirit of inde-pendence on the mossy moors of Rondane and the rocky peaks of Jotunheimen.

CHAPTER FIVE

Cadet Training in Christiania: 1893–1894

Herman reported to Krigsskolen (literally, "war-school") for military duty in September 1893. He was in great shape. He had passed his *artium* (school leaving exam) in the spring, and school now lay behind him with all its general preparation for life. He had had a thorough initiation into outdoor experience. Next would come serious training in how to cope with crises, with difficult situations, and with all kinds of people.

To him this year in Krigsskolen would be not so much training in how to make war as in how to survive. He saw it as developing a positive attitude, not a negative one, one that would sharpen his sensitivities, make him more aware of neatness and order, of physical fitness, of planning for action and carrying out those plans, and of working together with others. He had no intention of following a military career, but he was sure that the qualities that made a good soldier would make a good citizen – and so he turned up that morning, along with fifty other boys, to enlist as a cadet for officer training. They came from many different parts of Norway, all raw recruits, but strong and healthy, and eager to begin what would be for them an entirely new way of living.

In the back of his mind stirred the memory of the day eight years before when he and Johannes had watched in small-boy wonder the soldiers drilling on horseback outside Akershus. The moment had now come when he was to *be* one of those soldiers, although he realized it would still be some time before he would be assigned a horse.

As the new cadets lined up that first day, they were told some of the early history of Krigsskolen, how it had been founded in 1750 as a free mathematics school under His Majesty Fredrick V (at the time King of Denmark and Norway).

The initial years had been difficult. The courses were rigid and unimaginative. There was little *esprit de corps*. The number of students dwindled from thirty-five to sixteen. But in 1769, with the appointment of Peter Blankenborg Prydz as director of the school, there had come a complete revival of discipline and a renewal of the whole operation.

The recruits were told that Prydz had been a real martinet. He had demanded – and received – supreme dedication from everyone, and his aim was to develop their hearts as well as their morale. The director's personal habits were Spartan: he was always an "early bird," never in bed after sunrise, even in the daylit summer months. His every hour was well ordered. He ate sparingly, smoked strong cigars, and drank cold tea. And he was a stickler for discipline. Nothing escaped his eagle eye. No one could so much as borrow a pen or a jack-knife from another cadet, for each was expected to be entirely self-sufficient. In the last analysis, his doctrine was that the strength of the whole army depended upon the collective strength of individuals. In his twelve years as director, Prydz managed to transform Krigsskolen into a very efficient machine.

Training in those early days a hundred and fifty years before Herman's own time had been long and hard, but over the course of time the routine had been somewhat modified. Hours were altered, lessons adapted to suit changing conditions, and more and more emphasis was placed on physical fitness. But much of old Director Prydz's strict philosophy remained at the core of their training, and the new recruits came to look upon Krigsskolen as a real challenge and a great responsibility.

In that year, 1893, cadets from out of town were provided with living quarters in the barracks, but for want of space those who came from Christiania continued to live at home, and consequently their army routine was to a certain extent imposed upon their families. Every morning at six o'clock Herman had to be ready for inspection. This was the responsibility of a senior cadet, who appeared at that hour precisely at the front door to check him over. Herman had to have his boots polished, buttons shined, gun cleaned, and all his equipment laid out on his bed before him, sparkling and in tip-top shape. This cadet was being trained in the training of others, and he was very particular, for *he* would later be checked on how well he had checked on the others.

When the inspector was satisfied that all was well, and had gone off to report, Herman fortified himself with a big breakfast in order to be ready for whatever the day might hold. Then he marched the two miles to Tollbugaten with his pack on his back. It was important to look smart and business-like, for the honour and public image of the whole corps depended on each cadet.

Once he had arrived at Krigsskolen, his day continued with physical training, intended to limber up cadets' bodies and clear their lungs. After that, they had classes and lectures on all sorts of theoretical subjects until three o'clock; then more foot drill, the long march back home to Eilert Sunds Gate, dinner there, and plenty to study in preparation for the next day. And so it went throughout the fall.

By Christmas, Herman was ready for a holiday. His cousin Anders Beer and his friend Asbjörn Nilssen went up to Norefjell with him by train for a week of skiing in that beautiful timberline country, lying about one hundred kilometres northwest of Christiania. There they would set out in the early morning to cover long distances above the treeline, despite the short winter hours of daylight.

Making their headquarters at the same place were three young medical students, who were doing just what Herman and his chums were doing — testing themselves and their equipment for possible longer trips in the future. These men kept very much to themselves, and were out in all kinds of weather. They were strong and eager, intent on outdoor living, and they put particular emphasis on strenuous training. Their leader was a strapping six-footer, twenty-one years old, and at that time just another unknown student in search of adventure. He had, however, a hawk-like face one could not easily forget, with an aquiline nose and hooded eyes. Thirteen years later, in 1906, when he returned from his historic first trip through the Northwest Passage, his name would be on everyone's lips, for this was none other than Roald Amundsen, who six years after that would lead the first successful expedition to the South Pole. How well the boys remembered him from those snowy days on Norefjell in the wintry blizzard!

With the New Year, Herman was back at Krigsskolen for more drilling and lectures from Monday through Saturday noon, but the cadets were usually off duty from Saturday afternoon to Monday morning, and they managed to get in some excellent training on skis in Nordmarka during this spare time.

There was one weekend that Herman remembered very vividly. Asbjörn, Victor, and he had skied in to the farm at Bonna that Saturday night, and there they had a very good time with the lively young girls of the family. This was not exactly training, he had to admit, but it had its compensations. Then, after a hard Sunday's ski run, they were gathered beside the peis with its crackling fire, singing lustily, when he suddenly realized how late it was, and that he was due home for inspection at six o'clock that morning. He knew it would take a minimum of four hours of hard skiing to cover the necessary distance, so he hopped onto his skis and ran full out, just as though he were in a real cross-country ski race. And so he was, for he had to get there before the inspector!

In fact, he had just managed to reach his house and stack his skis when the inspector arrived. Long weekend ski trips were not on the approved Krigsskolen agenda, for everyone was supposed to rest up in order to be ready for the next week's work. And here the inspector saw those fresh tracks, at six o'clock in the morning, and the snowy skis standing at the door. He was not amused. He checked Herman's hastily assembled gear, and noted that he was not as composed as usual. But he finally decided not to report the escapade – this time. Instead, he issued a solemn warning, assuring Herman that he would be much more critical in future. This one day he would close his eyes to this transgression, for it seemed he was secretly impressed by the distance Herman had covered. (It turned out he was a cross-country racer himself.)

That was a wonderful winter, full of adventurous small trips and interesting studies, but behind it all there was still the comfortable atmosphere of home. Herman often recalled how they used to sit around the dining-room table for dinner at night – Far at the head, with Herman on his right and Johannes on his left. Then there would come Agnes and Helga, little Otto, their youngest brother, and then Mor, and completing the circle were Elisabeth and Fred. It was a cosy, happy family, and they had much to share as they sat there talking over their hopes and fears and aspirations. Herman little realized at the time just how much this intimate family life had come to mean.

In May his training resumed, and this time he went at last to live in the barracks at Akershus. Theoretical studies were over. Now would come the practical application of what they had been learning. Later in the summer they would be out on manoeuvres, camping in the open and leading a rugged army life, but first would come intensive training with the horses, and to that he had been looking forward with great anticipation.

Each cadet was assigned his own mount, for which he was entirely responsible. He had to curry him in the mornings and keep him in the finest condition. He had to feed and water him, and ride him through many complicated drills and exercises. Herman loved it. He called his horse Sleipner after their faithful old Sleipner at Ekeli.

The cadets had been back in barracks only a short time when there came a brief holiday in June at Pinse (Ascension Day, a national holiday). Herman couldn't wait to get back into Nordmarka to see some of his old friends. This was hiking weather, not skiing weather, and as usual he headed far back into the country, this time to visit his special girlfriend, Marin Val, on the farm where he had spent the previous summer.

It was a strenuous trip to get there, and a great reunion, but the time was all too short. He stayed as late as he dared, knowing that he had to be back at Akershus at four o'clock to curry his horse. At last he left, and hiked fast all through that summer night along the old wood trail. It was not difficult to see, for in Nordmarka the summer night is brief – it is really only twilight, lasting from eleven o'clock in the evening to one o'clock in the morning. Then it is dawn again. He "borrowed" a boat to row the length of Langlia, leaving it hastily at the far end of the lake and hoping the farmer would forgive his unknown night intruder. Then he hurried on down the valley and finally arrived at Akershus at the last possible moment.

He chuckled as he told the story to his family later on. "It was exactly four o'clock and I went to work immediately currying

Sleipner and preparing him for the day's activities. However, I was not in very good shape. My energy was completely used up. I had had no sleep for two nights and had covered many kilometres in Nordmarka as well. To say the least, I was somewhat light-headed when inspection time came round.

"We mounted according to command. We rode in formation. We cantered. We trotted. We halted. We formed a neat line. We stood to attention. And then, while the officer was examining each cadet in minute detail, I suddenly toppled – to Sleipner's great surprise, and to that of everyone else. I had simply fallen asleep right there in the saddle.

"There was a rude awakening as I struck the ground. The shock, on contact, thoroughly woke me up, and I scrambled to remount. The weather, however, had been exceptionally warm, and this mishap was mercifully put down to "the heat" and "general fatigue." Somehow I managed to get through the remainder of the day with no further misfortune. But that night, let me tell you, I *really* slept!"

The summer manoeuvres that followed were a great experience. At first all the cadets camped, eight to a tent, at Sandvika on the fjord near Christiania. Herman cherished for many years a photograph taken on the spot of himself and his seven tentmates caught in an extremely relaxed mood, their uniforms casually unbuttoned, taking their ease. However, life in army camp did include all the necessary work of pitching tents, drilling and marching, and eating and sleeping in temporary quarters in all kinds of weather. And this was only an introduction ...

Several weeks later they had to break camp and transport everything out to Gardermoen, away north of Nordmarka, in new country. There they once more set up their camp with military precision. In a welter of soldiers, horses, smells, and activity, they sweated their way through the dust and the dirt. There were mounted exercises and route marches in the heat of noon, and mosquitoes buzzing hungrily about them in the night. This gave them all a grasp of army life under varying conditions. They realized that, in a way, it was only glorified play-acting, but it was a splendid experience, and altogether something they would remember for the rest of their lives.

Suddenly it was all over. No more drilling. No more classes. Examinations were finished, and they graduated, all of them, each with a plumed hat and a commission as lieutenant in the Royal

Tentmates at summer manoeuvres, Sandvig, Norway, 1894.
Herman, second row, centre.

Norwegian Army Reserve. This military training had consumed a
full year of hard theoretical and practical work and concentrated
effort. Now Herman was free to go to Germany to start his studies
there, but this time things would be different. He would have *status*.
He was an officer in the Royal Norwegian Army Reserve, and as

Herman Smith Johannsen, Lieutenant,
Royal Norwegian Army Reserves, c. 1894.

such he knew he would be looked up to by all his fellow students in Berlin.

The previous fall, in 1893, Mor had taken the whole family down to the photographer for a family portrait. Far and Mor were seated sedately, surrounded by their seven children. Far wore his uniform as a Kommandör in the navy, and Herman stood proudly behind him, buttons shining, as the new cadet. Agnes and Johannes were there as high school students. Then came Fred and Helga and Elisabeth, still in elementary school. And finally there was little Otto, youngest of the family, perched soberly in front in his sailor suit, surveying the future.

This time, a year later, the children were lined up in descending order according to age. Herman was first in line, wearing a business suit, for now he was about to go to Germany for five years of college. Then there was Johannes, resplendent in his midshipman's uniform, about to leave for two years at sea. There was Agnes, just graduating from high school, slim and pretty, and preparing for a teaching career; then Fred, now suddenly much taller; Helga and Elisabeth, both fast becoming young ladies; and at the end of the line young Otto, still in a sailor suit, but definitely growing up. They were altogether a fine-looking family.

In the space of that year, things had changed utterly. Far was leaving for two years of naval duty in the Caribbean, Johannes and Herman too would soon be gone on their own adventures, and Mor would be left at home with the younger children and a student boarder to help her with the housework. The little house on Eilert Sunds Gate would suddenly seem very empty.

CHAPTER SIX

Student Life in Germany: 1894–1899

From the time that spring when he passed his "artium" in Christiania, there was never any doubt that Herman would continue his education. Far agreed that there was an expanding need for engineers, and that he should get the best possible training in this field. Once he had his diploma in mechanical engineering, perhaps he would go to America for more practical training.

During the last half of the 1800s all kinds of possibilities were opening up. In America, Samuel Morse had developed the telegraph, in which the alphabet was reduced to a series of electronic symbols that could be tapped by hand and sent as electrical impulses. These, when received, could be decoded and written down as a "telegram" (or "long distance writing"). Such messages had already become an important part of the business world.

In Canada in 1876, Alexander Graham Bell had managed to convey the actual sound of the human voice over a distance of many miles with his "telephone." Some of these early instruments had already found their way into Norway, where, no longer just a curiosity, they were beginning to be widely used.

In the United States, Thomas Edison, a young telegraph operator, had discovered in 1879 that an electric current could be used to illuminate a light bulb, which led to his invention of the incandescent electric lamp. By 1882 New York City had installed the world's first public illumination by electricity, and throughout America there was much activity in seeking additional uses for this new source of power. Who knew when electricity might even be used to power the streetcars in Christiania, putting all those good horses out of work? These inventions were reported in the Norwegian press and eagerly talked about, but the inventors were usually "lone wolves," and not directly connected with any educational institutions. They worked on their own.

The very best place in Europe for higher studies was Germany. With their passion for theoretical knowledge and their close attention to detail, the Germans were the acknowledged leaders in technology, and it was to Berlin that serious students streamed from all over Europe, from North and South America, and from Australia. A German background was essential; it was the basis for everything else.

When Herman set out in August 1894 to register at the Königlische Technische Hochschule (the engineering school in Charlottenburg, now the University of Berlin), he took with him all the equipment he would need for the next nine months, including, of course, his trusty skis. He went by boat from Christiania to Warnemünde, and then by train across the endless flat miles of northern Germany. He sadly observed that it was not "ski country." However, on the boat he met another Norwegian student, Ditlef Linto, also on his way to Berlin, and the two of them teamed up together as newcomers in this strange new land. Whether or not they would ever be able to use their skis remained to be seen.

They arrived at the huge Lehrter Bahnhof like two bewildered children. They gazed up at the great arched ceiling, which soared on steel beams above the arrival platform. It was vast and overpowering, a real engineering feat. Would they ever be able to create structures like that?

When they finally picked up their bags and threaded their way out through the high portal, they found themselves in the midst of a swirl of activity on the banks of the River Spree. Laden barges were moored at the riverbank as far as the eye could see. Cranes and derricks swung overhead, ready to load or unload their freight along the quayside. Drums and casks and barrels lay piled ready for pick-up by the horse-drawn wagons that trundled over the cobblestones and across the massive stone bridge, which spanned the river. There was plenty of action here, and it was all fascinating,

Student days in Germany, 1894-1899.

but sight-seeing would have to wait. The boys had to find the university and register there without delay.

They found the main university building, out in the suburb of Charlottenburg. It had an impressive high entrance hall, encircled with galleries that led off into corridors, with classrooms and laboratories opening off the corridors. They attended hastily to the necessary formalities, paid their fees, and then set about house-hunting, for there was no official student housing in those days, and everyone had to find private accommodation. As foreigners, they were anxious to find a boardinghouse as soon as possible, before the rush of other students would commence.

They began their search as close to the university as possible, and before long had the good fortune to find a very pleasant home with Frau Berenson on Englischestrasse. There were already two young German boys in residence, but she still had room for Herman and Ditlef, and here they established themselves for what turned out to be five happy years. Frau Berenson was very hospitable, and made them feel quite at home. They came and went as they pleased, but there was always a warm *gemütlich* (friendly) homelike atmosphere in which they could share whenever they wished. A number of other Norwegian students joined them at Frau Berenson's later, including Herman's cousin Anders Beer, until at last they were nine from Norway who made their headquarters with her. They were enrolled separately in medicine, architecture, or engineering, and they soon settled companionably into student life in the big metropolis.

The atmosphere at the university was stimulating. In those days many brilliant people came and went, either as staff or as students, and one could feel the excitement in the air. Guglielmo Marconi, the Italian inventor, was one of these. He was experimenting with wireless communication, hoping to be able to send messages that could be picked up by an unlimited number of receivers. When he came to Charlottenburg, he was delighted to demonstrate his invention there with one of the professors. It was a momentous day when they succeeded in sending a message from one end of the building to the other.

And there was Rudolf Diesel, a brilliant young German student from the Technische Hochschule in Munich, where he had been a protégé of Carl von Linde, the pioneer in electrical refrigeration. Diesel was older than Herman and the others, but they were well aware of his experiments "to make an engine as large as a hut, or as small as a hat," and of his desire to construct a machine that would run easily on any available fuel, "whether whale oil, coal oil, palm oil, or even surplus butter." The students all felt that the trend towards smaller machines and cheaper fuels was of the utmost importance.

Diesel was striving to make an automatic apparatus that would free the engine-user to do something more than merely tend his machine. His dream was to make it possible for independent artisans or craftsmen to compete with large industries, using smaller engines as their source of power. The large steam engines used by heavy industry were, Diesel insisted, oversized, much too expensive, and great wasters of fuel. He worked very hard on his idea, and by 1896 he successfully demonstrated what he called an "internal combustion engine." This, he claimed, was 75 percent more efficient than the old familiar engine run by steam. He went on to become a millionaire, and was hailed throughout Europe as the pioneer of a new age. His invention was destined to supply power to oil fields and pipelines, to automobiles and factories, and a fine future was predicted for him.

Unfortunately, however, despite his genius and his almost overwhelming success, he became increasingly despondent and withdrawn, and eventually, on a trip across the English Channel, Rudolph Diesel simply disappeared; he fell overboard and was drowned. His death was a great loss, for he was in the midst of a most promising career. Diesel had, in fact, a tremendous influence on the rest of the students, and many of Herman's later years were spent in promoting some of the remarkable internal combustion engines that came to bear the name of this former colleague.

Herman found university life very much to his liking. There were students from many countries, and they found that they had much in common, quite apart from their studies. In their free time they walked for miles and miles around the city, exploring every nook and cranny. They admired the splendid Brandenburger Tor spanning Unter den Linden, the thoroughfare that ran through the heart of Berlin. They were awed by the new Reichstag, the parliament building that had just been completed in 1894. And they investigated many of the parks and palaces, churches and museums. These would remain for years among their fondest memories of this great city, but most of all they were to remember the friendliness of its people.

However, there was one thing that Herman keenly missed in his new life, and that was the strenuous exercise to which he had been accustomed in Norway. And so it was with great excitement that he greeted the first snowfall of winter, which transformed Berlin into something that looked more like home. Out came the skis, which he had brought with him for just such an occasion. Here at last was a real chance to stretch his legs. Jubilantly, he set out for the Grünewald, a beautiful, though flat, forested area nearby where he could at least make tracks in and out among trees.

To get to Grünewald he had to ski along the Kurfürstendamm, which at that time was really only a country road, and he happened to pass a schoolhouse just as the children came pouring out for recess. He waved cheerfully to them, and they of course came running, clamouring to see what he was doing on those "crazy sticks." Herman demonstrated briefly by gliding back and forth a few times, and they milled excitedly around him, making quite an uproar.

Suddenly a policeman appeared. "What's going on here?" he asked sternly.

"I'm just skiing," Herman told him. "I'm on my way to the Grünewald."

"You're obstructing traffic!" the officer replied. "No one can obstruct traffic, no matter what the excuse. That will be a three-mark fine!" And he handed him a ticket for "disturbing the peace." Herman removed his skis, shouldered them, and walked soberly on to the Grünewald. What a blow to his Norwegian pride!

❦

Every Saturday evening the boys from Frau Berenson's, looking for a change of scene, used to gather at one or another of the many *Kneipe* (beer halls) on Friedrichstrasse. There they would sip their beer, and order meatballs, pickled herring, or some other German speciality. A long plain counter ran the length of the room. Behind it stood rows of shelves bearing bottles of homemade gooseberry, strawberry, or currant wine, the particular herbal liqueurs produced by the house. In front of the counter were neatly scrubbed and polished small tables, and here they would establish themselves. Customers would drop in for a beer, or a snack, or a conversation, for the Kneipe was the focus of the neighbourhood, where regulars got together to exchange news or gossip, and where newcomers were also welcome. It was a place for general camaraderie.

One evening they had their photograph taken as they posed in the doorway of one of these beer halls, beer mugs and cigars in hand. Another time they were photographed as they played out a scenario in a "railway station," in which Herman appeared as a vagabond with a huge sack on his back, saying goodbye to the rest of the gang as they crowded in the window of a make-believe railway carriage. They always found something new and amusing wherever they went, and they sampled the fare and the atmosphere of many different pubs. They had plenty of fun, and played many a prank, but for the rest of each week they stuck pretty well to their studies.

Early in his first year Herman had met Gerhard Humbert, an upperclassman who was very interested in a student fraternity, the "Berolina," which had been established in 1886, and had as members a very friendly group of predominantly German students. They were a convivial lot, and took a great interest in Herman's tales of military training in Norway, and especially in the fact that he would return to Norway in the summer to go on "manoeuvres." Humbert took him closely under his wing. When Herman returned to university the following fall, it was Humbert who was instrumental in getting him to join Berolina, where as a foreign student he found a warm welcome among those future doctors and chemists and engineers. Each new member was automatically given a permanent number, in chronological order of his induction. Humbert was Number 25, and Herman became Number 50.

Berolina brought him into immediate contact with young men from all over Germany. His new status as a fresh young officer in the Norwegian army reserve had, as he had anticipated, a great deal to do with his induction into Berolina, and this experience helped very much to make him feel at home with his new fraternity brothers. Among them were many who were to be lifelong friends. Their motto and rallying cry was *Nicht rasten und nicht rosten* – "Never rest and never rust" – particularly appropriate for a mechanical engineer.

It was a time-honoured custom in the fraternity for each member to have his own "beer name," a nickname that he kept for life. Herman's was "Jonas," derived presumably from Johannsen. Humbert's was "Stoff," and Stoff and his wife in the years that followed came to personify for Herman much of the wonderful friendship he had found in Berlin. The fine pewter stein they gave him as a Christmas present in 1898, with the date, their names, and the crest of Berolina engraved upon it, was one of his most prized possessions for the rest of his life. It had a cover that opened when a lever on the handle was pressed. At Berolina, if the cover were inadvertently left open when the mug was set down on the table, anyone could clamp his own empty stein down upon it, and thus claim a refill for himself, at the expense of the stein's owner. This could lead to all sorts of interesting results.

Berolina had a *Corpshaus* (headquarters), where the members would meet regularly for general conviviality, to drink beer, share a meal, and often sing far into the night. Although Herman was almost completely tone deaf, he thoroughly enjoyed joining in the songs, and his voice added to the volume, if not to the musical effect. Each member had his own songbook with words and music, and many were the pleasant hours they spent together in carefree comradeship. The covers of these songbooks were studded, front and back, with metal lugs, which effectively prevented the books themselves from touching the tabletop – a clever protective device for times when these surfaces might accidentally overflow with spilled beer.

The winters rolled by, with classes and labs and plenty of work, but every summer, as part of his required practical experience, Herman was expected to take a job in which he would be exposed to real life situations in his chosen field. Among his jobs was one in the summer of 1896 as a machinist's mate on a boat taking a cargo of steel rails, and two new streetcars, to Alexandria, Egypt. They loaded in Hamburg, stowing the rails well down in the hold. The streetcars were fastened securely crosswise on the deck, and the ship took off down the Elbe, through the English Channel, and along the coast of France.

It was an eventful journey. Herman often told the story in later years: "As we started across the Bay of Biscay, a fierce storm blew up, and we soon encountered heavy, mountainous seas. The ship heaved and tossed, and before long some of those steel rails began to shift ... It was a terrifying experience to listen to those loose rails go rattle ... rattle ... bang ... BOOM against the ship's side, as we lunged to starboad down a wave, and then to hear them go rattle ... rattle ... bang ... BOOM against the opposite side, as we lurched up the next billow. There was absolutely no way anyone could go down into the hold to secure them, and we had an anxious time of it, fearing they might punch a hole in the vessel's side.

"Suddenly, another problem claimed our full attention. With the constant rolling and tossing of the ship, both of the streetcars, which we had thought to be very securely fastened on deck, began to work loose from their moorings. Before the situation could be remedied, each of them, one after the other, simply broke loose and rolled back and forth until they broke through the railing, and sank like two great stones to the very bottom! That certainly lightened our load, and as the storm abated we limped into port at Bordeaux. There, at last, we succeeded in securing the rails. We made what repairs we could, and went on to Alexandria minus two major items in our cargo, but with a graphic account of the perils of our stormy passage which, we hoped, would satisfy the insurance brokers."

One of the crew members on a trip the following year was a Libyan Arab, whom Herman got to know quite well. This friend showed him around in various ports as they returned along the Mediterranean coast, picking up and discharging cargo. "Among the ports at which we stopped," Herman recalled, "was Benghazi, in Libya. This was the home town of my Arab friend, and as we had some shore leave, he invited me to his home for a meal. This was an interesting experience in itself, but most surprising of all was a picture hanging in a place of honour on his wall. This showed the crew of a Norwegian vessel on which my friend's father had sailed as a crew member a number of years before. And there in the middle of the picture was *my* father, who had been an officer on board! We had a copy of that same picture at home at our house."

One of Herman's shipboard duties that summer was to keep the propeller shaft well oiled. To accomplish this, he had to stoop low to enter the place in the stern of the vessel where the shaft was turning. There he would straddle the shaft as it revolved, and, holding a lamp in one hand and his oil can in the other, he would wait for the rats to run out between his legs before he went about his oiling. "Those rats always seemed to gang up in there where it was dark and warm," he said, "and my coming was always a surprise. Somehow, I found this was one of the less attractive aspects of that job."

And then in 1898 there occurred a marvellous opportunity. Ever since his early school days, Herman had followed the adventurous careers of Fridtjof Nansen and Otto Sverdrup, the revered heroes of all the Norwegian boys. He recalled how as youngsters they had pretended they were skiing with them, "over the frozen wastes," as Nansen and Sverdrup made their famous crossing of Greenland in 1888. Later, Herman had seen the successful conclusion of the First Fram Expedition, after the ship, which had been frozen fast in the ice north of Siberia, had drifted for more than three years across the Arctic Ocean. It had finally broken loose from the ice near Spitsbergen, and had returned triumphantly to Norway in 1893. Now, in 1898, Otto Sverdrup, who had captained the ship for Nansen, was preparing to lead the Second Fram Expedition. This would explore the islands west of Greenland in Canada's far north. He would be gone from 1898 until at least 1902, and was looking for crew members. Herman was sorely tempted to apply, since just at this time (as he was completing his third year of study), Far had encountered financial difficulties, which made it doubtful that Herman could return to college the following year. Had he been accepted on Sverdrup's expedition, it would at least have assured his living expenses for the duration of the voyage, and it would certainly have provided him with plenty of the adventure he craved. On the other hand, four years of Arctic life would have postponed the completion of his college education for the same length of time, and his entire future would have been affected. It was an extremely tough decision to make.

In the end, Far did find the necessary money for Herman to continue at university, and his dreams of going on the Fram had to be put aside. Just how his life might later have unfolded had he actually gone on that expedition he would never know, but he always felt that the choice he made then was a major turning point in his career.

Instead of sailing with Sverdrup, Herman took a summer job in a big steel rolling mill that belonged to the family of one of his college mates, Konrad von Borsig, in Essen. There, among the blast furnaces and the fuming ovens, he sweated profusely, and there he almost had his fill of the noise and the grime and the smell of heavy industry. But (as he kept telling himself) one must adapt to both the good and the bad.

All in all, his summer jobs provided him with special insight into the manufacture of commercial goods, the problems of short- and long-distance transportation, and the importance of cranes and derricks and hoisting equipment in every aspect of engineering. It was in this particular field that he finally found his specialty. Wherever he was to go in future years, the matter of massive weights and the means of moving them efficiently from place to place would always be among the problems that interested him the most.

Finally his university years were at an end. Herman received his diploma certifying that he was now, indeed, a qualified mechanical engineer. At Englischestrasse he and the Norwegian boys bade a fond *"auf Wiedersehen"* to Frau Berenson, promising to come to visit her whenever they should come back to Berlin. They had one more festive visit to the beer-hall. And at Berolina the fraternity brothers sang their last farewells, with vows to keep in touch as time went by.

The door was closing on five wonderful years of study, friendship, and experience. Now they would go their separate ways, out into the big business world to seek their fortune. Herman looked forward to the next stage of his life with great anticipation.

CHAPTER SEVEN

America, Land of Promise: 1901–1905

In December 1901 Herman sailed into New York Harbour on the steamer *Norge*. The twentieth century was just beginning and he had an irrepressible feeling that he was on the verge of real adventure. He was on the threshold of America, where everything was new and different: the people, the customs, the language, the whole country. It would take a great deal of adjustment, he knew, for him to cope with so much change, but he was willing, able, and eager to begin.

The voyage across had been relatively uneventful and he had thoroughly enjoyed his days at sea. It had been very pleasant to travel as a passenger for a change, and not to have to combat the rats in the hold. On the way over, he had thought often of Far, back in Christiania after his last stint in the Caribbean, and of the serious talk they had had before he left. Far had reminded him that as the oldest son he would be paving the way for his younger brothers who, Far hoped, would in time follow him to the "land of promise."

He thought, too, of Bestefar Herman Smith, and of his voyages some sixty years earlier with those brave Telemarkings, who were also seeking a new life in a new land. How transportation had changed since then! They had been almost two months crossing the ocean over the same route, but Herman had taken a scant two weeks, thanks to the powerful new diesel engines he had seen pioneered in Germany.

In his pocket was a letter of introduction to Alexander Brown of Brown Hoist Machinery Company in New York, from his agent in London. Herman was young and energetic, two years out of Technical University in Berlin. He had already had student apprenticeships in several major factories in Germany; he spoke English reasonably well; he had good European contacts, was fluent in German and the Scandinavian languages, and also had some knowledge of French and Spanish. He was pinning his hopes on the one contact he had: the letter to Brown Hoist. It was his dream that after a period of practical experience in America he would be transferred back to the Continent, in charge of some European branch.

Herman went straight from the boat to Mr Brown's office in downtown Manhattan, marvelling at the narrow streets and towering buildings. Such a lot of people – and every one of them in a hurry! It was not at all like Oslo or Berlin. Everyone here seemed preoccupied, and intent on his own affairs.

Not being exactly sure of his way, he stopped to ask directions of a young fellow coming towards him. He noticed how the young man kept working his jaws and twitching his face. "Poor fellow," he thought, "he must have some nervous disease." But as they talked it became evident he was chewing.

"Tobacco!" Herman surmised, and automatically stepped aside to be out of direct range. But the man did not spit. He swallowed.

Another man passed, making similar faces. "Funny," Herman said to himself. "What kind of people are these? They chew tobacco and swallow the juice!" That was his first encounter with the truly American habit of chewing gum, a practice that in all his years in the New World he was never really able to accept.

Mr Brown received him cordially, and they had a pleasant chat, but as it turned out there was no job opening at the moment in the New York office. However, Mr Brown did mention the possibility of an opening in the drafting room of his Cleveland office, where there had recently been a fire and they were seeking extra help. He gave Herman a further letter of introduction, holding out the hope that he would have a better chance "out there." So it was that on his very first day, one door had already opened, and had closed again. But a second door was about to open in Cleveland, nearly 400 miles away. Herman went out, excited by this new prospect, and determined to try his luck farther west.

Meanwhile, before leaving New York, he wanted to see whatever sights he could. There were tall structures rising flush from the sidewalk, making dark canyons out of the narrow thoroughfares. One twenty-storey building was compressed into an acute angle between two intersecting streets. In a European city such an odd piece of property would undoubtedly have been turned into a tiny park, allowing a little sunlight to filter down. But not in New York, where every square foot meant money.

He was overwhelmed by the Woolworth building, the highest in the world at that time. It tapered inwards towards the top, a huge tower of fifty-two storeys, visible many miles away.

But what impressed him most of all was the monstrous elevated railway, a rapid transit system that ran on double tracks raised on trestles high above the street. All day long, the trains hurtled by, their engines belching smoke and cinders as they hauled their crowded carriages, up and down Third Avenue, on a level with the third-storey windows, while down below in the shadows crept the ordinary traffic, apparently oblivious to the rush and racket overhead.

He strolled along the Battery, stopping to watch the busy tugs and ferries as they churned their way around the harbour, spouting soot and grime. And he went for a walk on Brooklyn Bridge, a soaring wonder that linked the foot of Manhattan Island with the mainland. It was streaming with horse-drawn vehicles, a few newfangled automobiles, some monstrous bicycles and many pedestrians like himself, all anxiously going somewhere. America was a busy country – that he could see. It was full of innovative ideas and exciting promises, and some crazy notions. But, definitely, New York was not for him. It was much too crowded, too impersonal, too big. What was that saying someone had quoted to him the other day? "Go west, young man, go west!" Well, thanks to Alexander Brown, he was on his way.

Herman sat up all night on the train to Cleveland, to save money and to see what he could of this new land as it sped past the windows. Cleveland, although not exactly the West, was partway there. And it had the advantage of being on Lake Erie. Although

Herman Smith Johannsen at 27; in Cleveland,
shortly after his arrival.

this was not to be compared with a Norwegian fjord, it was still
a good-sized body of water. He hoped there would be good rural
country in the neighbourhood, for if this was where he was to
settle for a while, he would need a place where he could get out
and stretch his legs.

He arrived in Cleveland to find that the fire at Brown Hoist had
been a real disaster. The old factory had burned to the ground,
and in this emergency, offices and drafting rooms had been temporarily set up in makeshift quarters, while a new factory was
being constructed on the ruins of the old.

The recommendation he carried from Alexander Brown turned
out to be very useful indeed. Mr Brown had written, "This is a
clean-cut young fellow of the type we need. He makes a good
impression." As a result, this second interview was short but

successful, and Herman found himself being introduced to Mr Wright, the chief engineer, who was in charge of the drafting room. He was to discuss the matter of salary with Mr Wright.

They went down together to look over the working area, and there Herman had a chance to size up the situation. It was obvious that there was plenty of work to be done. General conditions were certainly not good, but the new building would be complete in a few months, and better things were in sight. For the moment, many of the men were working in their overcoats to keep warm in the chilly drafting room, but Herman was optimistic, and it was good to feel that he was actually on the verge of a job. To be sure, the staff members were grumbling, but he felt he was as hardy as any of them, and looked upon such a temporary inconvenience as more of a challenge than a set-back. It would simply be up to him to "deliver the goods."

Cleveland was a thriving industrial city at that time. In fact, it had become the seventh largest metropolis in the United States, already boasting more than a third of a million citizens. Coal, iron, and oil were the basic raw materials, and its burgeoning factories, spread along Lake Erie, were churning out everything from machine tools, boats, wagons, and electrical goods to bicycles, sewing machines, and ready-to-wear clothing. Binding the whole together was a growing network of railroads, whose tracks radiated outward, far to the east, south and west.

Brown Hoist occupied an important part in this busy scene, doing business throughout the length and breadth of America. The railways were being further expanded. New mines were being developed. The lumber trade was booming. And all these industries required heavy machinery, such as steam shovels for excavating, lifts of all kinds, and cranes for transporting massive weights. Brown Hoist manufactured derricks and pile drivers and other equipment to serve all these many needs, and it was hard pressed to keep up with demand.

Mr Wright immediately brought up the matter of salary. Herman had been led to hope that he might earn $125 per month but, according to Mr Wright, this was out of the question. Wright observed that Herman's English was hesitant, and declared that at least at the beginning, until he became more familiar with

American ways, he would undoubtedly be a "slow drafter." He offered a starting salary of $100 per month. "Take it or leave it."

Herman had been planning to send home a portion of his pay, but at $100 a month it would be impossible. He considered turning down the job on the spot, but then he thought better of it. For the time being, it would be better to wait and see how things turned out. Once he had proved himself, he would be in a position to apply for a raise. He accepted.

He was shown to a drafting table, and assigned to "squad A." This was an invention of Mr Wright's, designed to promote competition and thereby increase production. It was easy to see that Wright was a power to be reckoned with, a kind of army sergeant.

Mr Wright, it seemed, was not at all popular with the men, who secretly referred to him as "Mr Wrong." He called himself an efficiency expert, but "slave driver" would have been a more accurate name. It did not take the newcomer long to get his number. True, Wright did stimulate the work, but he had peculiar means of gaining his ends. "Time is money," he would say again and again, and he was determined to squeeze every last minute of working time out of his men. He had a disconcerting way of moving silently about the drafting room in his rubber-soled shoes, peering unexpectedly over the shoulders of the men as they worked. At the same time he would nervously jingle the keys in his pocket. Whenever this jingling sound approached, pencils and rulers would fly into action, and everyone appeared to be intensely busy, although more often than not this was meaningless show, rather than evidence of real progress.

One of Wright's most hated innovations was his supervision of the washroom. Some of the draftsmen, he felt, spent too much time in the W.C. One man, it was true, used to spend some time, while sitting there, bringing his diary up to date! Wright decided to appoint a lavatory inspector; the man chosen for the task was the employee whose desk was closest to the washroom door. It was his duty to record the length of time each man spent away from his desk — in other words, he was a spy. This method, while it did discourage the journal-writing, failed to produce any other outstanding results, and Wright soon resorted to other tactics. He threatened to install a timing device on the toilet tank. After a due interval of pressure on the seat, a blast of cold water would be set off, which would certainly have shortened the stay of any malingerer! This would have been an ingenious solution, to say the least, but even though the system was never put into effect, it confirmed Mr Wright's reputation as a veritable "Simon Legree."

Herman found it hard at first to accept these new and petty ways. Wright's overbearing attitude was bad enough, but Herman also had to contend with some co-workers who assumed that Americans were superior to everyone else. Foreigners were automatically suspect, because they were "different." And in this respect Herman certainly qualified. Things here were not at all what he was used to. People were rough and ready, loud spoken, even rude. Where he came from, people bowed politely and shook hands when introduced. Here, they said, "Hi," and let it go at that. He had been to military college, where discipline meant self-discipline, second nature, not something enforced from outside. He had graduated from the Technical University in Berlin, and spoke English with an accent that was definitely not American. His manners and education, it appeared, were regarded as peculiarities rather than assets by those who had never ventured more than 400 miles from the Mississippi. Ordinary politeness seemed to make some of them ill at ease. "That Norwegian," said Mr Wright one day to a man in the head office. "What the hell is he after with all his fancy ways? You can't trust these foreigners. They're up to no good!"

But Herman stood his ground. He could work just as hard as the rest of them, harder in fact, and be a gentleman at the same time. He was certainly not going to lower *his* standards.

His letters home to Norway were full of amusing descriptions of what went on. "One day during lunch hour," he wrote, "while we were eating our sandwiches in the drafting room, I finally had a run-in with one of the boys, a young fellow, one of Wright's few devotees, who teased me about my 'curly hair and fancy ways.' I took his taunting good-naturedly at first, for I had found it best to ignore this sort of antagonism, but then he went a little too far – and I suddenly went for *him*. I had had enough. In the scuffle, I tossed him neatly under one of the tables ... I can see him there yet, peering out between the table legs ...

"'You just stay there a little while,' I said, 'and think things over!' The others looked on, enjoying it immensely. That fellow never bothered me again, and what was more important, the episode actually gained me the respect of all the drafting-room gang."

Later on, Herman wrote to Johannes, "Everyone here in Cleveland claims to be very 'sports minded,' but this is very different from the way we look at things in Norway. From the time you and I were very small, sport has always meant to us personal exertion and strenuous exercise both in summer and winter. Whether it was hiking, climbing, skiing, sailing or swimming, these sports always had about them a spirit of keen competition. Such activities always involved getting into an honest sweat, working off our energy, excelling in whatever we were doing, and above all having fun doing it.

"Here the attitude is completely different. Baseball is the common denominator, and this is primarily a spectator sport. You take your girl to the ball park on Saturday afternoon. You sit in the bleachers. You eat crackerjack. And you yell for the home team. Everyone talks baseball. In fact, it is said that you can walk down any street in Cleveland in the afternoon after a game and ask almost any stranger, 'What was the score?' and get the right answer because he was there himself. In fact, the most popular song here is 'Take me out to the ball game!' Everyone sings it. But while on Sundays in church they sing, 'Stand up, stand up for Jesus,' at the ball game they simply yell, 'For Christ's sake, sit down! Play ball!'"

Among the men in the drafting room there were two in squad A to whom Herman took a liking from the very start. Will Fewsmith and Locky Lockwood were obvious "live wires," and he was interested to learn that Locky owned a small sailboat, the *Flirt*, in which he and Will and some of their friends would sail up and down Lake Erie on summer weekends. They invited Herman to go with them sometime in the summer when the sailing season opened. During the winter, they said, they usually went skating on some of the frozen ponds around the city.

Herman had to admit that skating was a sport he knew very little about. He told them, though, that he had brought his skis with him and was looking forward to a big snowfall, although Cleveland, they assured him, was "definitely not in the regular snow belt." They were curious, however, for they had not seen skis before, and they could not imagine how anyone could get around in deep snow "with those awkward long boards on your feet." "When the time comes, I'll show you," Herman promised, and they let it go at that.

Meanwhile, it was difficult to find suitable living quarters. The first place he had tried, a rooming house near the corner of Wilson and Euclid avenues, turned out to be alive with bedbugs. He had to find something better than that! Finally, he rented a room from a motherly soul, Mrs. Agnew, who took in as boarders a number of young men from out of town who also were seeking a "home away from home." When Herman moved in, skis and all, she was filled with good-natured curiosity.

Unexpectedly, a big storm struck. Cleveland was plunged into a state of emergency, for the unusually heavy fall of snow completely disrupted everything. Streetcars were stalled, all ordinary traffic came to a standstill, and the city was virtually paralysed. But as far as Herman was concerned, conditions couldn't have been better – this was just what he had been waiting for. He rushed home after work, changed into sports clothes, shouldered his skis and took off for Wade Park, a wooded area not far away that had been given to the city a number of years before by a wealthy local millionaire. It was uneven ground, laced with little walking paths that were not completely hidden under the snow. Here he had a splendid time breaking in a real cross-country ski trail over the little hills and valleys. He had to admit it was not exactly Nordmarka, but under the circumstances it was not bad. In all of Cleveland, there was no one else on skis, so he had the Park all to himself that evening, and when he came home flushed and exuberant, to regale his fellow boarders with his triumph, they were properly impressed, and fingered his "boards" with growing respect.

The next day, Sunday, he was at it again. By afternoon, people had begun to come out of hibernation and were trudging along the snowy paths, battling the drifts and enjoying the winter air. They were amazed to see the ski tracks he had made last night, going up and down over the bumps and depressions where no paths led, and not a few of them were openly astonished as they watched him glide rhythmically past.

Topping a small rise, Herman saw in the hollow beneath him a crowd of young people, skating on a pond from which the snow had been laboriously shovelled away to make a skating rink. They were swirling around and laughing and thoroughly enjoying themselves as he slid down beside the pond to watch. And to his surprise, whom should he spot among them but his two friends, Will and Locky from squad A! They had seen him slaloming down among the trees, and with the whole group they clustered eagerly at rinkside to inspect those funny things he had on his feet.

Will and Locky made introductions all around, explaining that this was "the new man at Brown Hoist." The young people looked over his equipment with interest, and frankly shook their heads.

One particularly pretty girl said right away, "What fun that must be! Wherever did you learn to do that?"

"Well, she-ing is what we always do back home," he replied, enthusiastically mispronouncing every second word. He still had trouble with "sk." "Everyone does a lot of she-ing in winter in Norway." They looked at one another, both amused and amazed. "It's the only way to travel in Norway in winter," he explained. "You make use of the snow, instead of just pushing it away, as you do here."

"But can you really go places on those things?" asked one of the men.

"We sure can," Herman said. "All we need is a good pair of shes, some snow, a pole, or sometimes two, to push with, – and away we go!" He strode off a few paces, did a quick kick turn, and slid back to them.

"It looks so easy!" said the first girl, wide-eyed and clearly fascinated.

"And it is," he replied, rising quickly to the occasion. "Would you like to try?" Little did he realize at that moment that this was the beginning of a wonderful relationship, which was to last for almost sixty years. Alice Robinson, the young skater, was a kindergarten teacher. She was an only child, the daughter of a judge. Her father had been a young medical officer during the American Civil War, after which he had taken up up law. She lived with her parents in a house on Genesee Avenue, and, it turned out, was Will Fewsmith's "best girl." Two of the other girls, Carrie Kingsbury

Alice Robinson in 1899
when she was 18.

and Sue de Witt, were Alice's special friends, and with them were
Will's sister, Anna, and Margaret, Locky's girl. The three other men
were engineers, and altogether they were a lively and an interesting
lot. They invited Herman to join them some other evening, and
as he skied away he had the warm feeling that he had found at
last some compatible friends, for he was really beginning to feel
rather lonely in this strange new city. Thanks to Will and Locky,
it was not long before he was an accepted member of this com-
panionable group.

Meanwhile, things at the office were also improving. As the new
building neared completion, plans were under way for a gala affair,
a ball, which would take place in the new drafting room. There
they would celebrate the opening of the enlarged offices and the
completely modernized factory. The entire staff of Brown Hoist
was invited, including everyone from head office – the managers,
the field men, the secretaries – and, of course, all the "slaves" in
the drafting room, each with his own partner. It would be by far
the most important social event of the season, with an orchestra,
a catered dinner with wine, and dancing far into the night.

When the day finally dawned, furniture was moved aside, bright streamers and big balloons completely transformed the atmosphere, and everyone entered into the spirit with zest. Even Alexander Brown was coming from New York!

Herman's own social life at this point was at a low ebb. Most of the fellows living at Mrs Agnew's had girls of their own, whom they occasionally brought home to dinner. Mrs Agnew, herself, did her best for the others by inviting some unattached young girls from the neighbourhood to come in for the evening now and then "to liven things up." In fact, Herman had asked one of these girls to the ball. But when she told her parents, they put their feet down – hard! "What?!" they said. "Go to such a swanky affair with a foreigner? No way!"

The only other girls he knew, like Margaret and Carrie and Sue and Alice, were already coming with their own beaux. What could he do, short of missing the event entirely? Obviously, the answer was simply to go alone.

At the university in Germany it had been customary, for any formal function such as a special event at Berolina, to wear a "Prince Albert," a long dark coat with tails. He had his with him and, indeed, had been keeping it in perfect condition for just such an occasion as this. He got it out and carefully spruced it up. He polished his shoes with military precision, got a haircut, and dressed with great care.

And arrived at the ball to find that all the other men were wearing plain business suits! After all, out here in the Middle West, people were far removed from such European formality. Quite unexpectedly, he stood out as one of a kind, resplendent in his dress suit. He was, in fact, a sensation. One of the young ladies remarked breathlessly, "Why, he looks like a real Norwegian nobleman!" And that set the stage for a fantastic evening.

As for the girls, they were all simply beautiful in their long gowns with tightly fitting waists and bodices. Carrie and Sue looked especially lovely. But Alice! She was to his mind, absolutely the queen of the ball, and, truth to tell, he envied Will his good fortune.

The dinner was excellent, the music exhilarating, and the conversation, aided no doubt by the wine, was gay and amusing. Herman's English was slowly improving, but he still had an unmistakable Norwegian accent. However, he was in a particularly good mood that evening, and managed to contribute his own share to the festivities with stories and jokes. In fact, he was hailed as quite a raconteur. His tales of Europe and his travels in Egypt had the ring of truth. They were pleasingly exotic to these people, most of whom had never travelled much beyond the Sandusky River in Ohio.

After dinner, though dancing was not one of Herman's specialties, he was eagerly taken in hand by the girls, and the evening was a resounding success. It established him among his peers, and at last he began to feel at home in America.

❧

The Brown Hoist Machinery Company was particularly interested in a new furnace hoist that was being pioneered at one of the big steel companies in Pittsburgh. The raw iron ore, shipped all the way down to Pennsylvania from the Mesabi Range on Lake Superior, was being made into steel in huge blast furnaces whose belching smoke had earned for Pittsburgh the highly descriptive title of "Hell with the lid off." This was the source of some of those thousands of shiny steel rails that were being laid down across the plains and prairies of the west.

It was shortly after the ball, probably because Alexander Brown had been present and they had briefly renewed their acquaintance, that Herman was put in charge of drawings and engineering plans for the new furnace-hoist division. The promotion was certainly a welcome change. He had achieved a certain speed in the drafting room, but had recently applied to Old Wright for a raise and been refused. This unexpected new responsibility was definitely an upward step. He was anxious to do his best, especially since it would mean an end to his jockeying with Mr Wright.

He tackled the new job with enthusiasm, and when one of the new hoists suddenly broke down in Pittsburgh, he was sent immediately to straighten out the mess. Telegrams began to fly, and the affair was put to rights, but when he returned to Cleveland he made it clear that "I am not in this business just for the love of blast furnaces." He had proved not only that he understood

Bucyrus, steamshovel no. 4 used for clearing the route
of the Canadian National Transcontinental Railway, c. 1909.

machinery, but that he also knew how to handle customers. And
he got his raise.

By early 1903, business was becoming more and more competitive, and with the new factory in full swing it was evident that
the time had come to appoint a field manager, someone who could
go out into the hinterland wherever the action was, who could
size up the client's needs and recommend the best possible
machinery to do the job. Brown Hoist was finding it hard to locate
a young man who was free to travel about the country, often to
out-of-the-way places where conditions were primitive, accommodation poor, and the general situation somewhat risky. This
nomadic kind of life appealed to very few, and no one had as yet
shown any desire to leave the comfortable city and venture into
the unknown.

From Herman's viewpoint, however, what could have been
better? He had no immediate family ties, he was entirely free to
come and go, and he had the necessary mechanical expertise. He
also had an enormous interest in seeing the country. This, he
sensed, was a job with a future. No longer would he be tied to a

drafting table. He could be out of the office, enjoying fresh air and adventure in the course of his work. It was the very job for him. And his English was improving by leaps and bounds.

He applied and was accepted. And he soon found the job was a dream come true. Whenever a new inquiry would come to head office from distant parts, as for example from Ontario, in Canada, where the Temiskaming and Northern Ontario Railway was pushing its way up into the wilderness, and where the Grand Trunk Railway was opening farther to the West, he would be sent out to reconnoitre. This was a special kind of pioneering, and it brought him into contact with difficult conditions in many parts of the country, areas that he would not otherwise have had an opportunity to see.

From North Bay, for example, it meant going out ahead of the line of steel to check the terrain through which the railway would pass, to see where trestles had to be built over deep ravines, and to ascertain where great quantities of fill would be required to level the roadbed. It meant following the surveyors and really getting the feel of the land, as it alternated between spongy muskeg and hard, forbidding bedrock. He would then be in a better position to recommend the steam shovels, ballast unloaders, and track-laying equipment best suited to local conditions. And it would be up to him to make the sale to the railroad authorities. On this he would get a commission.

It was on one of these reconnoitring trips that he made his first contact with the Cree, through whose territory the railway was being constructed. His knowledge of Indians had been vividly coloured by the games he had played as a boy with his friends in Laurvig, when they chased each other around the rocky hillsides, playing "Indians and white men." In those games, all Indians were "bad."

He soon discovered that reality was very different. These Cree were real woodsmen, living almost entirely off the land. They were hunters, trappers, and fishermen, who roamed freely in the forest and knew all its secrets. They were shy people, reserved but curious, and understandably apprehensive about the frantic activity that was disrupting their homeland. Some, it was true, were employed by the railroad as woodcutters and handymen, but most of them clung to their old nomadic traditions, going about their hunting in the same way as their ancestors had for generations past.

Herman had a chance to visit one of their encampments during a trip that first winter, just as the men were setting out to follow their trapline on showshoes. He had (of course!) brought his skis with him, as this was the only way for him to get around in the bush, and the Indians were astonished to see how he managed to make his way through thick woods in deep snow. He had some difficulty in communicating with them, but they struggled along as best they could, and the Indians agreed to let him come along to visit their traps. To everyone's surprise Herman made as good time as they did, breaking trail on the level. Going uphill, he could almost keep up with them, but on the downhill runs he was far ahead. On skis, he was free to slide, while the snowshoers could only continue to tramp doggedly along. This was a revelation to them.

He was impressed, in turn, by their ingenious snowshoes, made according to a time-honoured tribal pattern of rawhide strips twisted and laced into a wooden frame. He had to concede that snowshoes were more practical when it came to working in deep snow around the traps, but the Indians agreed with him that for travelling the long stretches from one trapping ground to the next, his skis were faster and easier.

They taught him a few words in Cree, which stayed with him over the years, and continued to prove useful from time to time.

Eyinew naheyowao, for example, means "He is an Indian. He speaks Cree." *No tako tao* means "He is hungry," and *Akwu mechsisutak* means "Let us eat."

Herman remembered the Cree with great respect, and looked forward to meeting them again.

Between jaunts around the country, he would be back to Cleveland to catch up on office work and prepare for the next trip. On one of these occasions during the following summer, he was invited to go out sailing on the *Flirt*.

They were a jolly crew of six, including Margaret, Sue, Alice, Will, Locky, and Herman, and the little boat bounced along on the waves, tacking back and forth on the way to Put-in Bay in the islands off Toledo. The weather was beautiful, sunny and warm. Herman was happy to be back with these good friends. He could

Group on *Flirt*, 6 August 1904,
sailing on Lake Erie off Ricky River.
Alice Robinson, Will Fewsmith, Margaret Fahnestock,
and Locky. Photo taken by Herman.

see that they all thought a great deal of Alice – he gave them credit for that! – and he certainly agreed, but he kept his own thoughts to himself. For the time being he was content just to be there, saying quietly to himself, again and again, "She's all right!"

There were other trips after that, some of them north into Canada to the Muskoka lakes. They camped there several times in that lovely country, which reminded him so much of Norway. It was during one of these excursions that he began to sense a growing mutual interest between Alice and himself. "Let's say, there was no frost in the air. No violets yet, but things were moving!"

And just about this time there came yet another change at Brown Hoist. Will was suddenly, and permanently, transferred to Pittsburgh on a brand-new job. Just before he left, he said to Herman, "Please take good care of Alice for me while I am gone."

And that is exactly what Herman did.

❧

With his new job as field manager he began to realize that the United States was a very big country indeed. More and more inquiries were coming in from out-of-the-way places, and he would always be sent to investigate.

Some of these inquiries came from companies that were involved in a huge project: widening the channel of the Ohio River. They needed dredging machinery, drag-line cranes with grab-buckets, to remove the heavy silt that was constantly obstructing navigation. The material removed would be piled along the riverbanks to reinforce weak spots and to guard against perennial spring floods. The widened channels also made it easier for river boats to ply the waters downstream from Cincinnati to join the Mississippi some five hundred miles southwest of Cleveland, "as the crow flies." On the map of Europe that was just about the distance between Christiania and Berlin, but in America it was no more than one-seventh of the distance between the Atlantic and Pacific Oceans.

Other inquiries came from logging companies in Minnesota where machinery was needed for the forests north of Minneapolis, and from Colorado, eight hundred miles farther west, where hoists and ore-handling equipment were required for the mines at Lead-ville and Aspen. All this kept him constantly on the go, and as he criss-crossed the plains, mile after lonesome mile, he had plenty of time to think.

He remembered how in Cleveland, before he had made his first trip west, someone had said to him, "Watch out when you're out there! You'll be getting into country that's really wild. And it's not just the country that's wild, it's the Indians. The only good Indian is a dead one."

That attitude shocked him, for he had seen how the Cree in Northern Ontario still lived off the land, and how they made careful use of everything nature provided, wasting nothing. He admired their adventurous way of life, their ingenuity, their sim-plicity. He could see that the railway would definitely change things for the Indians in general, but in Canada there was still plenty of "bush" left in the north, and they were free to travel as far from the railroad as they pleased, into land as yet uninvaded by settlers.

In the United States, however, the situation was very different. "Civilization" was pushing westward with surprising speed, and the Indians were being overrun and shoved aside, their lands taken from them. Treaty after treaty between whites and Indians had been broken or changed, as new laws were made to accommodate the white people who were spreading across the country like a remorseless tide.

It was true he had heard lurid tales of how some of the western Indians, for example, had fought the railway gangs as they laid track for the Kansas Pacific Railroad in the 1860s. These tribes had done their best to stop the onward rush of the "iron horse," but they had lost. The railway had continued, and now this and other rail lines were spreading out across the western states. The buffalo herds, once so plentiful on the plains, were dwindling rapidly as the land became divided. The Indians were being pushed farther and farther from the land that had once been all their own. Their whole way of life was changing, just as the habitat was being changed. And meanwhile white settlers continued to break the sod, and white miners continued to stake their claims wherever they went, in the mistaken belief that all this land was theirs simply for the taking. The white people were winning through ignorance, as well as through sheer force of numbers.

Herman slowly realized what was actually happening. On his own trips west he was riding over the very trails that the Indians forty years before had tried so desperately to intercept and destroy. And here he was, engaged in selling machinery that was actively despoiling more territory, levelling the forests, excavating the soil, constructing railways, roads, and cities, and all this on former Indian lands now in possession of white men! His machines were helping to make possible all this "progress." They were actually changing the face of America forever, and he himself was an active participant in this enormous transformation.

As he rode the train, he had been reading a recently published book, *Indian Boyhood*, by O-hi-e-sa, a Sioux, who spoke eloquently of the way of life of his forebears on these open plains. O-hi-e-sa had been born to the old Indian ways, but had been adopted at an early age by white people and educated as a white man under the name of Charles A. Eastman. He had graduated from Dartmouth College in 1887 and received his MD from Boston University in 1890; he had then married a white woman, and was now actively practising medicine, but he was profoundly moved by the enormous change in attitudes that he saw taking place during his own lifetime, and he felt that this was something about which he needed to write.

Herman was deeply moved by the book, for he could sense that O-hi-e-sa stood poised between two worlds. On the one hand, he could see clearly the old Indian way of life, in which each mountain, river, bird, and animal had a spirit of its own, a world in which the Indians shared equally, and from which they took no more than they needed for their own survival. At the same time he could see the white man's world, scornful of these sacred attitudes, where men seemed always to be reaching farther and deeper into Nature herself in their constant search for personal and material gain. These were two concepts in mortal conflict, and the realization spread like a cloud above him. They were all caught in a trend that they were powerless to stop. Herman tried to console himself with the thought that this was the way civilization was going, and that he, too, had to make a living. He hoped that somehow the problems would all sort themselves out, but meanwhile machinery was needed, and it was his job to make the sales. For the moment he had to set his doubts aside, and keep doggedly on.

In between these trips he was back in Cleveland, where he saw Alice and her friends. Life on the road was strenuous, and he looked forward more eagerly than ever to those times when Alice and he could go for a little relaxation out to Gates Mills and other quiet places, and just sit and talk. He told her about his childhood, about Norway and Nordmarka, and she would always listen attentively to his stories. "Some day you'll have to see Norway yourself," he told her once. Her response was instantaneous: "I'd surely love to!" And he could see there were stars in her eyes.

Meanwhile, things were not going so well at the office. He had now been several years on these travels, and was seeing plenty of North America. Now and then there would be another inquiry from Canada, where he could once again get out on his skis if it happened to be winter, and he could visit with his old friends, the Indians. He was making sales all the time, but life was always unsettled. Brown Hoist was not as progressive as he could have wished, and it was apparent that the company was not interested in expanding into Europe. He could see his original dream beginning to fade.

It was just at this period that one of the competing companies, Browning Engineering, offered him a job in its sales department. Eric Browning, the boss, was a real "go-getter," and he *was* interested in the European market. So, after much soul-searching, Herman reluctantly submitted his resignation to Brown Hoist.

Then there was a flurry of excitement. Old Wright, the "slave driver," did his best to hold him. Wright even wrote him a letter, saying he was "one of the best engineers I've ever had in my employ," but Herman knew full well that didn't mean a thing. "I was the *only engineer* he had in his employ! The others were all just draftsmen. What a gas bag," he said. "Good riddance."

But squad A got together and presented Herman with a silver matchcase to commemorate his four and a half years with the firm, and this he treasured for many years. On it was engraved a jaunty motor car of the very latest model. This was enough to make a young man's head spin, for in 1905 Cleveland was becoming a recognized power in the automotive industry. The car on the matchcase was definitely a sign of things to come. "Some day," Herman mused, "I might even own one."

So, in October 1905, he signed up with Browning Engineering Company, and set his eyes on the busy years ahead.

His new job was definitely a cause for celebration, and so he took Alice to Hallowe'en dinner at the Hollenden Hotel, Cleveland's finest. She looked particularly lovely that night, and Herman was prouder than ever to show her off. This was one of their rare ventures into "high society," and he remembered how fascinated she was by all she saw, observing everything in minute detail, the décor, the orchestra, and their fellow guests. There were flowers on the table, and candles; the atmosphere was intimate and charming. The only trouble was that Alice was so busy taking in the scenery that he could hardly get any attention for himself. She was, however, having a wonderful time, and he let her enjoy herself to the full.

Then, in a pause between the soup and the entrée, while the orchestra was playing softly, he reached quietly into his breast pocket and took out an envelope. He placed it on the table before her. "You said you'd love to go to Norway sometime," he said. "What do you think of these?"

She took the envelope, and opened it cautiously. And there were two tickets on the mailsteamer *Pretoria* of the Hamburg America Line!

Alice was dumbfounded. She looked at him in consternation, the blood rushing to her cheeks. "But I didn't mean now!" she blurted out. "How could I go now? Oh, Herman!"

Only then did he realize what a blunder he had made. He had only meant to dramatize the fact that Browning was sending him to Europe to "scout out the markets on the other side." He had to confess that the second ticket was not for her at all, but for a colleague who was to go on the same ship. He had picked up both tickets that very day, and had thought it would be fun to tease her!

Again she said, "Oh, *Herman!*" but she was visibly relieved, and she quickly added, "I didn't see how you could really mean it, for we're not even engaged!"

"Well, that sure broke the ice," Herman declared emphatically. And then, pursuing his advantage, he put the question to her, "Don't you think it's time we really were?"

CHAPTER EIGHT

Postcard Romance: 1905–1906

It was hard to believe that he would not be seeing Alice again for nearly six months. This new job with Browning Engineering had certain advantages, but a long separation from his fiancée was not one of them. There was no denying the fear that someone else might step in and snatch her from him when he was not around to assert his prior claim. After all, had he not stepped in successfully when Will Fewsmith had been transferred to Pittsburgh? How could he know that Will, or someone else, might not now enter the picture while he was away? However, this was a chance he had to take, and he made up his mind that Alice would be reminded of him at every bend in his road. When he returned to Cleveland the next spring, things would definitely be different.

That was how it happened that the moment Herman found himself back in New York, he dashed off his first postcard. It showed a hobo with holes in his shoes, reclining in the shade of an old apple tree. He was reading the *Stock Market Report*, under which Herman had carefully inscribed, 'But feeling pretty lonesome! Best regards, HSJ.' There was also a brightly coloured picture of the *Pretoria* under full steam. "Nov. 4. We're just sailing out of the harbour with a German band playing. The pilot will take this ashore with him tomorrow. Goodbye. HSJ."

Then there came a gap, indicating the passage of time in transit, and at last there arrived a whole flurry of cards, all postmarked in London. They were delivered by the Cleveland letter carrier in a bundle, all held together with a rubber band! Now Alice could share with him the sights he was seeing. There was Piccadilly Circus crowded with horse-drawn double-decker buses, with ladies and gentlemen riding both above and below deck. There was Hyde Park Corner with more streams of horse-drawn traffic. There was Sunday afternoon in Rotten Row with hansom cabs, elegant horsemen, and ladies with parasols strolling along the boulevard. There was St Paul's Cathedral by day and by night. And Westminster Abbey, within and without. And finally Trafalgar Square, with the moon riding high over Nelson's Monument. Across the clouds Herman had written discreetly, "I always see the moon in London. Remember Put-in Bay? Well, it's the same moon shining over here!"

There were lots more postcards. "It's almost like being there," Alice declared as she entered them all chronologically in her album, allowing plenty of room for later additions as the months wore on. Meanwhile, Herman was busy calling on all the companies to which Brown Hoist or Browning had already sold machinery, and letting them know that "we are still very much in business."

In London he eagerly looked up Locky and Margaret Lockwood who had been married some months before in Cleveland. Locky had left Brown Hoist, and they were now well established in London. "We had a great time together last night," Herman wrote to Alice, "but we sure missed you!"

From London he went on to York, and then to Newcastle. On December first he sent a card from Glasgow, on the second from Belfast, on the fourth from Liverpool. "Leave for London tomorrow afternoon. Am having as good a time as possible, but rather lonesome. I just had a very good dinner here at the Midland Hotel, but do not feel quite as happy as the young fellow in this corner." The card showed an attentive young couple dining tête-à-tête in the Garden Terrace. "Hope to hear from you when I get back to London. Best regards, HSJ."

There must have been a satisfactory exchange of letters at this point, for the next card was dated December 8. "Arrived Brussels about noon today and met a cousin of mine with whom I will have a good time tonight. I haven't seen him for twenty years, not since he was the little boy peering over the railing beside me in that family picture from Bestefar Smith's house in Horten!"

"December 9. Went to Antwerp this morning and am now going back to Brussels on an awfully shaky train. Off to Paris tomorrow. Best regards."

From Paris there were cards from the Arc de Triomphe, and the Opera, and on December 12 from Cologne. "Had to stop here overnight," he said on a card of the great cathedral. "Besten Grüss, Herman." Then on to Bremen, and Kiel, and Copenhagen, from which there came a jaunty little catboat, across the sail of which he had written, "The Danish *Flirt*." And at last he crossed the border into Norway. What a joy it was to see those snowy hills again, and the evergreen trees crowding down to the fjord.

His arrival in Christiania had been conveniently timed to coincide with a special family event, the wedding of Johannes and Tul. Johannes was now a young naval officer, following in the footsteps of both Far and Bestefar Smith. All the family had managed to come together, with the exception of Fred who was studying in France, and who would, Herman hoped, come to visit him in Cleveland next year. Mor was in excellent form and just as lovely and warm as he had always remembered her, but it was a shock to realize that Far had never fully recovered from the stroke he had suffered three years before. What was most frustrating for him was the almost complete loss of his power of speech, although he was otherwise in fair health. He liked to go on long walks, and he listened with great interest to all Herman had to tell of his life in America. All the rest of the family were fine. There were Agnes, now teaching school; Elisabeth, newly engaged to Ole Christiansen; Otto, a lively young skier of fifteen; and Helga, who had been married in October to Christopher Meyer, another naval officer. It was wonderful to be all together again, and to see how their family tree was beginning to branch out.

Herman lost no time in contacting the American-based Norsk Kulkompani, which was opening some coal mines in Spitsbergen, the islands six hundred miles north of North Cape in Norway, and he was delighted to receive an order for several large cranes. It was a good beginning, and augured well for future business connections there. He immediately sent off a letter to Alice with the good news, followed by another barrage of postcards. Among these there were happy couples skiing on the hill above Frognerseteren, a cross-country racer dodging among the snow-laden trees in Nordmarka, and two sportily clad girls with tight-fitting white jackets and long flowing skirts skiing among the drifts at Holmenkollen. There was also a picture of a large party of young people with sleds and skis, some of them carrying flaming torches that scattered bits of burning bark behind them as they careened down a long winding road. "This shows how they coast and run skis here after dark," he explained. "This hill is four or five miles long in a single stretch."

But the prize picture of all was a lively winter scene near the old farm of Bonna, showing a horse pulling a sleighful of logs from the backwoods down to the lake "in preparation for the spring drive when the ice goes out." This was the Nordmarka he had known so well in his early youth, and this was the country in which Herman and a few others were planning a special Christmas ski tour. Across the bottom of this card his sister, Elisabeth, had written neatly, "Best regards from Elisabeth Johannsen."

On this trip there was, first of all, young Otto, eager for a last trip into the hills before taking off on a two-year voyage with the navy; then his sister Agnes and two of her girlfriends, Anna Rye and Tia Horn; and Herman himself, who was longing to set off on this three-day excursion, and recalling vividly the famous trip of ten years before, when Anders Beer, Asbjörn, and he had skied at Norefjell and had met Roald Amundsen in the blizzard.

This time the weather was clear and cold. The snow was sparkling. The girls all wore long woollen skirts that swept the snow, but didn't hamper their skiing ability in the least. They all used a single pole, but Herman preferred to use two. Somehow this gave him more balance, and a better push. Each of them also carried a knapsack with extra clothing against the cold, and emergency food, in case they should need it.

In 1905 long overnight treks through the bush were still the exception rather than the rule, and they had to break a fresh track for most of the way, each taking a turn in the lead. This was a new experience for everyone but Herman, and none of them had ever made as long a winter trip as this before. They found it exciting to have their brother from America as their special guide. For him it was like turning back the clock, for Nordmarka was just as invigorating and as reassuring as ever. It had remained pristine and unspoiled, so different from America, where civilization was stretching out its tentacles in every direction, turning once-wild lands into clamouring cities with alarming speed.

They settled into a good pace, and with familiar country around them, crisp new snow, and the smell of evergreens, the kilometres flew by. Their first objective was the farm at Bonna, where old

Hans Bonna and his wife still took in wandering skiers. With them were their daughters, Hanna and Valborg, "Nordmarka's Rose," whom he remembered so well from previous trips. They spent a cosy evening with them and he had much to tell of the forests and the mountains of America, and of how, despite considerable snow in many areas, the general run of people had no knowledge of the thrill of skiing. The Bonnas could see how delighted he was to be back again in their own Nordmarka.

Next day, in glorious sunshine, they skied on over the lakes and hills to Katnosa, where Fridtjof Nansen had trained. Magnus and Gunhild Katnosa welcomed them, and happily took them in for the night, just as they had in the good old days, and they were as interested as the others had been in his tales of America. The following day they went on through still wilder country, over Stubdal and Jurihaugen and on to Ringerike, to call on his old flame, Marin Val. There they found yet another warm welcome, and that evening he had to tell again the story of his exhausting trip back through the woods after his last visit to her, when he had barely made it back in time for military duty, and had fallen asleep on horseback at Krigsskolen! They all laughed, and swapped yarns until late in the evening, with Otto, Anna, Agnes, and Tia each contributing their share. The next day, sunburned, and proud of the distance they had covered, they caught the train home from Hönefoss, tired but very happy.

❦

Before Christmas, when Herman had first arrived in Christiania, there had been a series of letters waiting for him, bringing welcome news from Cleveland. The family saw at once how interested he was in "his girl." His sisters were especially curious. This time, however, there was a letter with a very different message. Alice's mother had had a sudden stroke, much like the one that had overtaken Far back in 1902. She had been rushed to hospital, and Alice and her father were doing everything they could to ease her, but the situation looked bleak indeed.

Herman immediately wrote as comforting a letter as he could. How thankful he was that she had turned down his "joking" invitation to come with him to Europe such a short time before, for she would have felt very helpless, stranded here in Norway at such a time. Her letters that followed held out little hope of improvement.

Meanwhile, Herman had a long and serious talk with Mor. She listened quietly as he told her how much Alice had come to mean to him over the last four years. Finally, Mor put her hand comfortingly on his shoulder and said, "I know, Herman. I know just what you mean. I think you have really found the girl who was meant for you. You need a woman who is understanding, and forbearing, and who can cope with difficulties when they come. Someone who can support your own enthusiasms, and who can share your load when things get rough. *She* needs someone who can take care of her, and comfort her, and rejoice with her." Then she added softly, "I give you both my blessing. You must bring her back to Norway next time you come. You may be sure we will all make her very happy here."

And, with that, he hugged her, hard.

But now it was time for Herman to be off again on his travels. People in Norway are used to saying goodbye, often for very long periods. In Bestefar Smith's time many a man would be gone to sea for several years, and here was young Otto about to set out on the full-rigged *Fortuna* as a sailor before the mast. They were glad to have had that wonderful trip together in Nordmarka, for it would be a long time before Otto would again have a chance to ski. The *Fortuna* would be sailing first to Australia, then to South Africa, then across to Newfoundland before coming back via Hamburg to Christiania. This would be his Great Adventure, and they all wished him well.

As for Herman, he set out resolutely through Sweden and down through Germany, with the usual trail of postcards marking his route. In Berlin he had a fine reunion with some of his old chums at Berolina, who took him out for a carefree evening at one of their old beer halls. There was lots of singing and good German beer, and they jointly sent to Alice a beautiful doublespread postcard showing the long column of a military parade headed by the Kaiser with his colour party and a marching band. "You can almost hear the oompah music," they wrote. This was followed by views of the Brandenburger Tor, the Reichstag, and the Tiergarten, and on most of these he managed to write some message in German, for Alice had learned some German in school, and he thought it would be fun to baffle the postman.

From Hamburg he sent a picture of the harbour, with a forest of tall-masted sailing ships and a view of the pride of the German fleet, the *Prussen*, under full sail, its five masts straining under forty-two billowing sheets of canvas. On this he wrote, "Imagine Otto on this! He sure would have a busy time here!"

In his old summer stamping ground in the Ruhr Valley, the "Pittsburger" district of Germany, he spent an interesting time with his college mate, Konrad von Borsig, who was working his way up through the family steel business. Next was Bonn, where with another classmate he sent off a comic card of the two of them in a simulated touring car, their bowler hats clamped down over their ears, as they "automobiled" at tremendous speed along the Rhine. Then to Coblenz, then Mainz, and at last, "Leaving for London tomorrow," he wrote, "Expect to sail from Liverpool on April 10." This was signed with a plaintive, "I wonder how you are?" but in London he found a letter saying that Alice's mother had died while he was crossing Germany, and he knew it would be a sad home-coming.

All was over by the time he returned to Cleveland. He could see, though, that in spite of her sorrow, there was joy in Alice's heart to have him home again. Those five and a half months had been a very long time for both of them, and communication had been further complicated by his being continually on the go, and by the time it took for mail to cross the Atlantic. Judge Robinson was taking his loss very well, and he and Alice would continue to live on Genesee Avenue until they could sell the house and move into smaller quarters.

Meanwhile, there was so much to tell of what Herman had seen and done, but most of all was the need to tell her how much he had missed her during all those months. "I know," said Alice with a quiet smile. "I somehow got the message, with every postcard – all the dozens and dozens of them! They surely made me feel as though I were really there."

"And next time, you will be," he said, holding her very close. They were sitting in her living-room, and his arm was around her, as he took from his pocket a small blue box that had been with him day and night ever since he had left Christiania. It was warm from the heat of his body as she took it in her hands. Slowly she opened it. And there, twinkling in the glow from the gas lamp lay a sparkling silver pin – a real *bunad* brooch – its six tiny dangling cups each catching and reflecting the gleam from the lamp.

"It's part of the national costume of Norway," Herman told her. "It was made by an old-time silversmith in Telemark. It means something very special, almost as if it were part of the soul of Norway itself, and I want you to have it as a special engagement present." He pinned it gently on her dress, and the tiny cups moved and twinkled with every breath she took. She put her hand to it, caressing it, and, smiling through her tears, she whispered, "I'll cherish it always!"

Then he told her the story of how, in 1842, when old Bestefar Smith had brought his first boatload of Telemarkings to America, one of the peasant women had taken this precious silver brooch from her own bunad and had given it to Bestefar in heartfelt gratitude for all his care in bringing them safely through storms and the raging fever.

He told her, too, how Bestefar had later given this very brooch to his young bride, as a symbol of something particularly precious. And now his mother had given it to him, as a gift for his Alice.

"So, you see," Herman finished happily, "history has a way of repeating itself. And now – after all these years – the brooch belongs to you, a legacy from Norway."

CHAPTER NINE

A Fresh Start: 1907–1908

It was one thing to be engaged, and quite another to rearrange their lives so that they could even think about getting married. Herman had as yet no great security to offer, and Alice had a continuing responsibility to care for her father, so they had to be content for a while with a very disjointed kind of existence. Alice kept on with her kindergarten teaching, and Herman continued to travel, but they made the most of every chance they had to be together. There were periods when he would be away for months at a time, and they were entirely dependent on the post office to keep them in touch.

These lonesome travels were spread out over more than a year as Herman moved back and forth across the United States, from the steel mills of Pittsburgh to the mines of the Rockies, wherever there were opportunities to sell hoisting machinery. Low freight rates were doing much to spread industrialization throughout the country, and many new branch lines were reaching into every corner of America. His fare and his expenses were paid, but the competition was intense, and he had to keep moving in order to bring in the business and earn his meagre salary.

He was thinking more and more about starting in business for himself. By becoming a "manufacturer's agent" he could represent a number of competing firms, not just Brown Hoist and Browning. It would be a big departure, for he would be giving up a steady salary and in future would have to depend upon commissions alone, but Alice was willing to take the gamble. He would set up a central office, and they would travel together. She could share with him the excitement of new sights, and he could begin to enjoy the comforts of a home of their own, even if it were still only a migratory one. So they finally set the "Day." The house on Genesee Avenue was sold. Her father would live in a home for the elderly, and they would be married on June 29, 1907.

As the Day drew closer, their excitement rose. The postcards continued in a veritable flood. From Milwaukee came one which said, "April 10. Good morning! It's 7 a.m.! S.L.Y.A.H.!" (S.L.Y.A.H. was their secret code for "somebody loves you awfully hard.") Finally, on June 15, his birthday, his message read, breathlessly, "Good morning again. This time it's 6 a.m. And from today IT'S ONLY 14 DAYS!"

And then the great day dawned. His brother, Fred, had recently arrived from Norway to get some experience in the Pittsburgh steel mills. He was to be Herman's best man and was delighted to be the first of the family to meet Alice. It was a simple ceremony, with only a few guests. Sue was there, and Carrie, and Alice's father, and some of the men from the office. Herman remembered very little of the service. He only knew that they were together at last, and were about to begin their own great adventure.

For their wedding trip they had planned something that would deliberately combine business and pleasure, and provide as much excitement as possible with a minimum of strain on their limited pocketbook. First they would stop at Niagara Falls, as so many honeymooners have done both before and since; then they would go on to Jamestown, Virginia.

Nineteen-seven was the year of the Jamestown Exposition, a major event marking the three-hundredth anniversary of the founding of the first white settlement in America. This very special celebration would put America squarely in the context of world history. Americans were justly proud of their three hundred years, but, Herman reflected, when you really came to think about it, it was just a flicker on the global scene. Three hundred years ago in Europe the Renaissance had barely ended, and the age of science just begun. The New World offered escape from the problems of

Europe, but when those first settlers landed in America none of them had any idea of what lay even beyond the near horizon, much less of how far the land extended.

The Jamestown Exposition was a great tourist attraction, advertised far and wide. Herman had hopes of making some good business contacts there, so it was with great anticipation that they set out. But they had another motive in going to Jamestown – a personal motive, for among the many foreign powers sending special exhibits was Norway, represented by the pride of her navy, the *Harald Haarfagre*. When they arrived, the ship lay at anchor in the bay, dressed in flags from stem to stern as befitted such an official visit. And among the officers on board were Herman's brother Johannes and his brother-in-law Christofer Meyer, husband of his sister Helga.

It was a wonderful reunion. They were received in style in the officers' mess, and there also, to their delight, was Fred, their best man, summoned down from Pittsburgh as a special surprise for this occasion. Alice glowed with pleasure, and made a great impression.

As the five of them sat together talking someone hurried in with the latest newspaper, bringing frightening news: the Norwegian full-rigged sailing vessel *Fortuna* had just sent out a distress signal in mid-Atlantic. Heavy seas and adverse winds had delayed her on her way from South Africa to Newfoundland, and she was constantly losing headway. It would be several more weeks before she could possibly make port, and meanwhile her food was running low. So there was Otto, their youngest brother, far out at sea and in difficulty. They vividly recalled old Bestefar Smith's story of how in 1824, when he was a twelve-year old boy, his sailing ship had been delayed along the Norwegian coast for eight days by a similar storm. This new situation was a strong reminder that life on the high seas was still dangerous for ships without auxiliary power. As for the *Fortuna*, a rescue ship soon reached her and sent food aboard by breeches buoy (a line slung between the two vessels). This would certainly be among the tales that Otto would some day recount to his own grandchildren.

After all the excitement of Jamestown, they set off to continue their honeymoon with two wonderful weeks on the edge of the wilderness in northern New York State. This was a totally different sort of experience. Friends had told them in glowing terms of a summer resort in the Adirondacks, which turned out to be the ideal spot. They went by train, winding in and out among countless rocky hills, lakes, and beaver dams, and finally they came to Sabatis, a small town where they hired a horse and buggy for the final drive up to Long Lake. There they were welcomed at a comfortable, old-fashioned retreat, with cabins, and daisy fields, and winding trails where they were able to absorb the full flavour of a real old-time Adirondack holiday. Alice took right away to this out-door existence, and Herman was proud of her. It was very different from the sheltered city life she had always known, yet she adapted quickly and happily. They climbed and picnicked with the other guests, swam, swatted mosquitoes, and had a glorious and relaxing time, and, as they watched the moon rising that last evening over Owl Mountain, they knew they had made the right choice. Whatever the future might hold they knew by the time they left Long Lake that together they would be able to weather whatever storms life might throw their way.

❧

Herman was now the representative of a number of very reputable firms, and his hopes were high. Their first stop was Montreal in Canada. Alice was sure they were starting out on the right foot, by beginning in what was after all a foreign country. To get herself into the proper frame of mind, her first purchase was a copy of Baedeker's *Canada*, on the flyleaf of which she proudly inscribed,
Alice R. Johannsen July 1907.
She leafed happily through the volume, which promised so much pleasure. Baedeker became their constant companion.

One of Herman's early moves in any new location was always to get a bird's-eye view of the surroundings. Their first destination was therefore one of Montreal's special attractions, the double funicular, which, starting near Park Avenue, ran straight up the cliff face on Mount Royal to the carriage road that encircled the top. This was where Herman learned that all her life Alice had been afraid of heights, a fear over which she had absolutely no control. However, even this early in the game, she shut her eyes, put her faith in her new husband, and hoped for the best as they stepped aboard that quivering electric cablecar and rode to the top, passing

Herman Smith Johannsen,   Alice Johannsen, Mount Royal, 1907.
Mount Royal, 1907.

the counterbalanced car as it descended to pick up the next load
of passengers.

At the summit, however, she was entranced by the view, for from
the Lookout they could see the whole city at their feet, and beyond
it the mountains that dotted the St Lawrence plain. Far away on
the southern horizon, they could see the hazy Adirondacks, in
which lay hidden their cosy little Long Lake. They sat on the
parapet overlooking the city, and took each other's picture to record
the event, little dreaming that some twenty years in the future this
city would become their home.

This was far from being Herman's first visit to Montreal. He had
passed through a number of times, and had sold machinery to the
Canadian Pacific Railway. In 1905 he had even joined the Montreal
Ski Club, just two years after its founding. In that year, Norway
and Sweden were peacefully separating. King Haakon had just
been made King of Norway, and the foreign consulates were being
reorganized. The Norwegian vice-consul in Montreal was, of
course, an enthusiastic member of the newly formed ski club, and
he convinced Herman that, as a Norwegian, he really ought to
join the club "for the good of the ski sport." So Herman was
already familiar with the pleasant cross-country trail that wound
over the wooded heights of Westmount, Outremont, and Mount
Royal. He remembered one particular evening trip that he and the

vice-consul had made the previous winter. They had ended with a straight run down Peel Street on their skis, across Sherbrooke, past the Mount Royal and Windsor Hotels, and finally down the last steep pitch to wind up for a beer at the Queen's Hotel next door to Bonaventure Station. The only heavy traffic they had had to contend with was an occasional horse-drawn sleigh and a few motor cars.

But this time, Alice and Herman had other things on their minds. They made the Windsor Hotel on Dominion Square their temporary headquarters, and while Alice and Baedeker explored the sights of the city, Herman went after business. First he called on the CPR Angus Shops, where he hoped to complete arrangements for the purchase of some machinery. There was always great activity in that vast enclosed shed, for this was where railway cars and engines were brought in for maintenance and repair. He was fortunate that day in getting an order (carrying an excellent commission) for a fine locomotive crane. It was his first sale after their marriage, and he felt that things were off to an auspicious start. He made a number of other calls in Montreal with future business in mind, but a pressing inquiry from Sault Ste Marie on Lake Superior was already hanging in the balance, so they packed their bags and a few days later headed confidently westward.

The change of scene was exciting and Alice kept her Baedeker close beside her as they went along. At the "Soo" Herman looked over the pulp mill, the Bessemer steel plant, the electric smelter, and the huge iron ore docks, and with another stroke of good luck, he sold a locomotive to the Algoma Steel Company. They then travelled on to Mackinac and Detroit, and so returned to Cleveland.

Now that he was independent, it was important to have an office, where he could coordinate all his contacts. The Mississippi Valley appealed especially as it was more or less equidistant from the farthest limits of his travels, and they finally selected St Louis, Missouri, as the most propitious location. Here he set up his headquarters, with a man in charge, a secretary, a telephone, a typewriter, and all his files. It was a modest beginning, but it served their purpose. They were really in business at last! In St Louis they also found themselves very pleasant permanent living quarters with Mrs Munroe, a motherly soul who ran a boarding house and who enthusiastically took them under her wing. They then set off on their travels. It was certainly good to have Alice with him. She joined in everything and kept his spirits high.

One of their first stops was Memphis, Tennessee, where there had been an inquiry from the army. The captain with whom Herman dealt was a very cautious man: he insisted that there be written into the contract a clause stating that "the company will grant a penalty payment for every cubic yard under 100 cubic yards per hour" that the machine he was buying failed to dig. He wasn't taking any chances.

"All right," said Herman, "but I'll make you a counter-offer. Would you be willing to pay us a bonus for every cubic yard over the stipulated amount per hour that you can dig?"

"Okay," answered the captain. "Why not?"

"So," said Herman. "Hang on." He immediately phoned Browning in Cleveland for approval. "Certainly!" said Browning. "Do what you think you need to, but by all means get that order!"

Herman drew up the contract, bearing both the penalty and the bonus clauses. He sold the machine, and got his commission. Several years later, when he again happened to be in touch with Browning, he asked casually what had been the final outcome of that affair in Memphis. Browning laughed. "You know," he said, slapping his knee, "We made almost as much money on that bonus clause of yours as the whole machine was worth. That sure was a good stroke of business. In the long run, it was a regular gold mine!"

From Tennessee they went on to Florida to sell hoists to the fruit growers, and from there it was only a short distance across to Cuba, where they looked into some interesting possibilities that were still opening up in the wake of the recent Spanish-American War. They felt it wise to keep their eyes on this situation while they pursued other business back in the states. As things turned out, this trip, though short, was a real eye-opener. They both fell absolutely in love with sunny Cuba – "las isla mas hermosa del ardiente sol" (the most beautiful island under the ardent sun) – as the Cubans sang so fervently about it.

Meanwhile, they learned by telephone from the office in St Louis of an inquiry from logging operators in Beaumont, Texas, so

Alice in her first year of marriage,
St Louis, Missouri.

that was their next stop. Alice got a tremendous kick out of riding
the cab of the private locomotive as they went up into the back
country, but Herman soon discovered that this was a really tough
area and absolutely "no place for a lady." So he sent her safely back
to Mrs Munroe in St Louis while he went after other leads in the
vicinity. At that time there was an epidemic of yellow fever raging

in Louisiana, but he managed to sell a crane in New Orleans, and escaped without getting ill himself. And so it went, with many smaller trips in between.

Then came a big call for steam shovels on the Panama Canal. That, too, was no place for Alice, what with both yellow fever and malaria running rife. She stayed on with Mrs Munroe while Herman journeyed alone down into that muggy hotbox of a country, for the opportunity was too big for him to miss.

It is claimed that in Panama there are only two seasons: one is the season of storms and wet weather, and the other is the rainy season. The lush green jungle flowed endlessly over the rocky hills, and the air was stifling.

The Panama Canal was a truly enormous engineering feat, created by Ferdinand de Lesseps. The French engineer had earlier masterminded the Suez Canal, which linked the Mediterranean Sea with the Gulf of Aden and thus saved India-bound vessels the extra mileage of a trip around the tip of Africa. Similarly, the Panama Canal would give direct access from the Atlantic to the Pacific Oceans by cutting a mere forty miles through the narrow isthmus of Panama and eliminating the eight-thousand-mile journey around South America. It was essentially a matter of digging one nine-mile canyon, the Culebra Cut, across the Continental Divide and another six miles long at the Atlantic end; and then dredging a channel through Gatun Lake, which lay between them. This was an undertaking that would consume almost eleven years. When it was finished, ships would be raised through a system of locks on the Atlantic side to a height eighty-five feet above sea level. They would then cruise through Gatun Lake, to be lowered through another system of locks to sea level on the Pacific side. The project, begun in 1904, was already in its third year.

It had been from the first a matter of hacking out the jungle along the right of way, then clearing off the topsoil and removing millions of tons of rock before new construction could begin. Much of the early excavation work was done by thousands of hand labourers with axes, picks, and shovels, fighting their way through hordes of malarial mosquitoes. The loss of human life had been immense during this early part of the program, and the finished canal would be forever a monument to their memory. No wonder the operators wanted more heavy machinery, to dig faster and more effectively in that soggy soil. Some of the original machinery was already wearing out. Replacements and newer models were needed, and the canal was not yet half finished. That was where Herman's Bucyrus Erie steam shovels, his backdiggers, and his clamshell buckets came into play.

He came back to St Louis with fascinating pictures of the countryside and of his machines in action. But he also came home with malaria. This was the first of many bouts that would plague him over the years. Whenever the summer weather was hot and muggy there was a chance his malaria would strike again. Alice nursed him through this and all the subsequent attacks, but they decided that Panama was definitely not their kind of climate. From then on, whatever machinery he sold down there was strictly by "remote control."

As an antidote to Panama, they decided to concentrate for a time on the much healthier climate in the high country of the western United States, where he could renew his mining connections in the vicinity of Denver. They stopped at the Antlers Hotel in nearby Colorado Springs, where Alice was happy to relax and enjoy the scenery while Herman went up into the mining country for about a week.

Imagine his surprise on his return to find that some enterprising friends, also staying at the Antlers, had persuaded Alice to accompany them on muleback to the top of Pikes Peak. She had thoroughly enjoyed her unexpected adventure, and felt it a great achievement to have reached the summit, 14,108 feet above sea level, on the back of a mule. "It was a perfectly easy trail," she told him, "and I felt much safer on the mule than I did in that cablecar on Mount Royal! You see, the mule wasn't mechanical!" Her lack of confidence in mechanical things was something Herman simply could not understand. "Aren't you the wife of a mechanical engineer?," he asked her in disbelief. "I know I am," she admitted reluctantly, "but, you see, a mule is so much more natural." And Alice bragged for years thereafter about her muleback journey to the top of the Rockies.

The more they travelled in the vastness of the United States, the more convinced Herman became that he should not entirely give up his foreign connections, not only because in America there was definitely a market for foreign machines, but more especially because he had recently heard from his old friend, Konrad von Borsig, that he was thinking of opening a branch office in Japan. Alice and Herman talked this over carefully, and they felt the idea was at least worth investigating. The lure of new places was always strong in him, and Alice was game for new adventures. So, that fall they decided to make a quick trip to Germany to look into the Japanese proposal, and at the same time to visit the family in Norway.

In Berlin they met some of his old fraternity brothers, including of course Stoff and his wife, and they went to call on Frau Berenson, with whom the Norwegian boys had lived so happily during their college years. Alice practised her high school German and made a great hit wherever they stopped, but their visit to von Borsig, the real purpose of the journey, turned out to be a disappointment. His agent in Hamburg, through whom the Japanese project was to have been handled, had unfortunately gone bankrupt, and the negotiations had come to an abrupt end. Herman, however, took this philosophically. "That's the way things go in life," he said. "You work towards a certain goal, you make plans. And suddenly the dream fades. But, just as surely, when one door closes, another always seems to open in some unexpected way." So he and Alice went on to Norway, the richer for this German experience, but eager to investigate any new possibilities that might arise.

Their arrival in Christiania was very exciting and a rather for-midable event for Alice, who found herself the centre of attraction and curiosity. She was an only child, and it was quite a new experience for her to be plunged into the heart of a large family, with all the hubbub of a strange language, new faces, and new customs. Johannes and Tul in Horten, and Helga and Elisabeth, the two married sisters, in Christiania, were eager to show off their new homes, and Otto, returned from his long voyage on *Fortuna*, was full of stories of his two years at sea. Many cosy evenings were spent gathered around tall paraffin lamps in the family living-room, the girls and Mor at work on their knitting or embroidery, and Far looking on in silent contentment. They laughed as they recalled many childhood adventures, and Alice, who was picking up more and more Norwegian phrases, was delighted to practise on everyone.

Herman made the most of the opportunity to renew old acquain-tances, look into business possibilities, and seek new contacts. He was especially interested in Uncle Nikolai Beer's stone quarries, where tons and tons of granite paving blocks were being produced. Herman could see a large market for them in America, where the growing number of motor cars was creating a steady demand for harder and more durable road surfaces. Refreshed by this European experience, he and Alice returned to America, all the more eager to take up the life that awaited them there.

CHAPTER TEN

Caribbean Adventure: 1908–1911

Among the firms with which Herman had been associated for several years was Liggerwood Manufacturing Company, whose head office was in New York. This was the company that, through Brown Hoist, had sent him up to Canada in 1902 to sell hoisting engines and ballast unloaders to the Grand Trunk Railway. Such engines could cost anywhere from $5,000 to $20,000, and in the proposed arrangement with the company, as manufacturer's agent he would receive a percentage commission.

Another firm he had been working with was the American Hoist and Derrick Company, which was developing a sugar-cane unloader of special interest in Cuba. The Cuban American Sugar Company also had an office in New York, and whenever they needed hoisting equipment they would contact Liggerwood or American Hoist, who then referred them to Herman. It seemed logical that Herman should move his head office to this new territory, and go after Cuban business right on its own home ground. Sugar prices were high at that time, Cuba was eager to export, and there were many individual plantation owners scattered throughout the island, all needing machinery. Furthermore, as there was very little competition for the products he had to sell, it would be pretty well up to him to make his own contacts and get the business going. It was exactly the kind of job that appealed to him – lots of adventure and excitement, a more or less untouched market to develop, and, as he spoke reasonably good Spanish, no language barrier. So, they opted for Cuba.

While Herman went down to Havana to get things started, Alice returned to Cleveland to be with her father over the Christmas holidays. When she rejoined him, Herman had found a delightful boardinghouse that catered particularly to foreign residents in Cuba, La Maison Royale, operated by an old-country Frenchman, Monsieur Lefebvre. It was out in the Vedado, a pleasant suburb of Havana, and was a relatively new, vine-covered, three-storey villa with two penthouses on the "woof," as Madame Lefebvre called it. In one of these Alice and Herman set up their living quarters, as well as a temporary office in which they installed a big roll-top desk and his shiny black typewriter. They also had a lovely view out over the blue waters of the bay.

The other boarders were a mixed but interesting lot. There was a young bank clerk who "batched it" in the other penthouse. There was an American fertilizer agent and his social-climber wife. There was Grandma Webster, a pleasant elderly woman who took a special shine to Alice; a Jewish couple from New York, banana dealers; and a kindly young doctor and his wife from New Orleans. And there were two elderly Spanish bankers, the Banta brothers. The Bantas volunteered to teach Alice Spanish "with a real Castillian accent." They felt she needed help, for one day, when the elder Señor Banta was about to depart on a short journey and Alice wanted to wish him a *buen viaje*, or a *bon voyage*, she had wished him instead a *"buena vieja,"* which meant a "nice old woman." To this Señor Banta replied with a twinkle, "Thank you, my dear, but I really prefer them young!"

All in all, they were an unlikely but congenial "family" and they got on well with each other, despite differences in origin and point of view. Their common denominator was the English language, and the Maison Royale became a happy base of operations for Herman and Alice for the next three and a half years.

Herman had been to Cuba a number of times before, selling locomotive cranes to the plantation owners, but to Alice it was all new and different. She wanted to get the feel of the country, to sample the customs, and to experience the way of life.

She was especially interested in the houses, with their open windows protected by beautiful wrought-iron grilles to let in the air and to keep out intruders. She was astonished, however, to learn from M. Lefebvre that, only the week before, he had left a wrapped-up birthday present on a table near an open window in the front room. He was planning to take it to his son in boarding school in Cienfuegos, but when he returned to the room shortly afterwards the package had disappeared without a trace! He could only conclude that it had been ingeniously "lifted" through the window grille by a thief. It was common practice, he told them, for light-fingered folk to insert a pair of extensible tongs through the grille. They would then open and extend these tongs so that they could quietly "pinch" whatever likely objects might lie within their range, draw them to the window, and then make off. Alice found it reassuring that, living as they did on the "woof," they were at least beyond the reach of such passing entrepreneurs.

The idea of a "siesta," or period of midday rest, was also new to her. Business came to a complete standstill for two hours each noon, and everyone would relax for a quiet snooze. They would resume activity when the afternoon heat began to abate.

Herman decided to take Alice with him on a reconnoitring trip down to the eastern end of the island where they could get into the back country. The scenery there was of great interest, but this was to be no mere sight-seeing tour. It would be a real initiation into life in rural Cuba.

They set off in high spirits, taking the train the eighty kilometres across the island to the port of Batabano on the southern shore. There they boarded *La Reina de los Angeles* (the *Queen of the Angels*) – a local passenger steamer that stopped at various outports and fishing villages along the Carribbean coast. They could get on and off whenever they chose, to visit plantations in a given area, then pick up the vessel later on when next she passed.

Alice was overwhelmed by the scene at dockside as they strug-gled up the gangplank, threading their way through swarms of people of every conceivable colour of skin. From the upper deck they looked down on a sea of wide-brimmed Panama hats, for all the passengers sported some kind of headgear to shield themselves from the blistering sun. One woman balanced a great basket of fruit on her head as she came aboard. Another clutched a brace of cackling live chickens, which she swung firmly upside down, holding them by the legs, their wings flapping helplessly as they protested this indignity with loud squawks. The boatswain stood at the top of the gangplank, screening the passengers one by one, and separating those who really had tickets from those who were mere spectators. Finally, with a toot of the horn the ship moved off, leaving the crowd on shore to disperse as quickly as it had assembled. Much the same scene was repeated at each village thereafter as they moved slowly from port to port.

As passengers in first class they travelled in comparative style, and were served a sumptuous dinner in the galley, while lesser folk with their assorted baggage were crowded unceremoniously on the deck. At mealtime at each place-setting there would appear a stack of six or more clean dishes, piled one upon the other. As each course was served and eaten, one more plate would be taken away, until, with removal of the final plate, the meal was definitely at an end.

Their first stop was Cienfuegos, where at the local livery stable Herman hired a little victoria, a four-wheeled, two-seated carriage with a box on the front for a *calesero* (driver), and a collapsible hood that could be raised or lowered against the sun. With this they could move around among the plantations, and they found it a convenient and pleasant way to travel. They were making this trip early in the new year, at the height of the sugarcane growing season, a time when the cane stood some ten feet tall in fields that extended for acres and acres in every direction. Every now and then a gentle breeze would stir the surface of the fields, sending lovely long undulating waves of green out to the farthest reaches of the horizon.

Alice found the large sugar plantations, or *ingenios*, fascinating. They ranged in size from five hundred to ten thousand acres, the larger ones being entirely self-sufficent, with living quarters, repair shops, a hospital, and a refinery all of their own, while the smaller ones shared a community mill. It was quite a sight to see three or four hundred black *trabajadores* advancing in a long line against a standing wall of green, their razor-sharp machetes flashing in the sun as they attacked cane after cane, first decapitating the growing end, then slashing the stalk at its base, leaving the eight-foot lengths to lie wherever they fell. They were continually urged on by an overseer, who cruised constantly back and forth on horseback along the line of workers.

Hard on his heels would come a continuous supply of slowly moving ox-carts, whose noisy drivers collected the cut canes. These carts looked for all the world like the tumbrils used during the

French Revolution to transport victims to the guillotine. The canes collected in each cart would be bound together using welder's chains, one of the products Herman sold, and the carts would then deliver these cumbersome bundles either directly to the owner's refinery, or to a branch of the railroad for further transport. At each unloading point a big overhead crane would be set up to lift these chain-bound bundles, and such hoists and derricks were Herman's main stock in trade. All this activity was completely new to Alice, who took great interest in everything she saw.

As they moved about the country they stopped at numerous plantations, large and small. While Herman talked business with the owner, Alice would have a look around. She often made friends with the children who abounded everywhere, and she soon found out that language was not really a barrier as long as they had a mutual curiosity and a sense of humour. As a result, she and the children got along famously.

One day, while Herman was discussing mechanical matters with the administrator, she set off to explore a little community of thatched-roofed cottages, where pigs and people wandered indiscriminately in and out. Later she posed, smiling, in the doorway of one of these for Herman to snap her picture, before they went on their way. Soon afterwards they both began to feel suspiciously itchy, and it became obvious that they had unknowingly acquired a fine cargo of fleas. So, stepping behind a screen of canes in a nearby field (while the *calesero* discreetly withdrew) they stripped to the skin and vigorously shook their clothing to remove any lingering insects. Then they moved on, more confidently, to a less flea-filled rendezvous.

It was at Manzanillo that they visited a number of big plantations, among them one called Media Luna, or Half Moon. This was owned, surprisingly, by a Scottish family, the Beatties, who hailed from Glasgow, and were naturally predisposed to anything that came from "bonnie Scotland." As Herman's welder's chains were of Scottish make, he was more or less assured of a sale at this plantation, and Media Luna became a regular port of call on all his future travels.

They were delighted when the Beatties invited them to spend the night. Alice found the idea of sleeping under a palm-thatched roof appealingly romantic, and although they were vaguely conscious of certain mysterious rustlings in the thatch during the hours of darkness, they slept well and awoke refreshed. The cause of these nocturnal noises was dramatically revealed next morning, however, when a large black snake dropped unexpectedly beside the dining table at breakfast! Mr Beattie hastened apologetically to pick up the snake and return it carefully to the rafters, explaining that it lived up there, where it did an excellent job of keeping the rats at bay. The snake was quite harmless, he assured them, and was really kind of a family pet. Alice, however, was hard to convince.

A few days later, on visiting Niquero, where the American navy was doing some work, they were again hospitably invited to spend the night, this time on board a navy ship. The prospect was far more inviting than the local hotel, and they were convinced the navy harboured no snakes in its thatch! However, the ship did have rats, which entertained them during the night by roaming the beam above their heads, and they found themselves becoming more appreciative of Mr Beattie's amiable rat-catching snake.

The country hotels in some of these small communities were rustic, to say the least. One of them boasted the forerunner of modern air-conditioning. As a means of counteracting the stifling heat, the bedroom walls rose to a height of eight feet, above which they were topped by a system of open wire netting to the roof. This space, continuous over all the bedrooms, assured maximum cross-ventilation. It was also acoustically efficient. The occupant of the adjoining room turned out to be a fearful snorer, who kept up a terrific, intermittent racket all night long. Thanks to the "air-conditioning" system, this sound was broadcast throughout the house, and every so often, when Herman could stand it no longer, he would bang on the wall with his shoe to awaken the culprit, who would stop abruptly, grunt, snort, and turn over – and then begin all over again, this time in a different key!

Alice and Herman shared many a laugh. Alice was quick to adapt, and by the time they reached Guantanamo she was ready for almost anything. In the Oriente, the easternmost province of Cuba, where there were large plantations of bananas and sugar cane, the distances were greater, and in order to move around more easily Herman hired three old saddlehorses, – one for Alice, another for himself, and the third for a local guide. On these mounts they travelled up and down among the canefields, fording streams where necessary, and generally getting to know the country. Alice wore a divided skirt, which allowed her to sit astride her horse without getting her skirt hung up on the horse's neck or rump. With her Panama hat and dashing kerchief she cut quite a figure, and Herman was proud of her.

They would ride from plantation to plantation, often going out into the fields to see the men expertly wielding their machetes. They watched the cane being loaded into the little "carettas" in bundles bound with welder's chains, then drawn by horse or oxen to a branch railway line that ran directly into the field. Here one of Herman's unloaders would be set up – a tall mast of girders with a swinging boom – to lift the bundles from the carts and place them crosswise on the train, four bundles to a flatcar. Then they were off to the mill, where another crane would lift the bundles, unchain them and dump them into a hopper, from which the loose canes would travel up a conveyor belt and into the factory for processing.

This mechanical inspection was a hot job in the broiling sun, but it gave Herman an idea of parts that needed replacing and spots where additional machinery might be set up. By being actually on the ground, he was able to recommend more efficient ways of handling the crop, and the farmers and mill owners were pleased. They appreciated this personal attention, and he almost always got an order of some kind.

Alice was particularly interested in what happened to the cane once it entered the mill, so they were given a special tour of one of the larger installations. They saw the raw cane as it was fed by the conveyor into the crusher, whose rollers squeezed out the juice. This opaque liquid was then filtered through heavy, perforated colanders where any loose matter was removed. The juice was then pumped into huge 450-gallon clarifying tanks and kept at the boiling point by means of steam, which was generated by burning the crushed cane. A further series of filterings, boilings, and evaporation reduced this liquid to a thick syrup. This was then pumped into a vast array of inverted, cone-shaped *hormas*, or forms, which fitted into a series of frames covering the entire second floor of the purging house. There might be as many as twenty thousand of these inverted *hormas*. Here, as the hot liquid cooled, the sugar would slowly crystallize, leaving the remaining liquid, or molasses, to drain by gravity through a hole in the end of the inverted cone. A system of troughs and channels collected this juice and led it into huge 1,500-gallon vats grouped on the floor beneath. From there the molasses would be packaged in various grades for sale.

The crystallized sugar left behind in the *hormas* was consolidated into loaves or *pains de sucre*, in which form it could be sold directly to the consumer. However, new technology in crushing and further refining these cones made it possible to package and sell the sugar in many grades of granulation varying from pure white cane sugar to heavy golden brown. Alice was sure she would never taste sugar again without seeing this entire process unfold before her eyes.

All in all, their exploration of rural Cuba lasted some two months, by which time they were glad to escape the mosquitoes and other inconveniences and return to civilized life at Maison Royale. Herman had accumulated a fair number of orders and made some useful contacts. Their Spanish was improving, and Alice had a great deal to relate to their fellow boarders around the dinner table.

Meanwhile, Herman set up an office on Obispo Street, where he could follow up on orders as he received them, and initiate new contacts with entrepreneurs in Havana. Like many places of business in the neighbourhood, it was adequate but unpretentious: hardly more, really, than a "hole in the wall," it had heavy wooden shutters that could be raised during the day, then lowered and securely locked at night. But it was a business address, which increased Herman's confidence in the importance of his undertakings, and relieved the crowded atmosphere of their living quarters at Maison Royale.

They found that there was quite an English-speaking population in Havana, whose social life was centred around the Havana Country Club with its beautiful, palm-fringed golf course. Here they met several other young couples who, with their children, became their fast friends. Among these were Hornsby, manager of the Royal Bank of Canada, and Fred Ross, manager of the Bank of Nova Scotia (called by the Cubans the *banca del bacalao* – the codfish bank). Through these men Herman and Alice met many other members of the business community, all of them playing their part in developing the country. Herman even learned to play a little golf, though he was inclined to be more interested in the big land crabs that sometimes pilfered their golf balls on the fairway than he was in the game itself, which he tended to dismiss as mere "pill-pushing." Still, it was a diversion, and Alice, too, took up the game.

One of the most active of the big developers was an old acquaintance, Sir William Van Horne. Back in Montreal Herman had sold machinery to Van Horne, for the Canadian Pacific Railway. After leaving the CPR, Sir William had gone out looking for new worlds to conquer, and had discovered the sugar business in Cuba. He was already building a big sugar refinery near Camagüey. This was served in part by the United Railways of Cuba, a line that had been built as far as Santa Clara a number of years before, using English capital. Sir William had been quick to see the possibilities of extending this line another eight hundred kilometres, all the way down to Santiago, and had in fact set about building his own railway, which he called the Cuba Company. The United Railway line and Sir William's new line would together provide connecting links between plantations and sugar refineries from one end of the Island to the other. Meanwhile, Sir William was also constructing several beautiful big new hotels which, together with these railroads, would bring about an upsurge of tourism in Cuba. This was the beginning of something new, and in this Herman, too, hoped to play a rôle.

Social life in Havana, however, had unexpected drawbacks: the bubonic plague, for example, which was linked to the large number of rats that ran about everywhere. In downtown Havana the police at one point ordered all furniture to be placed in the middle of the street for spraying. They then used fire hoses to flush out the houses, including Herman's tiny office. These were drastic measures, but they seemed to help.

One day Herman was sitting in his newly rat-purged office on Obispo Street when a plantation owner from Cienfuegos came in to see him. His name was Miguel Arango, and he was in desperate need of a locomotive. He owned a large plantation near Camagüey, and he wanted to buy a locomotive to haul the cane from his far-flung fields to his refinery. They talked a while, and Herman suggested a Baldwin locomotive, or possibly one from the American Locomotive Company.

"I've tried them both," said Arango, "but apparently they're too busy to bother with an unknown person like me. Can you find a locomotive for me from someone else?"

"Well," Herman said, "I have a good connection with the foremost locomotive builder in Germany. Would you be interested in something from there?"

"Certainly," said Arango. "I want one as soon as you can get it."

Herman cabled to Konrad von Borsig, and was delighted to receive his quick reply: "Okay. Have one for immediate delivery."

In due course, the locomotive arrived by ship, complete with a German-speaking mechanic. Herman had meanwhile arranged with the United Railways for a "right of passage": permission to run the new locomotive under its own steam over United Railway tracks all the way down to Santa Clara, a distance of 250 kilometres. It was to be done at night to avoid interrupting existing schedules. United Railways supplied him with an engineer, a Scot who spoke English with a strong Scottish burr; the fireman was a Spanish-speaking black Cuban. With the German-speaking mechanics, and Herman, a Norwegian, acting as interpreter, it was quite a ride. He found himself speaking German to the Spanish fireman, Spanish to the Scottish engineer, and English to the German mechanic, but otherwise the journey went without a hitch, and the locomotive was duly delivered to a delighted Miguel Arango.

Another time, Herman had occasion to go down to Oriente Province alone. He travelled to the end of the United Railway line, then changed to Sir William's Cuba Company, which was not as yet in full operation. He hired a horse at one of the small towns near his destination, and took it aboard the train with him, leaving it in the baggage car. It was night, and when the train pulled to a halt at the place where he was to disembark (there was as yet no station, only some kind of a flag stop) he tossed his saddlebags off the train into the ditch, then turned to go and get his horse from the baggage car. However, another passenger had already jumped unexpectedly from the train, and in the pitch dark, the flying saddlebags connected with this invisible traveller, and a string of Spanish oaths welled up from the darkness.

"*Caramba!*" yelled the unseen man, and there followed a number of very uncomplimentary remarks. Herman sensed trouble. The accent, however, was not Spanish, and on a hunch, Herman called down to him, "Can you swear in English?"

"I sure as hell can!" came the answer, in English, but the accent sounded neither English nor American. Then, inspired, Herman asked, "Are you by any chance a Norwegian?"

"Why, yes," stammered the man below.

"Where do you come from in Norway?"

"Horten," he replied.

"Well, I'll be darned," said Herman. "I was born in Horten myself!" The man, it seemed, was on his way to Baracoa, to work on a banana plantation owned by a Norwegian.

Herman guided his horse cautiously down out of the baggage car, and stood beside him in the dark as the train pulled away. Then the two abandoned passengers took up once more the acquaintance that had begun so inauspiciously in the ditch. "It sure is a funny world," they agreed, as they shook hands. And with that they turned and, Herman leading his horse, they walked up the road together, talking fondly of Horten.

Each year as fall approached there were storm warmings of hurricanes, which the Cubans seemed to take as a matter of course, but which Alice found very exciting. In any one season there might be six or more of these storms, some more serious than others, which would blow in over the Caribbean from the southeast bringing gales and high tides. Trees would be uprooted, tiles dislodged from roofs, and anything not firmly battened down could become a flying, lethal weapon. They remembered seeing roof tiles fly through the air like birds on the wing. No one ventured outside in such a storm, for such airborne missiles could cut a man in half.

After one such storm the streets of the Vedado were liberally strewn with lumber and barrels and parts of fences that had been swept about by the tide. There they lay, stranded wherever they had come to rest as the waters receded. Later, when the storm was well past and the sun came out again, the streets were a veritable obstacle course until salvage crews had cleared away the wreckage. Things were restored almost to normal in a surprisingly short time. Alice was impressed to see one of the work teams pick up a fallen palm tree and simply plunk it back into the hole from which it

House where Herman and Alice lived in Cuba.

had toppled. They pushed it into place, and poured in some earth. It took root again, and later flourished.

Obispo Street was quite another story. At one end, flanking a large hotel there was a long colonnade that overhung the sidewalk to protect passersby from the sun. Here the flood waters rose, converting the colonnade into a covered canal. The water was hip-deep, and the numerous guests of the hotel were spectacularly marooned on the upper balcony. From there they had a grandstand view, as enterprising citizens paddled makeshift rafts up and down the street, or formed a human chain as they helped pedestrians to cross a nearby intersection.

The author and nurse in Cuba.

When the flood at last subsided, road conditions were found to be deplorable. In those early days of motor cars, when the new-fangled contraptions were beginning to sell at a surprising rate, it was obvious that good, solid road surfaces were becoming more and more important, both in the city and for longer stretches in the surrounding countryside. Herman could see a promising market for paving blocks from Norway, and he immediately got in touch with Onkel Nikolai. But Onkel Nikolai was ahead of him; he already had a representative in Cuba, and so Herman lost out on that first big order. Eventually, however, the other representative left the job, and Herman finally got the agency himself, and kept it for a long time.

Herman's business in Cuba flourished for several years, and with good luck and careful management it seemed likely to continue. However, every summer, when the weather became almost unbearably hot, he would be stricken with a recurrence of the malaria he had originally contracted in Panama. It seemed possible that the Cuban climate was no healthier for him than the climate of Panama.

When spring 1911 appeared Herman and Alice were faced with a new problem. A child was on the way – due to be born in April. Although they looked forward with joy to the baby's birth, they were not at all sure that Cuba – glorious land of flowers and sunshine that she was – was the country in which they wanted to rear a family. For various reasons, therefore, it seemed wise for them to move back up north, and Herman was trying to arrange things so that they could get established in New York. The Cuban office was going well, and he could put someone in charge there. He felt that with his family centrally located in New York, he could still maintain the office in Havana and continue at the same time with the many contacts he had built up in the United States. He also hoped to reopen his connections in Canada and thus develop a strong manufacturers' agency serving the Atlantic seaboard. Now, the imminent arrival of the baby brought things to a head.

❧

How he swelled with pride when he visited the hospital, and saw two nurses standing in the upstairs window, as though in some theatrical balcony scene, holding up the tiny fair-haired child for him to see. She was the only white baby in the entire hospital, *la rubia Americana,* "the little blond American" they all exclaimed. And she made quite a sensation. Not to mention the sensation she caused at Maison Royale when they returned there, complete with Sarah, a delightful black nurse who posed proudly with her little *rubia* beside the fountain in the garden.

But then it was Alice's turn to be ill. She made a very slow recovery after the baby's birth, and that caused a drastic change in their plans. Early in July, Alice and Herman, accompanied by their new daughter in a clothes basket, sailed for Norway where Alice could recuperate in the care of Herman's mother, while he returned alone to New York to get things going there.

Before they left Havana, Herman went to register the baby and pick up her birth certificate. They had decided that if the child were a girl, she would be named after both Alice and Herman's sister, Elisabeth. The official asked, "And what, Señor, is the name of the infant?"

"Alice Elisabeth," he told him proudly.

"But that is impossible, Señor!"

"What's impossible?" asked Herman, taken aback.

"She must have a Spanish name. This is a Spanish-speaking country. Her name must be Alicia Isabela."

"Not on your life!" Herman told him. "There are no Isabelas in my family. And my wife's name is Alice – not Alicia."

But the official was adamant. "I regret, Señor, but that is the law." So, there was no birth certificate.

In high dudgeon, Herman went to the Norwegian consul, who happened to be an old schoolmate of his from Christiania, and the consul issued a letter stating that "On April 11, 1911, in Havana, Cuba, a daughter, Alice Elisabeth, was born to Alice Robinson and Herman Smith Johannsen, and this document shall serve as an interim certificate of birth." And that, as Mor used to say, was that. They would get the whole thing regulated later on in Norway, when the baby would be officially baptized. There, at least, they would not have to make any apologies for her name.

The journey overseas was somewhat complicated for Herman, the new father, with an invalid wife and a new baby, but they made it successfully, and as soon as they had settled down with Far and Mor, and Alice Elisabeth had been duly admired by all the family, Herman took off for Nordmarka.

How good it was to see Slagtern again, to drop in on Bonna, and to visit Katnosa once more. He had not realized how much he had missed this country during the last four years. It was warm here in summer, but not intensely, all-pervadingly hot, as it had been in Cuba; and he had to admit that to him waving palms and blazing poinsettia plants were no match at all for tall, cool ever-greens and fields of buttercups and daisies. He was a northerner, he decided, and always would be.

Alice, who had been struggling valiantly with Spanish, and who, thanks to the Banta brothers, had developed "a real Castillian accent," now found herself faced with an entirely different language. As she was probably going to spend a year or more in Norway, she followed family advice and engaged Fröken Reimers to teach her the rudiments of Norwegian. Thus began a series of weekly sessions; which not only helped her through her convalescence, but blossomed into a warm friendship. Fröken Reimers would appear at the house with a vocabulary and a series of anecdotes that Alice would master to the best of her ability, not only learning to recite these stories fluently in Norwegian, but also to write them down, using all the special idioms, and it was not long before she was quite the star of their family gatherings.

"Do tell us, Alice, about Herr Thompson and his dog, Rover." they would plead, and Alice would cheerfully oblige, reciting the story in fine elocutionary style, about how Herr Thompson with his dog had gone one day into a seafood store and had asked if the lobsters were fresh.

"'Certainly,' said the storekeeper. 'If you don't believe me, let your dog wag his tail over that big one there and see what happens!' When the lobster felt the dog's tail brush over him, he seized the tail firmly in both his claws, as only a lobster can. Rover, strongly resenting this treatment, bolted immediately for the door and for home, bearing the lobster with him.

"'Whistle for your dog!' shouted the storekeeper. But Herr Thompson was quick to reply, 'You whistle for your lobster, and see if he comes back. Meanwhile, I think Rover has caught me a very tasty supper.'"

When winter finally came around, it was quite a new experience for Alice to go on a Sunday *tur* with the entire family, taking the *trikk* (electric tramway) up to Holmenkollen for a day's outing. At Majorstuen, the trikk terminus at the edge of the city, they would stack their skis upright in racks along the outside of the carriages. Sleigh riders would stow their two-man sleds in the same way, dismantling the twelve-foot steering poles into two sections, and placing them in a separate rack. Then they would all climb aboard and ride up through the snow-laden trees to the summit, watching the city diminish in size as the trikk twisted back and forth in its long journey to the top. This was not a suspended cable car like the one Alice remembered from Mount Royal. It was a three-car train in which they could sit comfortably on wooden seats and admire the view. The trip took over half an hour.

They would then retrieve their skis and set out, Alice and Tul and the other women wearing long black skirts that swept the snow. For those who did not venture very far on skis, it was exciting to watch the bobsledders as they careened down the road back to Christiania, trailing their long steering poles, and squealing hilari-

At a skiing hut in the woods, Christiania, Norway,
December 1911.

ously as they rounded the turns. It was a good six kilometres
downhill back to town.

As Christmas approached, the entire family was plunged into
preparations for the festive season, a much more involved and
personal operation than Alice had ever experienced back in Cleveland. There were weeks on end of cooking and baking, and she
revelled in the traditional dishes and cookie recipes that Mor called
into play. Each section of the family had a special rôle in these
celebrations, and when the season finally arrived, everyone trooped
from home to home according to a well-laid and time-honoured
plan. On Christmas Eve everyone gathered at the grandparents'
for a festive dinner, to share their presents, and best of all, to sing
and dance around the Christmas tree. On Christmas Day itself all
were guests at another home, and on Second Christmas Day, at
yet a third. There were also visits to and from friends. Altogether
it was a wonderful succession of parties, and by the end, all that
vast store of accumulated Christmas goodies had vanished before
the onslaught of the hungry hordes. And then everyone went
skiing.

All that fall Herman had been travelling about in Norway, lining up equipment for sale in America, for his new business was to deal with exporting and importing. Immediately after Christmas he returned to the States, leaving Alice and the baby in Mor's care. They would follow at the end of the summer, by which time he would have everything ready for them in New York.

It was good meanwhile to know that his two Alices would join in the annual family summer holiday up on Lake Mjösen. Herman remembered nostalgically how Johannes and Karl and he had steamed up the lake on the little paddlewheeler, *Kong Oscar*, twenty years before on their way to Jotunheimen, and how they had seen the rich farmlands extending right down to the water's edge. One of these farms was called Skumsrud, and the Smith-Johannsen clan had established the custom of renting it for the summer season. In all, there were some sixteen adults and their accumulated offspring who assembled there, and while the fathers came and went depending on their job demands, the wives and children would remain in residence to enjoy the novelty and excitement of life on the farm. This, Herman could see, would be an excellent way to imprint on Alice Elisabeth some of the values in life which he had come to respect in his own youthful days in Horten and Laurvig, and the farm at Skumsrud became for her the real cornerstone of her later life in the out-of-doors.

The farmhouse was spacious and airy, with traditional "ginger-bread" scrollwork framing the wide veranda and tall windows, which could open wide to let in the summer sun. Over the cowbarn there was a huge hayloft in which the youngsters could play, and all sorts of wagons and things for children to climb upon, while a young nursemaid, hired for the summer, kept order among them. Meanwhile, Far and Mor had gone to stay at another old-time farm higher up in the mountains where they could rest and relax, far from the hubbub of grandchildren, and where they could enjoy the evening peace and quiet beside their own *peis*, the cosy soap-stone fireplace that occupied a corner of the old log cabin.

It was a summer that was long to be remembered. Alice herself became more and more at home in the Norwegian language, and Alice Elisabeth was starting to walk and talk. But at the end of August, when the families returned to the city, both Alices bade farewell to Norway with all its happy memories, and embarked at last on the steamer for New York, where Herman waited eagerly for their arrival.

The story to this point has been based on family letters and reminiscences, but now I (who was the baby Alice Elisabeth) can add to it my own recollections of my father's life.

CHAPTER ELEVEN

Success and Frustration in New York:

1912–1922

It is strange to rummage about in the recesses of one's memory, to recall events that lie half-buried at the dawn of one's own time. I remember nothing of that trip across the Atlantic, nor of our arrival in New York, nor of how overjoyed my father and mother were to see each other again, but I do have a flicker of memory of the moment when Dad led us proudly into our new, but as yet empty, apartment on Fort Washington Heights with a view over the Hudson River. As a toddler of a year and a half, I tripped excitedly down the long hallway to look out of the window. I can see it yet – the empty flat, the shiny floor, and the bright window at the end. Suddenly, I fell over my own feet, and my head bumped hard against the wall. I felt a flash of pain and at once began to wail. The next thing I knew was Mother's astonishment over the egg-sized lump that rose abruptly on my forehead.

I cried long and loud. And to make matters worse, I would have nothing to do with the strange man who tried so hard to comfort me. Who was this creature who didn't look at all like my own comfortable grandfather back in Norway, with his lovely white beard. This man had no beard at all!

Mother was devastated, but Dad was patient. "Don't worry," he said calmly as we huddled together on the floor of that empty flat. "She'll come around all right. Just ignore her for a little while, and we'll see." He turned his head and continued to talk to Mother. After a while, without looking at me, he let his hand quietly touch my knee, then took it away again and continued his conversation. Several times he did this, and I became interested. Then he looked at me, and grinned, but again he turned his head away. I was definitely intrigued, and before long, I had reached out my hand and tentatively touched him, too. He smiled, and poked me gently, and I poked back, and before long we were laughing together like old comrades, my lump almost forgotten.

"Just like a young puppy," said Dad. "Leave him alone at first, and let him sniff you over. Before long he'll come to you of his own accord."

So many times in later life I have watched Dad make friends with children, first arousing their curiosity and giving them confidence, then disarming them completely. He had a wonderful way with youngsters. To him age was no barrier at all. As time went on, the bond between us grew stronger and stronger.

Ever since he had come back from Norway, Dad had been busy. He had set up an office at 50 Church Street in New York and was "getting things in shape." He had been back and forth to Cuba a number of times with some success, and he had been up to Montreal to check on prospects with the Canadian Pacific Railway, but orders were slow in coming in across the country. Right from the start, he had had a hard and trying time. There was so much competition in New York, and he soon discovered that the city was full of big business sharks who were always out to "get the other guy."

"It's really kind of a jungle here," he told Mother. "More of a jungle than I ever sensed in the heat of Cuba. Here, business is really bloodthirsty. But we'll make a go of it. At least now I can come home to you, and we can get out and go for a walk on weekends on the Palisades and breathe some fresh air."

True to his promise to his own father back in Norway long ago, Dad had offered to help any family members who wanted to try out life in the United States. As a result, we held "open house" for years for numerous wandering relatives. That fall, it was Onkel Otto who came to live with us. He was back from his life at sea, and had been lured, as Dad had been, to seek his fortune in America. Dad was delighted at the chance to have his help in the office at 50 Church Street, and they worked hard together. Then came Andreas Hoyer, whom I called Onkel Andy. He lived with us while he worked for a time on the big new subway. We became a cosy little family.

❧

After a year or so, we moved from the apartment in Fort Washington Heights to another place called Cragmere Court. Things were better now for Dad. Business was running more smoothly. Onkel Otto's fiancée had come over from Norway, and they were married and were settling down. Onkel Andy had moved on to other things, and we were now a family on our own.

This new apartment house, while not exactly in the country, was in an area that was gradually building up, and there were still some open fields to be seen. Across the road was a big sandpit, where still another apartment was about to rise, but so far there was only a large hole in the hillside and some odds and ends left by the contractors.

Unexpectedly, New York was blanketed by a fall of new snow, which changed the appearance of the whole world. All the ugliness was covered up by a beautiful white carpet, a most unusual occurrence for New York. Dad could not have been happier. He could hardly wait to get out on his skis, for this was his first real chance to introduce me, his Cuban daughter, to the joys of winter.

I remember how he bounced me lightly up on his shoulders and how we struck out over the open fields, my feet dangling over his chest, my arms wrapped securely around his neck. I could feel the surge of every step as we whisked over the new snow. This was really the life! We both shouted with happiness. It was great to sit up here on his shoulders, to feel the wind in my face, and to see things from an entirely new perspective. We strode out over the open land, and climbed to the top of the little rise above the sandpit. There we looked down, and way below, I could just see a little "something" peeking out above the snow. "Hang on tight," said Dad, as he kicked off. "Here we go!" And down we went.

Somehow, one of Dad's skis caught in the submerged "something," which turned out to be a coil of wire left behind by the contractors, and before I knew what was happening, I was sailing through the air as though shot from a cannon. I landed upside down in a snow drift. It was quite a shock, but Dad extricated his ski and came quickly to dig me out. He brushed me off, and before I could protest, I was settled once more astride his shoulders, and we were climbing up again. "Every once in a while, you fall," said Dad, "but then you just get up and try again. This time we'll look for a place where there are no hidden wires!" And this time we did not fall. We rode safely to the bottom, and we did it again, and again, and again. That was a very good lesson, which has always stuck. "If at first you don't succeed, then try, and try again. Never give up. When things go wrong, just pull yourself together – and try *once* more. It's bound to work."

It was while we were living in Cragmere Court that Bob was born. I had been shipped off to visit family friends in New Jersey when the big moment finally came, and when I returned I found that, inexplicably, I had a baby brother. This was exciting, and I was proud to go for walks with Mother and Dad and the new baby in his carriage, but I decided that babies were a terrible lot of work, and I hoped he would be more fun when he grew older.

About this time we also acquired a touring car, a monstrous green Winton Six. It was a car that reminded me very much of the picture on the silver matchcase Dad always carried in his pocket. He would show it to me, and laugh as he said, "This picture has now come true, ten years after my friends in squad A at Brown Hoist gave it to me." I thought his friends must have been very clever to have foreseen this so very long ago!

The car made it much easier for us to get around, and during the next two summers we would motor out to Shelter Island, located in the "lobster's claw" of Long Island, some 160 kilometres east of New York City. What an expedition that was, a whole day's journey in which Mother, the baby and I, plus all our gear for the summer, would be piled into the car, and Dad would drive us out over that long, bumpy, dusty road. All too often we would hear a loud BANG! – and we would pull over to the side with a blowout. "We always manage to have at least two flat tires on every trip," Dad would say, resignedly, "but I guess that's only to be expected." And he would somehow make a joke of the situation as he wrestled with the spare.

Those were wonderful summers, with Dad commuting by train on weekends, leaving the car safely with us on the island during the week. He would arrive with all the other business husbands on Friday evening in Greenport, taking the ferry over to Shelter Island. All the wives and children and babies would be down at the pier to meet them. There was a great flurry when the boat docked, and Dad would be among the first to leap ashore, ahead of the flock of more sedate business men. "Just like in Norway when the coastal steamer comes in," he would say. "Everyone comes down to the dock to watch the excitement." And we would walk back to Bowditch's boardinghouse, with me riding happily piggyback and Mother pushing Bobby in his carriage. Then we would plan the next day's activities.

Sometimes this would mean taking the car down a side road to some high dunes at the island's end. There, hand in hand with Dad, I would slide deliriously down the steep dunes to the sandy shore. "It's almost as though we were really skiing," he would remind me, "but at least on skis you don't have to take the sand out of your shoes at the bottom!" And we would crawl up once more, and slide back down. It was marvellous fun.

At other times, we would go for a cruise in the *Aeolus*, the little catboat that Dad kept at the Shelter Island dock in care of Captain Griffin. Dad and Mother and I, with the baby in his carriage, would go down to the pier with our lunches and sweaters and all the other necessary equipment, and there Captain Griffin would have the boat ready and waiting for us. Sometimes we would invite another family to go along for the ride, and Captain Griffin would sail us right around Shelter Island, or we might go way out in the sound, to one of the other islands, before turning back.

Aeolus, Mother told us, was the Greek god who was famous for his "bag of winds." We thought it was a fine name for our bouncy little craft with its billowing sail.

Once in a while we would anchor in the reedy little bay where Captain Griffin had his Red Fox Inn, a tiny one-room cabin where he stayed with his cronies in hunting season. One time he took us ashore there and showed us the cabin. We went inside, and he pushed aside a strip of carpet to reveal a trap door in the floor, with a concealed iron ring for a handle; beneath it lay a dark, sandy cellar. That, he told us, was where they kept their venison! Carefully replacing the carpet, he added mysteriously, "Just in case the troopers come by." It was very exciting!

During our last summer at Shelter Island I became aware that the United States was at war. I knew that Dad was anxious about certain ships, which were carrying cargoes of paving blocks from Norway to Cuba. Dad's fear was that they would be sunk by enemy submarines. It was reassuring to know that the father of one of my little friends from Shelter Island was in charge of a submarine chaser, a big grey boat stationed over at Greenport. We used to see it as it sped up and down Long Island Sound on test runs. I wasn't too sure what a submarine was, but I had a mental picture of a procession of Dad's ships dodging back and forth at sea, pursued by submarines, and these in turn were hotly pursued by chasers. Eventually the ships must have reached Cuba safely, as we heard no more about submarines, and the chaser was still to be seen as it cruised up and down upon the sound.

In the fall, we motored back to New York again on another puncture-filled journey. Dad and Mother had been looking for a suitable place for us, where we could really settle down. Apartment rents were high in the city, and school would soon be a problem. Business was improving, the office in Cuba was doing well, and they felt they could begin to expand a bit. The car and the sailboat were both expressions of their improving finances, and they now wanted to invest in a real house of their own.

We would drive out into the country on weekends to go "exploring," as Dad used to say, visiting houses that were either still under construction or else had a For Sale sign out in front. Sometimes there would be a watchman on duty, who would take us around, and sometimes a person who lived there would show us through. Mother was always interested in how many bedrooms and bathrooms they had, whether or not there was a fireplace, and if the stairs were steep, while Dad always wanted to see the furnace room, and look over the garage. To me it was all a game, and I was delighted to poke around in these exciting places, pretending each time that this was where we were going to live.

Eventually they decided on a house in Pelham, one of the suburbs. Dad could commute into the city daily, while the family could enjoy the country air. This was one of the "bedroom communities," only half an hour by train from New York, and in 1916 we moved to a new brick house with a beautiful green-tiled roof, at 31 Benedict Place.

I have very clear memories of that house. It had a big entrance hall with a tall grandfather clock, and a living room with a cosy fireplace. Beside it was a roomy sunporch, with plants and a goldfish aquarium, where we would play on rainy days. There was a large dining-room, a big kitchen, and a breakfast nook where we children had our meals. Upstairs were four bedrooms, three bathrooms, and a sewing-room, and on the top floor, two maids' rooms, and another bathroom. It was quite a change from Cragmere Court, and Mother had a wonderful time furnishing it. We had to have two maids to look after it – Ruth, who was a wonderful cook, and Inga, who did the housework.

The house stood on a hill, and the road turned around in a big circle just beyond our property, and went back down the hill again, so there was never any through traffic. It was a great place for kids.

One of Dad's first moves was to build a playground in the side yard: a big wooden framework from which dangled a swing, a set of rings, and a removable turning pole. There was a big sandbox, too, for the smaller children, and it soon became a mecca for all the youngsters in the neighbourhood. They would congregate here and play to their heart's content.

Occasionally on Saturday mornings Dad would come out into the yard to see what we were doing, and there he would be immediately besieged by the small fry, whose favourite pastime was to have a "parade." At that time everyone was very war-conscious, even small children of my age or younger. Dad would line us all up, each one brandishing a broom, a rake, a shovel, or just a plain old stick. Then he would give the command, "Shoulder arms!" and march us down the driveway. "Left, right, left, right! Company halt! One, two!" There we would "About face!", and file back up the driveway again. "Left, right, left, right!" It was great fun, and Dad pretended he was back in Krigsskolen again.

But most fun of all was when he would lead the troops in a "cavalry charge." With legs outspread as though mounted on horseback, he would brandish his imaginary sword above his head as he led the attack, cantering down the driveway – slashing to left, slashing to right – and ending up again at the sandbox, where he would rein in his phantom steed. After that, he would disappear once more into the house, leaving us to canter about the yard, shouting commands to each other as we expertly wielded our own imaginary swords.

At the time, it never occurred to me that Dad was unusual – that other fathers never joined us, as he did, in these games. I suppose it was a welcome diversion for him from his regular business worries, but to me and the neighbourhood children, he was an outstanding hero.

For a number of years some Norwegian friends, Alf and Mia Hjort, had been luring Dad and Mother up to the Lake Placid Club in the Adirondacks for a short winter holiday; we children would be left in the care of a nanny while they explored the possibilities of this new territory. After a few visits they decided that Lake Placid, a small town in the midst of honest-to-goodness wilderness country, with lovely mountains and lakes, lots of snow in winter, and limitless trails in summer, would be the ideal spot for a family summer vacation. And so the next year – 1918, shortly after Peggy was born – we set off for Lake Placid.

The trip was a real adventure, a two-day motor journey from Pelham, punctuated by an overnight stay in a big hotel in Albany and several blow-outs as we navigated the rough mountain roads. Our first Winton Six had been traded in for a newer model, a sedan, and this was loaded to the brim. The engine tended to overheat on the long uphill climbs, and we often had to stop to let it cool. Dad would pull up beside a roadside stream and drain the radiator, putting the hot water to splendid use by warming the baby's bottle and thus ending her hungry howls. Then, after we had wolfed down our sandwiches, he would refill the now cool radiator from the babbling brook, and we would be off again, engine, baby, and family all quietly content.

After many miles, we came to the spooky, winding road through Wilmington Notch, a dark narrow route through a wild gorge at the base of Whiteface Mountain. The road twisted and turned many times before it finally emerged from the forest. Then it climbed a long hill rising higher and higher until suddenly we could look out across the golf course, and there was the Great Range spread before us. Here Dad stopped the car, and we all climbed out to savour the view, with every mountain standing out in solemn procession along the skyline. There was the sharp peak of Whiteface behind us, and tree-covered Sentinel Range nearer at hand. Then came Cascade, with the open slide on its flank, which looked like a startled fawn. Behind it were the High Peaks themselves: Wolf Jaws, Gothics, Saddleback, Basin, Marcy, Colden and MacIntyre. These were "real live mountains" as Bobby used to say, and each had a personality of its own. We took a long look, and then drove on excitedly over the last few miles to the Club.

That first summer we rented "Bywood Loj," one of the cottages belonging to Lake Placid Club. It was nestled in the pine woods. There was an icebox on the front porch, where the baby's formula was kept, and a hole under the veranda from which a mother skunk would emerge in the evening, followed by a troop of lesser skunks. They looked, I remember, like a toy train, with the big engine leading in front, and identical little passenger cars behind. Bobby and I were cautioned to make no unexpected moves, lest we prompt "offensive tactics," and the nightly reappearance of the skunk family was among the highlights of the summer. Never once was there an "accident." They were very circumspect and well-mannered; they went their way and we went ours. The experience was a splendid lesson in co-existence.

Dad, however, yearned for the distant hills. One day, after due preparation, he set off at five o'clock in the morning on what was to be a truly epic journey. Although he always maintained that one should never go climbing or hiking alone, he was in a quandary, for despite an earnest attempt the day before, he could find no one willing to accept his challenge to climb Mount Marcy in a single day, walking all the way, including ten miles to the foot of the mountain, and ten miles back. Dad decided to go by himself anyway, having first raided the front porch icebox for bread and butter and cheese, and a bottle of Peggy's formula.

It was a beautiful June day, with strong sun, no wind, and only a few mosquitoes as he set off across the golf course, long before there were any players in sight. He went on across the Ausable River, up through North Elba, across the farm fields and into South Meadows, where Marcy, Colden, and MacIntyre rose comfortingly near.

At South Meadows lived Abe Fuller, a north-country character who farmed a lonely patch of ground at the foot of the mountains.

Abe seldom had visitors at his farm, which lay "way off the beat," as he used to say. Dad came marching in with his pack on his back at eight o'clock that morning. "Hi!" said Dad. "Nice day!"

Abe agreed, slowly. "Hi. Sure is. Whar're ye from?"

Dad put down his pack and explained. "Lake Placid. I left at five this morning. I'm heading for the top of Marcy."

"By gosh!" said Abe. "Thet's a long ways. Ye all alone?"

"Yes," said Dad. "Couldn't find anyone to go with me. Want to come?"

"Wall, no," said Abe reflectively, "don't know's I do. I'm kinda busy here, anyways." He looked across the young crop just showing in his field. "Ye can cut in over thar," he said, " and foller a lumber road till ye come to Marcy Dam. Keep on goin' till ye come to Marcy Brook. Turn left and go on to Indian Falls. There turn right and foller up over the shoulder of Marcy till ye come to the top."

"I knew from the map," said Dad, "but I really need to stretch my legs. I live in the city in wintertime, and I'll never get used to city living. I grew up in Norway, and there we have real mountains – like yours."

Abe thought this over. "When 'er ye comin' back?" he asked.

"Tonight," said Dad. "I've got to be back in Placid this evening."

"Wall, I'll tell ye," said Abe. "Come back here after ye've ben to the top. We'll give ye supper. Ye'll be hungry by then. How about a chicken?" There were a number of scrawny fowl scratching about in the yard. Dad thought this a great idea. "Jest a minute," said Abe, and he went inside, reappearing with his rifle. "How bout thet one?" He took aim, and fired. BANG! The chicken fell over, headless. Abe picked it up, its wings still flapping. "See ye later," he called. "Hev a good climb!" And he disappeared into the house.

Dad went on, through the deep forest, out through small clearings, across the stream and up Marcy Brook. Everything smelled so good, so fresh. This was really living. The birds sang, the stream tumbled over waterfalls, and the trail led up and up. Finally he came to the cut between Little Marcy and the peak itself. There he could see clearly the bald mountain top rearing above the timber line. This really began to look like his kind of country.

As he approached the verge of timber, the trees became shorter and shorter, until finally he reached the top and stepped out into another world, carpeted with blueberry bushes, juniper, and crowberry, and he could see far, far away. In the distance lay the village of Lake Placid, the open golf course, and the intervening country through which he had walked that morning. Down at his feet lay South Meadows and Abe Fuller's farm, where he was sure the chicken would be waiting for him for supper. He ate his bread and cheese, and relished Peggy's bottle. There was not a living soul in sight. He had the whole world to himself.

Far below on the other side of the mountain he could see the Ausable Valley while, across Panther Gorge, Haystack reared his head sharp and clear. Far down the valley, flanked by other mountains, rose Giant, scarred by massive slides. It was a soul-stirring sight. At last he shouldered his pack and began the descent.

It was four o'clock when he came again to Fuller's, and Abe and his wife were out to meet him. They led him into the house, past the big incubator in the parlour, filled with hatching chicks. They sat down to the chicken, roasted to a turn, with potatoes and vegetables from their own garden. It was an excellent feast, and the two men had a wonderful time swapping yarns. When dinner was over, Dad thanked them heartily as he left a little "something" to cover the cost of the meal, and promised to drop by again next time he passed. Then he set off on his homeward way, back to Lake Placid.

He reached Bywood Loj long after dark. The kids and the skunks were all in bed. It had been a lovely day, he told Alice. His legs were definitely stretched, and as he lay down, content, Alice said softly, "I'm glad you're back!"

"So am I!" said Dad, as he gathered her close.

❦

Now that there was plenty of space in our house and we had a guest room, other relatives came from Norway to visit with us. There was Tante Jeanette Platou, one of Dad's little girl cousins, whom I knew only from that old picture taken on the steps outside his Bestefar's house, Ekeli, when Dad was ten years old. Tante Jeanette stayed with us for almost a year, and helped to look after us children.

Another of our Norwegian relatives, Tante Anna Hoyer, Onkel Andy's sister, was a concert pianist. She loved to come out to

Pelham for Sunday visits; after dinner, she would perform for us on Mother's grand piano. She played her own music, then ran through all sorts of funny little Norwegian children's songs and the family would sing with her. As time passed it became evident that Peggy was the musical member of the family, for she would happily climb into Tante Anna's lap, placing her hands carefully on Tante Anna's own as she proudly "helped" her to play, and the look of joy on her face was a sight to see.

Most exciting of all was when Dad's mother, our Bestemor, came over from Norway. She arrived in New York on her seventieth birthday, escorted by Dad. Our Bestefar had died in 1913, and now that the war was over and the seas were once more safe for travel, Dad was happy to have Bestemor come to us in America and see for herself how well we were. She stayed with us for a year in Pelham, and we still cherish the portrait taken of her with us three children. Dad took her back to Norway with him when he went over on a business trip in 1920, for then he had hopes of setting up a branch of his New York office in Christiania, with his brother Johannes in charge.

The Norwegian navy was reducing its staff, and Johannes was delighted to take on a civilian job. He spent several months in New York learning the machinery business from Dad and Onkel Otto, and then he returned to Norway as purveyor of steam shovels, locomotive cranes, winches, and buckets. At first it seemed an excellent arrangement, but the new business partners had not counted on fluctuations in the currency; they had not foreseen that the American dollar would go up and the Norwegian crown would go down, nor that business would be slow anyway after the war. More important still, it gradually became clear that Onkel Johannes, as he himself admitted, "was never really cut out to be a salesman." Although he opened an office and travelled around to many places which he hoped would have use for heavy machinery, he soon discovered that he was not meant for the business world. So, at the end of the year, the Norwegian office was closed, and Johannes with a sigh of relief rejoined the navy.

At this time a wave of nationalism was sweeping Norway. Christiania, the capital, had been named in 1624 after the Danish King Christian IV, who at that time was King of Denmark and Norway, but now many citizens were in favour of changing the name to

The Johannsen family, 1918: Herman, Alice, Robert, Alice, and Peggy.

something with more of a "Norwegian" ring. "Oslo" was the name chosen, meaning "mouth of the river Lo" (the Lo is a stream that discharges into the fjord at that point) and "Christianiafjord" became "Oslofjord" to match. Even little Laurvig changed the Danish spelling of its name to "Larvik," by which it is known today.

Just before taking ship back to America, Dad called on the Norsk Kulkompani, the large firm that operated the coal mines in Spitsbergen to which he had sold some heavy machinery for Browning Engineering back in 1905. This company functioned with American capital, and Dad felt the time was ripe for replacements. He was disappointed, however, to learn that the purchasing agent had just sailed north to spend the winter in Spitsbergen. On the spur of the moment Dad decided to take the next steamer north himself, hoping to intercept the man at one of the ports along the way. Meanwhile, he would enjoy the scenery along the coast where his father and his grandfather, to say nothing of numerous others of his ancestry, had sailed in generations past. Furthermore, he could picture to himself just how the coast must have looked to Nansen and Sverdrup as they returned from their First Fram Expedition in 1893.

At Hammerfest, the northernmost port on the mainland, he still had not overtaken the purchasing agent. Spitsbergen lay a thousand kilometres farther north, but having come this far, it seemed pointless not to continue as the ship was going there in any case: it was to be the last scheduled voyage of the season. At Spitsbergen she would turn south again with the least possible delay in order to avoid being caught in the pack ice. Sailing so far north at the onset of winter was risky, but it was a risk well worth taking, he felt, so he stayed on the ship.

Everything went well. Dad managed a good sale at Spitsbergen. Then, while waiting for the return trip, he was invited to go with some of the men from the coal company to visit one of the sights of the region, a huge bird colony, where in the nesting season thousands of seabirds circled and screamed overhead. Although this was not the best time of year, it was nonetheless an unforgettable experience, and a further unexpected bonus was the chance to purchase the skin of a freshly killed polar bear, which had been considered a danger to the settlement. This he hurriedly arranged to have salted, then packed in a large barrel for shipment by the last boat of the season to Gunther's, a furrier in New York, together with a note requesting that it be made into a rug "without delay."

Just as the ship was about to sail, Otto Sverdrup, the man who had skied across Greenland with Nansen in 1888, who had been one of the great heroes of Dad's youth, came down to the pier. Dad had almost sailed with Sverdrup in 1898 on the Second Fram Expedition, which would have interrupted his student years in Berlin. What a coincidence that he should actually meet this famous man at last, and here in Spitsbergen at that. Sverdrup had made his headquarters in the north for a long, long time, and, as he told Dad, he was beginning to feel a little restless. "I've spent fifty years of my life battling the Arctic seas," he said, "and now I'm about ready to go south to warm up."

"Why don't you come down to Cuba with me?" Dad suggested immediately. "I can guarantee that will warm you up in a hurry!"

"A great idea," said Sverdrup with a chuckle. "I might just do that. I own a banana plantation in Baracoa on the northeast coast. I should go down and look it over." Dad told him of the time, ten

Swedish Coal Company quay with *Braganza* in Spitsbergen.

Coal packet at the entrance to Swedish coal company mine
at Spitsbergen, 1920.

years before, when he had encountered that surprised Norwegian
– in the dark, in a ditch, near Baracoa – and they had a hearty
laugh together.

But then it was sailing time for Dad, and his ship began, none too soon, its race with the pack ice. The weather looked seriously threatening, and it was obvious that a real storm was brewing. They sped south, but the ice soon closed in, and before long, there they were, frozen fast, with a solid mass of ice floes extending in all directions.

The storm, meanwhile, developed into a real hurricane. Everything not securely fastened to the deck was damaged or torn away. The wind howled for several days, and when it finally subsided, Dad and some of the men climbed down onto the pack ice to walk around. Things looked pretty much as they must have looked to Sverdrup and his crew as they had drifted northward towards the Pole almost twenty-five years before. The storm, however, one of the early ones in the winter, had weakened the ice, and before long a lane opened in the frozen mass and the ship managed to work its way slowly free, to limp into Kirkenes in northern Norway for much needed repairs.

Here it was possible to pick up another southbound steamer, but Dad first took advantage of being in Kirkenes to investigate the large iron mine that was then reopening after the war. There he had the good fortune to sell some more machinery, and he left well satisfied with all the unexpected adventures that had befallen him on his totally impromptu expedition to the north.

Weeks later, when Dad finally returned to us in Pelham, it was exciting to hear all these wonderful new stories, but by far the most dramatic one for us had to do with that huge polar bear skin, of which the furrier in New York could find no trace. After many futile enquiries by Dad, a mysterious, unidentified barrel was finally located in a corner of their warehouse, where it had been set aside because it had such a terrific smell. Somehow, all the documentation had been lost in the course of its having changed ship three times *en route*, but when the barrel was finally broken open, there lay the missing polar bear skin, fortunately discovered in the nick of time, just as the barrel was about to be discarded. In spite of this near misfortune, and in spite of the smell, the skin was successfully tanned and made into a handsome rug, and when it was finally delivered to us in Pelham and unrolled on the floor of the sunparlour, it made a tremendous impression on all the many friends who came to admire it.

The local children were particularly thrilled. Each one of them firmly believed, and just as firmly declared, that "Mr Johannsen himself had shot the bear when he was up last summer near the North Pole," a slightly exaggerated version which, I must say, Dad himself did little to correct.

Anyhow, the bear proved it. They had seen it and touched it themselves. And of lesser stuff than this are legends made!

CHAPTER TWELVE

Health and Happiness in the Adirondacks:
1922–1928

After twelve years of relentless struggle, there came at last a time when Dad had had enough of New York. He was tired of competitive jostling in the big city, the hot, dirty streets, and the callous striving to get ahead; it was like jumping through a perpetual quagmire, hopping from hummock to hummock, trying to avoid the mudholes, fighting to stay on top. He remembered the *myrs* back in Rondane – boggy ground where it was difficult to navigate among the lurking danger spots. The hummocks – the business orders he managed to get – seemed to be getting farther and farther between. There were always people caught in the mud around him, trying to undercut him, struggling to grab his spot, forcing him to jump on, and on, and on. There were even the unscrupulous, who sought to gain advantage through lawsuits.

Why was he there at all? Why had he not kept his eyes on the far hills? He knew from past experience that the longest way around is often the shortest way to one's destination; that what might seem a difficult and circuitous route often turned out to be the one that would take a traveller to the distant hill without his ever entering the boggy *myr* at all.

"Enough of this," he said to Alice. "I can't stand this rat race any longer. What I need is to find a place where I can do business in a more congenial way, where I can earn a living and at the same time continue to *live*."

Pelham had been a lovely place when they had first chosen to live there. There had been woods and places where one could take a Sunday walk in peace, but now it had become much too civilized. One was never far from the sound of motor cars, the smell of gasoline, the sight of new houses going up. Mother agreed with him. He longed for the freedom of wide spaces, where he and Alice could bring up their children according to a different set of values, a place where there was fresh air and a more relaxed way of life.

They had long been thinking of a move to Canada. In Montreal, the business atmosphere was less cut-throat then in New York. There he would still be able to pursue his old contacts with railroads and lumber companies, some of them going back twenty years. Montreal was more cosmopolitan, less of a melting pot. Furthermore, to the north of Montreal lay the Laurentian Mountains, a relatively unexploited territory of forested hills, with cosy little towns in the hollows, very much like his beloved Nordmarka. Living there could be his ultimate goal. Meanwhile, he had managed to accumulate a comfortable "nest egg." Now was the time to begin to spend some of it, to branch out and get something more out of life than mere money.

Otto, on the other hand, was quite content to stay on and continue his business and family life in New York, taking over that office on his own. His responsibility would be to diversify and adapt to changing conditions, while Dad, with a man in charge of the Cuban office, would concentrate his efforts on Canada, where the markets were more open, and where he could continue to sell the hoists and heavy mining, lumber, and construction machinery with which he was so familiar. Meanwhile, he would establish his family for a number of years in Lake Placid, where they already felt at home from several previous summer visits, and where they would have all the fresh air they needed. The house in Pelham could be rented to others, and eventually sold. When the children were closer to college age the family would move on to Montreal, but these formative years in Lake Placid were to be part of a well-calculated plan. Dad would drive the 200 kilometres from Montreal to Lake Placid on weekends to share their wonderful country life. From Friday night to early Monday morning he would have the wilderness at his doorstep, and his children would grow up strong and healthy and independent.

Ever since 1919 Dad had had a post office address in Montreal. Now, in 1922, he set up his new office in the Keefer Building in Montreal, and took a small apartment on Bishop Street where he "existed" during the week. Otto Platou, another Norwegian cousin who was just getting established in Montreal, moved in to share the apartment with him. It was an excellent arrangement.

In 1922 Lake Placid Club was, according to its brochure, "an informal university in the wilderness, a meeting and working area that combined civilization with leisure and beauty, access to the vitalizing forces of nature, and contact with many of those contributing to the nation's growth."

But the Club was far more than that. It was really a community in itself. There were three clubhouses – Forest, Lakeside, and Theanoguen – and a fourth, the Agora, with a full-scale theatre and concert hall, chapel, and seven-storey guest quarters, was under construction. There were eighty-odd cottages, some built for summer, others also equipped for winter. These were clustered on a thousand acres of partly forested land fronting on Mirror Lake and extending as far back as Cobble Hill, and down to the Ausable River. The Club had its own post office, general store, and pharmacy, its own garage, maintenance shops, laundry, and bakery. It had a network of farms that produced dairy products, eggs, and vegetables for its thousand or more guests. And it had seemingly endless sports facilities, including two eighteen-hole and three nine-hole golf courses, a putting green, twenty-one tennis courts, and a fully equipped boathouse and swimming complex. In winter, its tennis courts became one vast skating rink, portioned off into two full-scale hockey rinks, with other special areas for figure skating, general skating, and curling, the whole surrounded by a huge speed-skating track. The golf courses became ideal for those who were learning how to ski, and the surrounding countryside offered trail-skiing and bushwhacking at its best. Lake Placid had everything.

A number of well-established authors and artists made their home at the club. There was T. Morris Longstreth, well known for his books on travel and the great outdoors, who had written the brochure on the Club. There were people like Paul King, a distinguished Adirondack artist, whose paintings were in great demand. Every summer a dozen or more members of the Boston Symphony Orchestra came to the Club, giving seven classical concerts each week. There were also well-known actors and actresses who came from time to time as Club guests, and appeared there in various theatrical productions. There were golf and tennis idols, champion skaters, skiers and dog racers, many of whom gave lectures on their skills or hobbies, or participated in competitive or exhibition events, which in turn drew other famous people. The Club was a constant parade of celebrities, summer and winter.

We children accepted life at Lake Placid Club as a completely normal way of living. We were not concerned with the cities to which our friends returned. The Club for us combined the desirable qualities of city dwelling with all of the advantages of life in the country. It was in fact a very exhilarating place to be, and we could only feel sorry for our many friends who, between visits, had to go home to Toledo or Philadelphia or some other big city.

During the four previous summers we had become used to the Lake Placid way of life. Now that we lived permanently in Midnol, one of the Club's winter cottages, we joined avidly in the continuous program – the annual Indian council fire in the fall, the Christmas pageants, the druid ceremony at the New Year. We learned to ski and skate, and participated enthusiastically in every masquerade and ice carnival. We loved to take part in the traditional costumed special events, which required the help of many "extras". Certain important Club figures always took the leading parts, notably Godfrey Dewey, son of the founder of the Club (Melvil Dewey, inventor of the Dewey decimal system), whose red-and-green court jester's costume with its belled cap and curly-toed shoes set the tone for the Christmas season. He led all the participants (and sometimes there were hundreds of us) on a merry hunt for the Yule log on the day before Christmas, and again on a song-filled pilgrimage on Christmas morning when we were all disguised as "waits" (carollers and itinerant musicians). Parents, grandparents, and children of all ages took active part, and all were issued with special multi-coloured hooded capes, which were easily tied on over our outdoor clothing. Transformed into a throng of medieval characters, we sang lustily as the jester, playing his guitar, led us along the snowy paths of the Club grounds from cottage to cottage amid softly falling snowflakes; pausing from time to time, we sang

"Away in A Manger," or "We Three Kings of Orient Are," or "Good King Wenceslas." It was a vivid, unforgettable event, and many families came back for it season after season.

Dad, however, was not particularly impressed with all this "theatrical stuff." His great interest lay in winter sports, and the Club soon found that he had many useful connections. In fact, he was instrumental in helping the management in 1922 to obtain Örnulf Poulsen from Norway as the first winter sports director, and later, Mikkel Wettergren, another Norwegian, as a ski instructor. Club members and their guests had a wide choice of activities presided over by this sports staff who had to cope with a mass of city folk, many of whom tended to cling together on well-beaten paths and were apprehensive about venturing too deep into the woods. Dad, on the other hand, was all for luring anyone who would follow him out into the "hinterland," to travel over winding forest trails where they could see the tracks of fox and deer and rabbit. We, his children, had ample opportunity to do this, but the average run of Club guests "had not been brought up the proper way," as Dad used to put it. "They don't know what they are missing when they run around a speed skating track. They should get out and explore! They should savour the real life that lies all around us here in this wonderful mountain country."

Winter sports had been popular at the Club from the very beginning, when, in 1895, Melvil Dewey first bought "Bonnie Blink," an old farm house. It was later converted into a boarding-house, and later still incorporated into Lakeside Clubhouse. At first, these sports were referred to as "frolicking in the snow," but by 1924 skating, skiing, and dog-sledding had become major attractions. Poulsen and Wettergren became responsible for all organized activities including races, gymkhanas, sleighrides, toboggan runs, and ski-joring (being towed, on skis, by a horse). Dad, however, was openly amused. "You should really concentrate on taking people out into the wilderness, away from all this civilized stuff," he would say. But his own children had great fun joining in all the events, accumulating as we did so a pin, a star, or a medal, to mark our way up the competitive ladder.

Right from the start, Dad was a stickler for keeping us in trim. Part of our daily routine was Walter Camp's "daily dozen," a series of Victrola records. Dad would put them on the gramophone, crank up the handle, and lead Mother and the three of us through arm-

Alice and Herman at Lake Placid, 1923.

swinging, toe-touching, and deep-knee bending to the tune of lilting waltzes and martial bands. This was a daily ritual that we all enjoyed, as much for the lively music as for the exercise. Then we felt prepared for whatever the day might bring.

Back in 1921, the "Snowbird" had been adopted by the Club as the emblem of its newly formed Winter Sports Association. Each winter season began with the special raising of the Snobird Flag, on which a pure white bird winged its way across a field of blue, set on a great banner of white. This flag would fly until the snow disappeared towards the end of February, and all winter sports events took place under its protection.

The most important of all these competitions was the International Ski Meet. There was always a seven-mile cross-country race followed by a ski-jumping competition on the Intervale Hill.

The four racers in the first 25-mile race.

However, with the advent of Örnulf Poulsen in the winter of 1922–23, a spectacular new dimension was added in the form of a twenty-five-mile race held on Washington's Birthday, this in spite of the criticism of many who felt that holding such a strenuous event would be not only foolhardy but actually "inhuman." Dad, however, called to mind the early opposition in Christiania to the first fifty-kilometre race run there in 1888, and now Poulsen assured everyone that the fifty kilometres had at last become the accepted rule in Norway. So Dad and Örnulf and a number of volunteers spent days that fall preparing the track – cutting underbrush and linking various lumber roads on the surroundings mountains.

The press reports of that event provide some interesting details: the *New York Times* wrote,

R.S. Wade of McGill University, Montreal, today won the 25-mile cross-country race, feature event of the third annual International ski meet of the Snobird's Winter Sport Club of Lake Placid. Wade's time was 4h 21m 20s.

A.N. Edson, Dartmouth College Outing Club, finished second, and H. Smith Johannsen, Norsemen's Ski Club, New York, was third.

RAPID TRANSIT OVER THE LAKE PLACID
SNOWS: H. SMITH JOHANNSEN

Herman carrying Peggy, *The New York Times*,
31 December 1922.

The race was regarded by judges as the first of its kind to be held in North America and a test of every phase of skiing skill, including endurance. It covered hills, woods, clearings, underbrush, and level ground, and twice crossed the west branch of the Ausable River, successful negotiation of the distance requiring good judgment on grades and general cross country efficiency.

Johannsen, third to finish, came in collision with a dog while crossing a highway some 300 feet from the finish, getting a hard fall and breaking his left ski. He regained his position on the right ski, however, and made the final dash down a steep slope on one foot, carrying the broken ski.

What the newspaper failed to mention was that all the other competitors were college men in their early twenties. Dad, at forty-eight, was already more than twice their age. And what no one could foresee was that in 1924 he would again compete, this time coming second. Or that in 1925 he would take fourth place, after having come fifth in a field of twelve men in the ten-mile competition!

Despite our family's preoccupation with skiing, Bob and I both took great interest in skating as well. Bob was keen on speed skating, which was the rage at Lake Placid High School. Some of the best speed-skaters in the Adirondacks, in fact, hailed from Lake Placid, and Charlie Jewtraw and the Shea brothers were the idols of all the young. They flashed around the huge natural rink on Mirror Lake on fifteen-inch blades, and ten-year-old Bob, not to be outdone, skated frantically on his own fifteen-inchers under the hopeful impression that the longer the blade, the better (eventually) the skater.

I went in for figure skating, and took great joy in the freedom of movement and the graceful swings of the waltzes and ten-steps we danced to the tune of Victrola records played at the Club rink. It was always exciting to watch the outstanding performers who came each winter from Ottawa, Toronto, and New York to compete in the international figure skating meets, and well do I remember watching breathlessly as Beatrix Laughran of New York trained there before the First Winter Olympics at Chamonix, France, in 1924. And there were also Maude and her sister Cecile Eustace-Smith of Toronto, who wore the shortest skating skirts I had ever seen. They were actually above the knees!

The summers at Lake Placid were also exciting and eventful. The semi-weekly tours led by a marvellous amateur naturalist, Abigail O'Brien, who used to take a group of Club children on rambles with butterfly nets and magnifying glasses and flower books, were particularly important to me, for she introduced me to the scientific side of nature. Dad was always interested in where and how the animals lived, but he cared little about what they were called. To him, a bird was a bird. Abigail O'Brien, on the other hand, taught me to call these creatures by name, and to observe the special places where one could expect to find a certain plant or animal. And she went one important step further. She awakened an enduring curiosity in my youthful mind, which added an extra dimension of interest to my subsequent trips in the wilderness during all the ensuing years.

In summer months, Dad would drive down from Montreal on Friday evenings and Mother would have food packed in readiness. We children would be fully prepared for camping, and would be sent to bed at sunset to be ready for the early Saturday morning start, when food, sleeping bags, and knapsacks would be speedily loaded into the car, and all of us would take off in a flurry of excitement for Adirondack Loj, ten miles farther into the wilderness. There we would take possession of one of the lean-to's at Hart Lake. We would unroll our sleeping bags on the fragrant balsam boughs, and help to assemble wood for the cooking fire. Dad was fireman, and Mother the cook, with such help as we might give her, although we tended to be more interested in rushing down to the lake to catch salamanders than we were in keeping house. Despite the often stubborn, smoky fire, she always managed to produce delicious meals even though her eyes were often filled with equally smoky tears.

An important part of those weekends was always some special "expedition," led by Dad, to the top of Mount Jo, out towards Indian Pass, or up the MacIntyre trail. Occasionally we would go on a berry-picking jaunt, spurred on by the promise of raspberry jam for next winter. I remember one time when Bob preferred to go salamandering, and Mother said, "That's all right, Bob, but the rest of us are going to earn our jam. If you don't want any, that's your choice, but we want to have plenty for next winter." And to Bob's eternal surprise, she kept her word. When raspberry jam appeared on the table that year, he never got a lick. "Sorry, Bob," said Mother, "you didn't earn any, so there's none for you!" It was a hard lesson, but one that stuck.

But most of all, I remember those wonderful summer evenings around the campfire after supper, toasting marshmallows and watching the sparks ascend. Then we would curl up in our sleeping bags to watch the stars come out as we listened to the chorus of bullfrogs and the distant hooting of an owl. These were halcyon days, and all of these experiences became woven forever into the fabric of our lives.

In the summer of 1924 the house in Pelham was sold. During our first two years in Lake Placid, we children had given Pelham scarcely a second thought, so occupied were we with our own new lives, but Mother felt somewhat nostalgic about Benedict Place when she went back to pack things up.

"It's not really as though we were burning our bridges," she explained. "We're really only consolidating." But I remember how glad we were to see our own old things again when they finally arrived in the big moving van.

We transferred very quickly then from the furnished apartment in Upper Midnol to the ground floor of Westgate, another winter cottage near the entrance to the Club grounds. There we had a little more room to expand, although it was still pretty much of a tight squeeze. However, all the bedroom furniture finally got in, and so did Dad's big wing chair in which he loved to sit comfortably in the living-room and smoke his pipe, and the little old-fashioned mahogany table which Mother had brought all the way from Norway with her when I was a baby. We found space for most of our things, and the residue went again into storage. But most important of all was the grand piano, which had to share my bedroom with me, leaving just enough space for my cot to fit into the curve of that massive instrument. The piano was Peggy's special domain, and here she used to practise by the hour.

So, Westgate was now home, as we settled again into the exciting round of life at the Club. And when winter came, we went back to school in the village. For us three Johannsen children, however, the most exciting times of all were really our special winter camping trips to Adirondack Loj. Dad would arrive by night train from Montreal, and we would drive out next day to the Loj by sleigh with some of the winter guests from the Club.

On our first such winter trip, I remember we could not see out of the windows in the ranger's cabin because of the build-up of our frosty breath on the inside. I remember, too, how we youngsters were almost flattened by the weight of those heavy horse-blankets piled on top of us to counteract the sub-zero temperature.

Then, there was that red-letter Friday when Dad returned from a business trip to Quebec where he had been with Sir William Price and a number of other men reconnoitring the Price Brothers' Timber Limits at Lac St-Jean. He brought home with him a six-week-old puppy, an Alsatian with droopy ears and feet out of all proportion to his body. He was so small I could hold him cupped in my two hands. "But," said Dad with an eye to the future, "he'll grow. We'll train him to be a real sled-dog, and he will go with us on all our trips."

Mother, however, was more concerned with the immediate present, and lost no time in making him a small coat of blanket cloth, which was held in place by a tummy band. "This will keep him warm until he grows a little older," she said. "After all, it's very cold when we have to take him outdoors." We named him Ken, after Kenogami, Québec, where he was born, and Ken soon became an integral part of our family life. Years later, we were amused to find that little coat tucked away in a box. Ken had indeed grown to match the promise of his enormous puppy feet. The blanket coat by that time barely covered his head, and he had become the handsome shepherd dog with alertly pointed ears and happy disposition who accompanied us everywhere. With the little coat, Mother had also laid aside a clipping from the *Lake Placid News* of 1925:

Mr. and Mrs. Ward M. Canaday and their young daughter, Doreen, Morris Gregg, Jr., Mr. and Mrs. Herman Smith Johannsen, Alice Elisabeth, Bobby, Peggy, and Ken, who is as eager for skiing as is any other member of this family, spent last weekend at Adirondack Loj. From there they took trips up the side of MacIntyre and across Hart Lake, and to the river through one of the most beautiful trails in this vicinity. Deer tracks were found in the heavy snow, and at one place they came upon deer at a water hole.

Even little Peggy, though only seven, kept up with the party and skied the three and a half miles from Wood's Farm to the Loj.

On Monday, Mr. Johannsen left for New York and will sail on Saturday for Cuba to be gone three or four weeks on business. Mrs. Canaday and Doreen, who have spent the winter at the Club and have taken part in some of the season's outstanding sports events, will return Friday to their home in Toledo.

One special expedition to which Dad always looked forward each winter with extra enthusiasm was with a group of hardy skiers from the General Electric Company of Schenectady. The previous year, the *Lake Placid News* had reported:

Four Schenectady men, F.L. Stone, C.V. Ferguson, A. Kennedy, Jr., and H.R. Summerhayes, with H. Smith Johannsen of Lake Placid Club, are camping at Adirondack Loj this week, using it as a base from which to take ski trips over Avalanche and Indian Passes, and into the high peaks which rise close by. The Schenectady men arrived Monday morning and went to the Loj by sleigh, carrying with them all camping equipment needed to replenish that kept at the Loj the year round. With them went Herman Sibley, Lake Placid guide.

Mr. Johannsen did not return from a business trip to Cuba until Tuesday morning, but donned his skis that day, and accompanied by his large police dog who runs in harness, skied the 10 miles into the Loj in the teeth of a blizzard.

The following day, however, the weather was ideal. It was the weekend of Washington's Birthday, with strong spring sun. Dad and Ken led the group up through Avalanche Pass to spend the night camping in a lean-to, which was an experience in itself. The next morning, leaving the guide to "keep house" at the camp, the five of them set out in deep snow to follow Opalescent Brook. They soon observed that the trailmarkers, which had been nailed to the trees at eye-height during the summer, were sinking lower and lower as the depth of snow rose. Finally, the markers disappeared completely beneath the surface, and so did much of the under-brush. The forest, in fact, took on a more park-like appearance, and the higher they climbed, the deeper the snow had drifted. The stream lay completely camouflaged, and only occasionally could they hear the water as it gurgled underneath. In fact, the brook bed had become a veritable highway, and only once in a while did a fallen tree trunk, lying across the stream under a blanket of snow, offer any major opposition to their progress.

They worked their way over from Opalescent Brook to Feldspar Brook, still climbing, and it was exhilarating at last to reach Lake Tear-of-the-Clouds as it lay nestled between the highest peaks. A thousand feet above them loomed the bold top of Marcy, snow-covered and trackless. The men took temporary shelter in the snug lean-to in the pass, where they had a welcome snack as they contemplated the summit. They were glad to rest a while, and absorb the noonday sun. It was strange to realize that they were

Timberline lean-to between Skylight and Marcy.

standing on the actual watershed between the southward flowing streams which, beginning in Lake Tear, would reach the Atlantic Ocean through the Hudson River, and the northward flowing streams that would be gathered into the St Lawrence system to flow out to the Atlantic through the province of Quebec. When they finally set out again, it was with the sensation that they were real explorers, as they zigzagged their way out above the timber line, between patches of ice and snow, to the very top.

Several years before, Dad had stood on the summit of neighbouring Haystack in winter on skis, in company with John Apperson, another Schenectady man who was a close friend of the present group. Dad and Apperson had made their way that time up from the opposite side of the mountain, from the Upper Ausable Lake, and had arrived at the summit just as the sun was setting. It had been a rough trip as there had been only the two of them to share the trail-breaking. Apperson's description had inspired the present tour, and Dad recalled the previous event to the men now standing triumphantly on Marcy's snowy dome.

"We stood there together," said Dad, "on the top of Haystack and looked over here towards the setting sun. The sky was a wonderful rose. To the northwest trailed the peaks of the Great Range, with Giant in the far distance. All the intervening peaks were basking in the sunset glow. High overhead rode the full moon, which we knew would give us plenty of light as we picked our way down again through the thick forest back to our Camp on the Upper Ausable.

"It was a sight neither of us would ever forget, for in that moment we saw the world below us as though it were frozen in time. There was no past, no future, just the present. And it was unspeakably beautiful!"

This year, however, the men had reached their objective much earlier in the day, and there was still plenty of light, but there were many places on the return trip to Avalanche Pass when each man wondered whether he could really have made it down successfully had he had only moonlight to guide him! The lean-to in the pass was a very welcome sight, and Herman Sibley, the guide, had a good hot meal ready for them. Their bones ached, but they were well content, and their own accounts of this day's exploits would live through many years of telling.

❦

Every once in a while the village of Lake Placid received certain visitors, whom for various reasons it was delighted to honour. Dad received a call one day from the village manager of athletics, who told him with some excitement, "We're going to have a special guest, a real athlete, this time! We thought you might like to take him on a good ski trip."

Dad, who was beginning to be somewhat hard of hearing, caught the name as "Hicks." "He's in great shape," the athletics manager went on, "and he sure can ride a mean horse! We're asking you to take him on a real North Country outing – perhaps up Sentinel Range, and down to Clifford Falls."

Dad was somewhat taken aback. "All right," he agreed, a bit hesitantly. "I'll do the best I can for him. I'm interested in horses myself, but I don't have one. The best I can offer is my dog and sled."

The manager laughed. "That's just fine," he said. "He'll love it."

"I don't know what this is all about," Dad confided to Mother as he was preparing for the day, "but I'd better be on my toes. Whoever Mr. Hicks is, he's someone very special – a real bear for punishment, they say."

The athletics manager arrived at the appointed hour, with Mr Hicks in tow. They shook hands, and Dad said, "Here's my dog, Ken. He runs well in harness, but I'll bet he's no match for your horse!" They had a good laugh at this, and set off briskly across the Club golf course and down to the Ausable River.

It soon became apparent tht Mr Hicks, splendid horseman though he might be, was not exactly an experienced skier. He was certainly game, however, and things went reasonably well, with Dad breaking trail in the lead, followed by Ken with his sled and the lunch, and lastly by the two men. Such a single file arrangement is not exactly conducive to conversation, but at one point, when they paused to catch their breath, Dad asked his visitor, by the way of breaking the ice, "And where did you say you live?"

"California" was the reply.

"Nice country out there," said Dad, "but it's far too civilized. Too many people. I like the wide open spaces. No canned air for me!" And then he asked, as kind of an afterthought, "What business did you say you're in?"

Mr Hicks looked somewhat surprised. "Oh, you know," he said casually. "Motion pictures."

"Good heavens!" exclaimed Dad. "All that hot air! No wonder you want to clear out your lungs. We'll have to give you a real good workout." And he headed off again, without pursuing the subject.

The athletics manager tried tactfully to fill Dad in on Mr Hicks, but he drew a blank. "I'm sorry," said Dad, "but I really don't know anything about motion pictures. They're all the same to me! Just indoor stuff."

They went on, following the woods road, up through the snow-laden trees. Conditions were excellent, the temperature clear and cold. At one place they came upon fresh porcupine tracks. "Well, I see he's still here," said Dad, somewhat apprehensively, as he launched into a vivid account of Ken's last adventure at this very spot, when the dog had tried to make friends with a porcupine – and had come off second best, with a snoutful of quills. This time, however, Dad kept the dog well in check. They ate their lunch and had a short rest, then went on over the crest and down to Clifford Falls, but Mr Hicks was beginning to tire, and Dad was glad to get him home safely at the end of the day, all in one piece.

"Well, now, what kind of a trip did you have?" asked Mother, as Dad unharnessed the dog.

"Oh, we had a good time, all right", said Dad. "But I couldn't get much out of that fellow Hicks. I think he enjoyed himself, but he sure didn't have much to say."

Imagine our astonishment when we read next week in the *Lake Placid News*:

Movie Star Takes to Adirondack Trails

TOM MIX TRADES HORSE FOR PAIR OF SKIS

Climbs Sentinel Range with H. Smith Johannsen

"*Wow!*" said Bob. "And to think you thought he was some Mr Hicks! Tom Mix! I'd sure like to have skied with *him!*"

It seemed incredible to us that Dad had never heard of Tom Mix, idol of the silver screen. "But *I* never go to the movies. I'm sorry. I'll have to do better next time."

"You don't deserve a next time," growled Bob, with feeling. "Tom Mix! *Wow!* I know plenty of folks who'd love to have had your chance!"

That was one story Dad would never live down.

In due course, when Örnulf Poulsen returned to Norway in 1926, he was succeeded at the Club as sports director by the Marquis Nicholas degli Albizzi, a Russian-Italian nobleman of fallen fortune but with astounding vitality and charm. The marquis became a fixture at the Club where his distinguished accent and flashing smile, to say nothing of his title, made him a great hit among the ladies. The marquis had been an officer with the Italian ski troops and had trained in Switzerland during the First World War, an experience reflected in his stunning posture and his dashing and carefree style on skis.

Unfortunately, his reckless abandon led to a catastrophe at the Intervale Jump one day, when he fell and, literally, broke his neck. A lesser man might have succumbed, but not the marquis. I vividly recollect his marching around at the Club for months thereafter wearing a remarkable brace, which consisted of a leather-covered steel "halo" that encircled his brow. This was in turn firmly welded to a ramrod that passed down his back and was securely anchored

The author and Jackrabbit at Hovde saeter,
Norway, 1926.

to a rigid frame strapped around his hips. This contraption effectively prevented any sideways motion of his head or neck and must have been extremely uncomfortable, but eventually it was discarded, and the marquis emerged from his harness none the worse for wear, and just as jaunty as ever.

It was in that same summer of 1926 that Dad had hurriedly to go back to Norway on a business trip. He was hoping to expand the Norwegian paving stone business in Cuba, and to my utter joy, he took me to Norway with him.

One of the first things Dad did was to take me on a wonderful three-day hiking trip in Nordmarka with his sister, Helga. The old familiar territory brought back to Dad so many memories of his youth, but for me the best of all was a marvellous two weeks I spent with Tante Agnes and some of her friends, up in the Rondane Mountains at the Hovde *saeter*. This was "Per Gynt country," and one day we walked the long trail in to Rondevatn, the lake that had inspired Edvard Grieg when he composed the *Per Gynt Suite*. Back at the Hovde there was a little old gramophone, on which we kept playing Grieg music over and over, and to this day, I never hear "Morning," or the "Hall of the Mountain King," without instantly seeing all those wonderful Rondane Mountains marshalled before my eyes.

When Dad came up to spend the second week with us, we climbed together in the neighbouring mountains above timber line, and one day, on top of one of these, we came upon a herd of some twenty "wild" horses, outlined against the sky. They were a truly beautiful sight, their manes flowing freely in the wind as they eyed us cautiously. It was the custom down in the valley to turn the farm horses loose after spring ploughing was over, and horses from several farms would often band together to roam during the summer months on the high moors beyond the treeline. In the fall, the farm boys would come up, armed with halters, to capture one or two of them, round up the rest and drive them all home again. This was always an exciting time. The herd sniffed the wind as they watched us, fearing their freedom was about to end. Then, suddenly, they wheeled, and thundered away into the distance. What a wonderful sight that was, to see them running wild and free!

Norway came to mean something very special to me that summer, and I returned to Lake Placid much the richer for all these experiences. Dad came home content, too, for he had succeeded in grouping together the larger Norwegian quarry owners into a combine, and was looking forward to developing a major road-building business in Cuba, using Norwegian stone.

When we returned to the Club, we found that Mikkel Wettergren had resigned as ski instructor. The marquis, however, warmly recommended a man with whom he had served as a climbing guide at Banff during a previous summer. And that is how Erling Ström, yet another Norwegian, found his way to Lake Placid. Erling was just the man for the job, bringing with him his terrific sense of humour and his natural skill on skis. He settled comfortably into life at the Club, where his name thenceforth became synonymous with the ski sport. When the Marquis left the following winter, Erling stayed on, happily, for eleven years in all.

Erling tells of his first encounter with Herman in his book, *Pioneers on Skis*. One winter day shortly after his arrival at the Club, he was returning from a short run when he saw another skier approaching with the unmistakable loping gait of someone from "back home." They naturally stopped to have a chat, and soon discovered how much they had in common: both had been (almost literally) born on skis, and both knew the hills of Nordmarka like the inside of their own pockets. Neither of them imagined then

Jackrabbit and Alice starting out for an overnight trip.

that their friendship, struck up so casually that day, would flourish for more than half a century.

Throughout these years, the Johannsen family had been gradually taking longer and longer cross-country trips. At last in 1928 a professional photographer, H. Armstrong Roberts from Philadelphia, prevailed upon Dad to have the whole family act out a winter camping trip, with full gear, for the camera to record. It was great fun, and we went through all the paces. First, we harnessed the dog, then set out, with Dad, Mother, the whole family, and the loaded sled. Then we were photographed finding a campsite, setting up the tent, and preparing a cooking fire, with Ken by this time dozing in the sun, his work finished. The next pictures showed Dad and Bob "waking up" in their sleeping bags in the snow, and last the long trek back over the golf course, with Ken in the lead, sensing that he was homeward bound. These pictures have appeared in many magazines over the years, and whenever we see them we remember that bright sunny day when we did our first bit of "play-acting."

We also remember, with sadness, that our pretend trip was the last one we would ever take with Ken. Several days later, Dad had already put the harness on the dog for another short tour, but had not yet hitched him to the sled, when he remembered something

Alice, Ken, and Jackrabbit; a home away from home.

left in the house and went in to get it. When he returned, Ken was nowhere to be seen. Inexplicably, he had wandered off on his own. We called and whistled, but to no avail, and finally we gave up. Dad said, "Never mind. He'll come back when he gets ready. He's probably got something else on his mind." But he did not come back.

It was a sad-faced friend instead, who came to the door next morning carrying something in his hand. "I found the two of them – my dog and yours – down by the railway track," he said. "They must have been playing there together last night and didn't hear the train as it rounded the bend. They were probably blinded by the headlight. Both of them were killed outright. I brought you this. I thought you might want to keep it – to remember him by." It was Ken's harness, still bearing the little Norwegian hand-woven bow that Mother had sewn to the collar, "so that people would recognize him as part of the Johannsen clan."

And so he had been, a real part of our home team, and a very important part of our lives. We would have other dogs, but there would never be another Ken. He was known throughout the Adirondacks, far and wide, as "the mountain-climbing dog." His demise was recorded in newspapers from Plattsburg to Syracuse. The ski hills, for us, would never be the same again.

Among all the experiences in which we children shared at Lake Placid, there was yet another that Dad wanted us to have, which had meant so much to him as a boy. Remembering his friendship with the young colt that used to follow him about the farm at Stollingen, how he and Harald Hals had "chariot-raced" the old manure cart, and how he had participated in the haying at Amundsrud, he felt that we, too, should be exposed for a brief period to life on a real farm. That was how we came to spend the following summer on a venerable old property at North Jay.

This was a comfortable old-fashioned farmhouse, with rickety barns and haymows and clucking chickens, but Farmer Jones and his wife were really more interested at that time in taking in summer boarders than they were in propagating livestock. Still, the property was located on a broad plateau that faced Whiteface mountain and the Great Range, with wonderful sunsets and lots of surrounding hills and exciting places to investigate, and we enjoyed ourselves to the full. With the children from a neighbouring farm we used to jump in the hay, play hide-and-seek among the out-buildings, and hold impromptu harmonica concerts in the barn on rainy days.

Meanwhile, time was relentlessly marching on. We had had six wonderful years in Lake Placid, and Dad and Mother felt that the time was at hand when the family should move on to Montreal. Dad had now closed out his office in Cuba, as business was becoming more and more difficult. It would be less expensive to have the family all in one place. We would give up the Lake Placid Club and all that it represented, Dad would relinquish his little apartment on Bishop Street, and we would take a house in West-mount where we could all be together. We would from now on focus our weekend attention on the Laurentians.

In September 1928, all our furniture was packed into two large moving vans, which came down from Montreal for the purpose, and the family climbed once more into the Winton Six for the momentous drive up to Canada. We crossed the border at Rouses Point, where we were recorded as an "immigrant family with all their goods and chattels." A new and exciting chapter in our lives was about to begin.

CHAPTER THIRTEEN

Going Broke in Montreal: 1928–1930

Only two hundred kilometres separated our new home from our former one, but Canadian history and culture were absolutely unknown quantities in the Adirondack school curriculum. When we arrived in 1928 we knew almost nothing about our new country. For us children Montreal was a Great Adventure. For Dad, on the other hand, our move to Montreal meant a major reorganization in his business.

New York was behind him. Now Cuba, with its hot sun and more relaxed point of view, was also a thing of the past. The good years of Dad's business in Havana had begun soon after the turn of the century when, with the end of the Spanish-American War, foreign capital had begun to flow into Cuba. Investors from the United States and Canada were helping to develop communication systems; Sir William Van Horne's railroad had done much to open up the eastern provinces, linking hundreds of plantations and offering new opportunities for crop movement; and Canadian banks had been eager to stimulate the exporting of codfish from the Maritimes to Cuba, as well as the importing of Cuban fruit, tobacco, and sugar to Canada and the United States.

And as long as sugar prices remained high, Dad's canehandling machinery and his durable Norwegian paving blocks continued to be in great demand. Even during the First World War (neither Cuba nor Norway was involved in hostilities) business had gone well. Then, in 1919, the bottom suddenly dropped out of the sugar market. Large companies went bankrupt overnight, purchasers defaulted on payments, and Dad was one of the many who were caught in the middle.

Just at this crucial point, five large sailing vessels arrived in Havana from Norway, loaded with paving blocks on consignment to Dad. And suddenly there were no buyers who could pay. Added to which, there was a strike on the waterfront in Cuba. The cargo was hastily unloaded onto the harbour shore, and Dad was left with $300,000 worth of material that, for the moment at least, was quite unsaleable. He represented Onkel Nikolai Beer at the time, and had to answer for the delay in payment. But he stubbornly kept his office going in Havana, and as the years went by he was able gradually to sell off this surplus stock by dribs and drabs.

Then, in 1926, there came a resurgence of hope, when the Cuban government announced its intention to build a surfaced highway down the entire 1200-kilometre length of the island. This, of course, was of the utmost importance to Dad. He left for Norway immediately to reactivate the interest. There, he had succeeded in forming a combine of major quarry owners, who would all share in the long-term profits. Back in Cuba, he was filled with hope and optimism, but just as the deal was about to be closed one of the Norwegian companies "jumped" the combine, offering a lower, still more attractive price on its own. The Cuban government hesitated.

Then, suddenly, all deals were off. Asphalt, a new type of surfacing material, had appeared on the market. Improved methods in refining crude petroleum, coupled with great advances in its application, had opened a whole new era in road construction. An American company held the patent for the special steamrollers that were used to smooth the new material into place and, as patent-holders, were able to offer the Cuban authorities a much lower price.

Dad could see the writing on the wall. Against this new technology, his old-fashioned hand-laid paving blocks stood not a ghost of a chance. In its own way, this was a variation on the calamity that had overtaken his old friends the Indians. They had been forced aside by the "iron horse." Now Dad was blocked by liquid asphalt and the steam roller. It was the end of a dream.

So, after twenty years, Dad finally withdrew from Cuba altogether. He closed his office in Havana and said goodbye to all his old friends. He would not forget the happy times in that delightful land, but from now on, he would concentrate his attention on Canada. He had had his foot in the Canadian door, so to speak, since 1919; here the climate was really much more to his liking, and furthermore, from a single office in Montreal he would be able to consolidate all his work with the Canadian lumber, mining, and construction industries. It would be another new beginning, but he was ready for the challenge.

The family's early days in Montreal, starting in 1928, were exciting. We children had been used to the open hills and trails and country roads of Lake Placid, and we found it an entirely new experience to explore the possibilities that now surrounded us in the city.

We rented a semi-detached house on Western Avenue, close to beautiful Westmount Park, where there were tall trees and a little stream that made it seem a little like the country, although the library, the conservatory, and Victoria Hall certainly added more than a touch of civilization. It was wonderful once more to have a house to ourselves, with two floors and a basement and a backyard, but we were surprised to find that this house shared a common wall with our neighbour on the right, and that only a narrow walkway separated us from the neighbour on the left. We were fascinated by the gas fireplace in the living-room. It was lined with shiny white tiles and had a fake "log"; its flames were fed by a gaspipe. To Dad it was a real eyesore. "Can you imagine a fireplace in which you can't even burn honest wood? I'll never get used to it," he muttered. We installed our beloved grandfather clock, unseen since our early Pelham days, in the place of honour in the entrance hall, and it was a delight to have Mother's grand piano once more dominating a corner of the living-room.

It amazed us to see "nannies," wearing strange headgear that hung down their backs like a nun's veil, pushing perambulators around in Westmount Park. In Lake Placid, which was after all a country town, no one had ever heard of nannies. When Canadians spoke, they pronounced some words in a curious way. They would say, for example, "I'll see you next Chews-day". And when they said, "Isn't it about time we went outdoors?" it almost sounded like *aboot*. They referred to a train timetable as a "shed-ule." They spelled and pronounced what we had always called "X, Y, Zee" as "X, Y, Zed," and when we were invited to a friend's house for tea, it turned out to be a full meal. But these were only minor differences, and we soon got used to them.

Transportation, too, was a revelation. In Lake Placid we had easily walked from one end of town to the other, but in Montreal, for a six-and-a-quarter-cent streetcar ticket, you could ride for miles – to the farthest edge of the city if you liked, getting off wherever you pleased. And where one streetcar line crossed another, you could ask the conductor for a "transfer," board any car you wished that was going on the crossing line, and ride on that to the end of the track.

Gradually, the family became part of the community. The Johannsens joined St. Matthias Anglican Church, and to our surprise Bob enrolled in the choir. We had never thought of him as having a "voice" but we thoroughly enjoyed watching him during the service, for we thought he made such funny faces as he sang. Being in the choir, however, greatly enhanced his prestige, and we were impressed with his angelic appearance in his white surplice and red cassock, and eventually, with the gold medallion on a scarlet ribbon he was permitted to wear in recognition of his steady attendance and good behaviour. Obviously the choirmaster knew nothing of his prowess with a pea-shooter from the vantage point of his upstairs bedroom window, from which he and his pals loved to harass unsuspecting young ladies and other passersby out for an evening stroll.

Ten-year-old Peggy became an avid member of the Girl Guides, taking great interest in her uniform and in all the activities of her "company." And when not otherwise engaged, she and her classmates would practise their athletic skills, turning cartwheels up and down across the front lawns of our nearest neighbours on Western Avenue.

An early snowstorm in the mountains brought my first introduction to the Laurentians north of Montreal. Dad had already told us much about the country up there, where one could ski from one village to the next, crossing through farm fields, climbing over fences, winding through maple groves, "bushwhacking" through the forest beside a quiet lake, and finally coming down to the next town. A special car for skiers used to be attached to the end of the regular Saturday train, but in 1928 the Canadian National Railway had responded to popular demand and had inaugurated the Sunday "ski special," a whole train with ancient, wicker-seated cars especially for skiers. The Canadian Pacific was quick to follow suit. One could then go up on either line, get off at a different station each Sunday, find one's way over the hills to another town, and catch the train home again from there in the evening.

On that first day, Dad and I took the ski special from the CNR Tunnel Station where in the early morning we found skiers converging from all directions bearing knapsacks, skis, and poles through the almost bare city streets. The snow in the mountains, however, was already deep and, as the train went through the tunnel under Mount Royal and over the flat plain behind the city, we worked our way through from car to car to see who else was on board. In one of these we were greeted by three lively young members of the Montreal Ski Club, Allan Tiffin, Art Gravel, and Emery St Pierre. They were heading for Camp Kanoraset above St-Sauveur. When they caught sight of Dad, they hailed him joyfully by his nickname "Jackrabbit," and excitedly urged us to join them. They had known Dad well from previous winter trips, long before our family had moved from Lake Placid, and they considered him, despite his age, as one of the "gang." I think this was the first time I became aware of Dad's special magic. He had a certain magnetism, around which all sorts of interesting enterprises seemed to form.

We all disembarked at St-Sauveur, a sleepy little village in a broad, open valley, where tiny houses clustered around a great stone parish church. A number of large red box sleighs were waiting at the station, ready to convey the more citified passengers away to their various destinations, and the wonderful country smell of those horses and the music of the jingling sleigh bells haunt my memory to this day. The scores of eager skiers, however, soon strapped on their boards and disappeared into the waiting hills under their own power.

We took turns at breaking trail through the fresh new snow as we crossed the valley and climbed together up St-Sauveur Hill, past the Lone Elm at the top, and down the other side to the little old farmhouse beside Lac Morin. Known as Camp Kanoraset, it was rented by the Montreal Ski Club; the boys had a key, and it did not take them long to build a roaring fire in the old iron stove. In a jiffy that cold and frosty cabin became a habitable house. This was where the Ski Club members, sometimes ten or twelve of them, spent their winter weekends, cooking up a tempting stew, singing and yodelling and planning together the next day's trip. If one of them happened to have a mouth-organ in his pack, so much the better, for their diversions were all home-made, and all the more fun for that. There was no night life in St-Sauveur in those days, even if anyone had had the energy to seek it out after a hard day's ski.

We consumed our hot tea and toasted our sandwiches around the glowing stove, while the boys recounted some of their adventures.

"Remember that time," Emery recalled, "when after dark we decided to play 'hare and hounds'? We were a big gang up here that night. The moon was full, the snow was fresh, and I said, 'Herman, you be the "hare." We'll give you a two-minute start. Then all of us "hounds" will follow your track and try to catch you before you can get back here to the house.'

"You set off at a great pace, down the gully, off through the deep woods. We followed as best we could, in and out among the trees, down and up again, and finally we heard you holler from way up beside the Lone Elm. Then you swooshed back down here to the lake. 'Just look at that jackrabbit go!' I shouted as we all streamed after you. But we never did catch you, and you sure had the laugh on us when we panted up to the kitchen door. Somehow the name 'Jackrabbit' has stuck, and I guess we'll always call you that!"

Today, in broad daylight, we still had a fair trip ahead of us, so after lunch we set out again across the lake on the trail to Lac Marois. There the boys turned aside with a whoop and a yodel to follow another route back to Kanoraset, while Dad and I continued to pick our way across lakes and fields and fences until we arrived, just as darkness was falling, at the crest of the Big Hill at Shaw-bridge.

From the summit, the North River Valley lay spread out below us, and the lights of the little village winked a welcome. Beyond, the hills blended softly into twilight, and above, the first stars began to glimmer. We took a long look. "This is such a cosy, friendly country," said Dad reflectively. "I think I could comfortably live here for the rest of my days."

Then we twisted our way down the broad open slope, crossed the icy river, and skied up to the CNR station just as the southbound train rattled its way across the trestle. It had been an exhilarating day, the first of many. We could hardly wait to tell the rest of the family all about it.

Dad was busy for some time after that, struggling in his office to line up customers for his cranes and hoists and shovels, but he finally reached the point where he felt he had had his temporary quota of "canned" city air and was ready to gather the family together for another Sunday expedition up north.

We set out, all five of us, including Mother, each with our skis on our shoulders. This time we boarded the CPR at Westmount Station, where we saw much the same scene as on the last trip. Everyone seemed to know everyone else. There was a great feeling of camaraderie, as small groups formed on the train and plans were made for the day's adventures. Our own objective this time was Laurentian Lodge Club at Shawbridge, and on the train we met several of Dad's older friends with their wives and children. Among them were Percy Douglas, president of the Canadian Amateur Ski Association, Mac Yuile, president of Laurentian Lodge, and Dr Wilder Penfield, the neurosurgeon.

Laurentian Lodge was an old two-storey farmhouse, located at the edge of Shawbridge beside a golf course. Some years before, it had been converted into a boarding house, and a living-room wing, with bedrooms above, had been added. A group of Montreal friends had purchased the house in 1923 to form the club, and here their families and other club members would gather to pass the winter weekends. A forest of skis lined the front porch. The floors creaked, the beds were lumpy, and the bathroom facilities were cramped, but the big fieldstone fireplace in the lounge was a great attraction, and everyone looked forward to the delicious meals provided by Leigh and Anna Harding, the genial hosts, assisted by their faithful helper, Harry Lawton.

Our arrival was greeted with happy shouts, and soon a lively group of parents and children was ready to take up Dad's offer to lead us on a trip in the back country through the Vale of Fallen Women (many female skiers fell on the tricky slopes of this trail – hence the name). Some of the less ambitious ones, including Mother, were content to putter around on the golf course, then return to the club to toast their shins by the fire, while the rest of us worked up ravenous appetites on the trail. Later we headed across the river to spend the afternoon eagerly climbing up and skiing down the Big Hill, doing jump turns and "gelandesprungs" and turning christies and telemarks as we vied with each other in the clear cold air.

Our family again went up to the lodge at Christmas for a glorious week, during which we had plenty of time to explore the hills and valleys. The two railway stations at Shawbridge – the CNR and the CPR – were the ones closest to "town," and therefore the least expensive for us to reach. The Big Hill was the centre of activity, and there from time to time Dad and his friends would set out a slalom course for everyone, in which we could individually run downhill around obstacles, against the clock, just as he used to do in his younger days in Norway.

Several years later, Mario Gabriel from Switzerland was hired as ski instructor, and his lessons provided an excellent foundation of ski technique for both youngsters and older people. To Dad, that kind of thing was all right in its place, and Mario was a good friend of his, "but," he maintained, "practical experience is worth more than any number of lessons on a hard-packed, flag-posted practice hill. Lessons are fine for those who have the money and the time to spend, but after you've found your 'ski legs,' then come with me on a trip in the bush. When you rattle down a lumber road, and suddenly meet head-on with a team of horses and a sleighload of logs, that's when you learn to ski in a hurry!" But it never occurred to him to charge for such trips. When asked, he would simply shrug his shoulders and say, "Why should I take money for something I love to do? This is a joy I can share with others, without its costing me a cent. There is a great deal I can't afford to do these days, but a love of skiing is something I can *give,* and that makes me really happy."

Throughout the season of spring skiing, when the sun was bright and one could wander in shirt sleeves, we explored even further north, sometimes taking the train as far as St-Margaret's. On such excursions I would have my school homework with me, and would try to make up for lost study-time during the two hours that passed as we travelled up and down on the train. It was a means of blending business with pleasure. I remember once getting a very successful mark for an essay on Scandinavian literature, most of which was composed between drips from the snowy skis stacked behind the wicker seats on the homebound CPR. "This shows hard work and excellent research," was the teacher's comment. Little did she know of the awkward conditions under which it had been written.

Dad, meanwhile, was trying to diversify his business by bringing in some less expensive equipment. He had acquired a new agency for a portable two-man chainsaw, which he felt was really going to revolutionize the forest industry. This endeavour took him up the Saguenay River and into the steep-gullied Pikauba country where he was to demonstrate his new machine to a gathering of experts. The saw was being transported by dogsled and would meet them at the appointed place.

The men were all equipped with snowshoes, and they looked askance at Dad with his ever-present knapsack and his skis. "You'll never get through our bush with those things on," they said. But Dad insisted, and they reluctantly set off. It was tough going, under crusty conditions, but as they traversed a long steep pitch, Dad, with his good Norwegian ski wax, could grip the snow by plunking his skis down hard with each step, to bruise the crust. The snow-shoers, meanwhile, slid helplessly sideways.

He remembered how, some years before, he had met with some men from the same company. On that occasion he had taken them up a steep hillside trail, to demonstrate an economical system of overhead cables for skidding logs from both sides of a narrow valley down to the river; from there in the spring the logs could be flushed downstream to the mill. The men had had considerable difficulty in navigating the steep slopes on their snowshoes, and he recalled how, when they had come to a long flat stretch, he had simply skated along, poling as he went, while the others plodded solemnly behind. When they at last caught up, they found him at trailside with a small fire burning brightly in the snow, his knapsack open beside him, and a pot of melted snow already boiling for tea. He had made his point, just as he had made it with the Indians years before, about the utility of skis for winter travel.

This time once again, Dad proved the superiority of skis over snowshoes. But the saw was a different story. The men were pleased with the way it cut, but found it disappointingly heavy and awkward. Such a two-man saw, they felt, was dangerous to operate in deep snow, especially under their local conditions with steep slopes and uneven ground. In fact, they were afraid of it. "Come back in a few years," they said with a laugh, "when you can show us a power saw about one-third the weight of this one, which a single man can handle on his own. Then perhaps we can talk business!"

If Dad could only have seen some sixty years into the future to the time when one-man chainsaws would be in common use, how he would have laughed at the dinosaur he was trying to sell. The idea itself was excellent, but the product was not yet good enough. He and his power saw were, in fact, far ahead of their time, pioneers, scouting new territory. The technology itself would take years to catch up.

Business in that spring of 1929 was fast disappearing. The large mining, lumber, and construction companies could no longer afford Dad's expensive big machines, no matter how good they were. They would repair their old machines until they could no longer be used, then discard them; or, worse still, they would simply go out of business. Even his smaller, relatively inexpensive, portable saw, which had seemed so promising at first, was not catching on. The outlook was discouraging indeed.

During all this time Father had watched his reserve resources slowly shrinking, but we children had no inkling that things were any worse than usual. He was always cheerful, although we did notice that he concentrated more and more on teaching us to be "independent." "It's important for everyone to be able to cope with hard times," he would say. "We don't really need all this civilization. It's better to lead a simple life. Exercise and a positive attitude are more important than new clothes and fancy gadgets."

It was the beginning of the Great Depression. Things were tightening up all over. There were "bread lines," such as the one I saw every day on my way to school as the streetcar made its way along Ste-Catherine Street, where block-long double lines of destitute men shivered in the cold as they waited their turn for a free bowl of hot soup and a crust of bread at an emergency food shelter.

From time to time we would read newspaper stories about New York businessmen, one of whom Dad had actually known during his years in that heartless city, who had finally given up. This man had tried to solve his problems by jumping out of a window and committing suicide, because he had gone bankrupt and had lost all his money. "But what on earth is going to happen to his family?" Dad asked in astonishment. "They will get his insurance money, of course, but what other good could he possibly do – dead? This is a time when families must stick together. Everyone has his own part to play, but most of all, we all need each other."

For our part, we took in a young Danish couple to live with us. Dagmar helped Mother with the housekeeping and cooking in exchange for lodging, while the husband looked everywhere for small jobs as a handyman. Our trusty old Winton Six had already been traded in for a smaller Studebaker, but Dad soon found that business was so bad he no longer needed a car at all – so it, too, was sold. We gave up our daily newspaper. We could get all the bad news we needed by radio. We would walk rather than take a streetcar, we never lit our fancy gas fireplace, and we spent absolutely no money on non-essentials, but instead saved every cent we could spare for occasional trips up north. To Dad's way of thinking, this was no luxury. "It's an absolute necessity both for our health and our peace of mind. People simply have to get out of the city once in a while and get their feet on the ground. They have to smell the pines, follow the animal tracks, and forget their business worries. After all, getting out into nature is really a kind of health insurance, and it's a lot cheaper than going to the doctor!"

With the arrival of summer, Dad and Mother were determined, no matter what the cost, to send the three of us to camp. Dad made things very clear: "I've taught you as well as I could how to take care of yourselves on land, how to find your way with map and compass, to build a fire without a match, to make an emergency camp, how to fish, and how to set a rabbit snare. Camp will round you off. It will teach you how to swim and canoe and take care of yourselves on the water, as well as how to get along with other people under difficult conditions. Wistfully, he added, "I wish I were going, too."

The first thing that happened that summer was a change in my name. It seemed that there would be two Alices in camp, which might lead to confusion. So while the other girl continued to be Alice, the campers christened me "Jo" (a short form of Johannsen). The sound of this name definitely appealed to me and it was soon adopted, not only by the campers, but by my entire family, including Mother, for we also had the confusion of two Alices under a single roof. From that time forward, I was known to nearly everyone as Jo, and the name has stuck with me over the years.

As things turned out, camp was a great success for us, because we decided to treat it as professional training. Bob, at camp Nominingue, covered miles and miles on rugged canoe trips. Peggy qualified for her bronze medal in life-saving, and was looking forward to her silver award. I won the cup for "best all-round camper." Then, as a means of proving what good physical condition we were in, four of us girls – Agnes Tennant, Merle Peden, Hilde Brabander, and I, accompanied by the footsore nature counsellor from England who was commandeered to accompany us as "chaperone" – hiked home from Lac Ouareau to Ste-Dorothée, following back country roads and covering eighty miles in three days. It was kind of a pilgrimage, which some of the farmers' wives with whom we chatted on our way assumed to be some special penance for wrongdoing. It was unheard of to walk, deliberately, such a long distance, "for no reason at all."

❦

In the fall, when we were safely home, Dad one day said quietly, "Do you suppose the camp would lend us a canoe some weekend so that you and I could get off by ourselves, and you could give me a crash course in canoeing? I'm embarrassed to have my children already proficient in something I myself have never had a chance to learn." And that was how Dad and I embarked one September morning on our first canoe trip.

We had checked the map and found what looked like an easy route for a pleasant, and not too long, round trip. It passed through several small lakes connected by a winding stream, and finally returned to Lac Ouareau.

Ignoring the fact that at the time Dad was feeling slightly unwell and had a very unpleasant boil on his neck, we set out, Dad paddling bow, I paddling stern, with our tent, sleeping bags and food stowed comfortably amidships. The leaves had begun to turn, and the far hills were glowing, though there were a few suspicious-looking clouds on the horizon. We coasted down the length of Lac Ouareau and up the Ouareau River, where Dad tried a stint in the stern as he practised steering. Then I took over again and we went on and up the slow, winding Pembina along one of our last summer's routes. We ate our lunch at the place where our planned route turned to the east, through territory that was new to me.

It took both of us to carry our borrowed craft, a heavy trip canoe, and after making a second trip to pick up our gear, we were glad to load up again at the next lake and turn south. The weather was definitely worsening. There were two more small lakes to be crossed before we could reach the shelter of a disused lumber camp, marked on our map at the dam at the far end of Lac Maribou. Dad had caught on at once to the paddling, and we made a good strong team, dipping in unison as the storm clouds gathered behind us.

It was nearly dark when we finally heard the water rippling through the Maribou dam; we touched shore just as the first clap of thunder rolled and the first raindrops began to fall. Hastily, we stashed our canoe upside down in the bushes where it would be safe from the wind, and scurried up to the camp with all our possessions.

The dilapidated cabin we found there would have been a spooky place even in the best of weather. The door was gone, leaving only an empty black hole in the wall, but we found a rickety built-in table under the paneless window, a bench, and a rough bed of boards crouching in the corner. I scrambled to dig out my flashlight while Dad pulled the stump of a candle from his pack and set it on the table. He lit it and, as we could already see the rain beginning to drip through several holes in the roof, we spread our tent out over the bed to serve as a tarpaulin, and quickly slipped our sleeping bags under the bed, as that promised to be the driest spot.

While I rummaged to assemble our supper of cheese, rye crisp-bread, a roll of Hungarian dried sausage, and raisins and chocolate to top things off – ppssfftt! – out went our candle, victim of a well-placed leak in the roof. So we made do with our single flashlight. We pulled the bench over beside the bed, and extended the tarp to include it, too, thus enlarging our sleeping quarters. Then we crawled into our cosy, dry bags, with our bodies under the bed and our heads projecting into the protected space, and gratefully consumed our meal. Finally, as the thunder roared and the lightning flashed, we thanked the good Lord that we were safe on shore, and before long fell fast asleep.

In the morning the sun was out again, but Dad's boil had burst in the night, making a nasty mess, so we had a quick session of first aid. When he was suitably patched, we set about our chores, and prepared and enjoyed a hearty breakfast. Then, in the cheerful morning sunlight, we lugged our canoe down below the dam and stowed our baggage.

In former days, when the dam had been properly regulated, the surge of water when the gate was opened would have flushed the logs downstream, but the system was no longer in operation. The water spilled lazily through the open gate, and the stream was discouragingly low. To make things worse, there was no portage trail. There was nothing to do but struggle down that two-mile stretch of trickling water, working the canoe back and forth among the boulders, pushing and shoving as we splashed through the shallow reaches, climbing into the canoe when we had to cross a deeper pool, and climbing out again on the other side. It was a back-breaking task, but we arrived at last at the place where our stream joined the free-flowing Ouareau River, and from that point on we took the regular portage route beside the rapids leading up to Ouareau Dam. There, we settled comfortably into our canoe once more and paddled the long scenic way down the lake and back to camp.

The whole itinerary had looked so easy on the flat map, with the chain of little lakes and the picturesque winding stream! It hadn't occurred to me to wonder whether it was really a viable route. We found out the hard way why it was never used by canoers.

But, all in all, it was truly an "educational tour." What with the troublesome boil, the thunderstorm, Dad's learning to paddle, and our man-handling of that heavy canoe down the unco-operative stream, we looked back on it many times as a memorable adventure. It taught us, above all, never to attempt such a trip without being in good health, and always to be as informed as possible about the route to be travelled – before setting out.

❦

In the fall of 1929 the Montreal Ski Club had rented the Old Red House, a Shawbridge landmark, as its winter quarters. Being in the village, it was far more accessible to ski club members than little old Camp Kanoraset had ever been. A number of the younger boys – Don Heasley, George Sumner, Doug Urquhart, Martin Chapman, and Alister Grant took on the responsibility of putting the house in order. Several of them had cars, in which they would gather a group of willing helpers to sally forth for a weekend of hammering, sawing, and painting.

Dad had become (as an antidote to his business worries) a very involved weekend member of the club, and so, of course, had we children. Along with several other girls, I often went along to cook and to serve as a "carpenter's help." The Old Red House soon blossomed once more under our combined efforts. When snow fell and driving was no longer feasible, we would take the train. Dad, as often as he could, would be with us and when competition season opened, he and other officials were there to manage the serious meets. We girls and other volunteers would go out to various checkpoints along the trail to serve as "posts." It was our duty not only to assure that every competitor had followed the entire route, but to administer first aid if necessary, and to dole out oranges to thirsty runners, according to need. Those were busy, happy days for all of us. Skiing, in fact, became a welcome escape from the grind of daily existence.

At Christmas there came a delightful surprise: Canada Steamship Lines was to open its Manoir Richelieu at Murray Bay with an

The Red House, Shawbridge, Montreal Ski Club, 1932.

international, intercollegiate winter sports competition, with the Red Birds Ski Club in charge of the events. As a special inducement to families to attend, the entire Johannsen tribe was invited to spend the holiday there "to provide local colour at all levels." This marvellous opportunity meant that Mother would have a week's vacation from housekeeping chores; we children were expected to encourage other children to join in all the festivities; and Dad would lead the more adventurous types on impromptu ski trips, in addition to which he undertook to lay out the eighteen-kilometre cross-country trail. He threw himself whole-heartedly into helping with all the arrangements.

The meet was a resounding success, and there was no doubt that much of the credit was due to Dad. The Red Birds were in a jubilant mood as their parlour car wound its homeward way to Montreal along the curving north shore CPR tracks, and the three co-founders of the Red Birds Ski Club – Bill Thompson, No. 1, Harry Pangman, No. 2, and Sterling Maxwell No. 3, – held an emergency summit meeting on the train. As a result, Jackrabbit was declared the first Honorary Life Member of the Red Birds and given permanent No. 27. When this was announced, the new honorary life member astounded everyone in the crowded car by standing on his head on the edge of the rickety card table and kicking his heels in the air to show his appreciation! "Not bad for a fifty-four-year old!" Bill Thompson later recalled, and a similar headstand was a feat which Jackrabbit continued to perform at annual Red Birds meetings for many years thereafter.

An important matter awaited Father's attention on his return. Convinced at last that there was really no hope of his ever returning to live in Norway, he had decided to commit himself to this new country, where he knew he would in all likelihood spend the rest of his life. After much soul-searching, he had applied for Canadian citizenship, and on 31 January 1930, he received his "papers," which definitely established all of us as "British subjects by naturalization," including Dad, Mother, and all three offspring, since we children were all still under age.

"In all those years, from 1902 to 1922," said Dad in a letter to one of his Canadian friends, "when I was in business in the United States, there were many who suggested that I become an American. But, America always wanted to 'swallow everyone whole.' It was a real melting pot, in which you were expected to forget all about where you had come from. Here, in Quebec, where I have had my business established since 1919, I feel I am more truly at home. Here we have two languages, the pace is more relaxed, and the Laurentians seem so much like the land of my birth. Furthermore, here I can keep my pride in my 'old country' and at the same time be accepted as a true Canadian." So Jackrabbit took the important step, which was to mean so much to all of us as the years slipped by. From then on, we rejoiced in the knowledge that we were all real Canadians.

Nineteen-thirty was also the year of persistent rumours about a large development to be sponsored by the CPR at Montebello on the Ottawa River. A private club, it was said, was planning to build a huge log lodge. Hundreds of men, mostly carpenters, were to be employed, working in the old Scandinavian tradition with axes and simple tools. Dad, now a "former Norwegian," was captivated by the whole idea, and hoped to sell at least one crane to aid in the construction. However, as it turned out, the sponsors already had a crane in hand. Work was to begin in February 1930, and sadly for Dad, this hoped-for sale turned out to be yet another lost cause.

To take his mind off this disappointment, Dad turned his attention to new ski country. One weekend in April, he and three other stalwart skiers – Harry Pangman (a veteran of the Second Winter Olympics at St Moritz in 1928), Stirling Maxwell, and Neil Stewart, all of them Red Birds – decided to reconnoitre the territory in Mont Tremblant Park. They took the Saturday train to St-Jovite, and spent the night at Tom Wheeler's Gray Rocks Inn on Lac Ouimet. Then on Sunday they broke trail across the Devil's River to the foot of Mont Tremblant, and climbed the mountain using the fire ranger's summer trail, the only trail on the mountain at that time, to his lookout on the summit. There they ate their lunch in spring sunshine and powder snow, and climbed the lookout tower for a breath-taking view of the entire countryside.

They then attacked the descent, bushwhacking their way down the mountainside, sometimes riding their poles, sometimes grabbing young spruce trees to check their speed, even straddling a small sapling to use as a brake or a rudder. "I think my first impression of Herman's skiing ability was formed on that trip," wrote Harry later. "Bursting out of the upper slopes in to a small clearing, he suddenly found himself straddling the fire ranger's telephone line which had suddenly come out from under the snow. As if this were a natural occurrence, he rode it for some twenty feet, getting higher and higher above the ground until finally, losing momentum, he flipped off, dropped some ten feet to the ground, landed on his feet and continued down the hill, albeit a bit bow-legged."

Eventually all four men skied out onto Lac Tremblant and looked back up at the mountain top, rising over two thousand feet above them. It had been quite a run, and it remained in the memory of all four as the answer to a request from the Ski Club of Great Britain, which had offered to award an impressive prize cup "for competition in Canada, if a suitable hill can be found."

"No doubt about it," they reported. "This is *it!*" And they proceeded to recommend that Mont Tremblant be the site for the first Quebec Kandahar Downhill Race, to be held the following year.

By May 1930, matriculation exams were upon me, and I had become totally immersed in my own problems. Times were hard for us, and I do recall that there had been some difficulty about the telephone at home, and that Dad had decided the telephone, too, was something the family could do without, but none of us were prepared for the final calamity, when it struck.

Peggy had come home from school late one afternoon to find Mother, sobbing uncontrollably in the living-room. This was absolutely unheard of. All of us assumed that, after years of ups and downs, Mother would always "bear up" no matter what happened. Bewildered, Peggy was trying her best to comfort her when Dad came into the house and with that Mother collapsed into his arms. "Oh, Herman," she wailed. "They've cut off the gas – and the electricity! We can't even cook, or turn on a light! Whatever is going to happen to us?" And the three of them sank down together on the sofa, stunned and unbelieving.

That was the scene that greeted Bob and me when we, too, came in a little later and heard the news. All five of us then sat staring blankly into space. We scarcely knew how to start to think. Everything seemed to be falling apart.

At last, Dad spoke, slowly, weighing every word. "I must say that although I've seen this coming for a long time, it's hard to accept the situation, now that it's really here. I was always sure there would be more orders, that business would improve, but now I can see that that simply isn't going to happen. I'll just have to face the fact that *no one* can afford to buy heavy machinery any more. I only know I have done my very best, but this seems to be the end of that line."

He drew Mother closer to him, and took Peggy comfortingly by the hand. "From now on, we'll have to depend on my knowledge of the wilderness, and on whatever I can do for the ski sport and for the people who believe in it. My greatest asset is that I am a "skiing engineer." I'll have to concentrate on that. But people are going to have to pay me from now on, if they want my help. Meanwhile, the most important thing for all of us is that we must not lose our faith – faith that somehow we will manage to weather this storm.

"In a way, you know, life is like a canoe trip. You have good weather, and you have bad weather, but for those who wait long enough, the sun always comes out again! At least, we have each other. We also have our health. And the five of us make a strong team. This isn't the end of the world. There are many other people in the same fix we are in.

"We just have to take stock all over again. Weed out everything we don't need. Sell some things. Find a cheaper place to live. But above all, we must stick together, keep our chins up, and adapt to all these changes, even if we don't like them ... At least we still have a roof over our heads."

He took a deep breath. "Now, let's all pretend we're on a canoe trip. We'll have a real camp supper – rye crisp and cheese and raisins. They don't need any cooking, and they always taste good. Then, we'll go to bed and we'll say our prayers. In the morning, the sun will shine. You'll see. We'll all feel better after a good night's rest. And tomorrow, we'll find a way! This whole thing may actually turn out to be a blessing in disguise."

And as it turned out, he was right. "A blessing in disguise" is exactly what it was.

CHAPTER FOURTEEN

Necessity Creates a Skiing Engineer: 1930–1932

It is surprising how an event that seems overwhelming can turn in a matter of days into a challenge, bringing with it new and unexpected strength. As Dad so often said, "It's always darkest just before the dawn."

During the previous winters, Jackrabbit had gradually become recognized in the rural communities up north as a promoter of cross-country skiing. These efforts were beginning to draw more and more city folk into the country, and this was seen as a boost to tourism. The CPR passenger agent had encouraged Dad's efforts, and had given him a pass that allowed him to board the train at any point along the Laurentian line. He could then disembark wherever he liked, scout the hills for a feasible ski route, and pick up the train again at another station on the homebound way. The CPR was well aware of Jackrabbit's earlier involvement in the development of skiing of Lake Placid; they knew he had given advice from the jumper's point of view, to the designers of the now famous Intervale ski jump. In fact, the company had already come to regard Dad more as an important figure in the lively world of skiing than as a supplier of material and equipment for the building and maintenance of railroads.

It was no surprise, therefore, that with its forthcoming major development at the Seigniory Club in Montebello, the CPR should turn to Jackrabbit to assist in planning some of the winter sports facilities on its huge eighty-thousand-acre domain. In particular,

Skiing engineer, 1931.

they wanted to build a championship-calibre jump, which would attract the most skilled ski-jumpers, and at the same time provide a thrilling "spectator sport" for Seigniory Club members and their guests. It dawned on Dad at last: here was a golden opportunity to augment his meagre earnings by really becoming, as he had said, a "skiing engineer."

But first there was the urgent matter of family living quarters. He and Mother located a small apartment, a third-storey walk-up, on Lansdowne Avenue not far from our old house on Western.

Dagmar and her husband found a place where they could live inexpensively in Verdun, and we gave them some of our furniture to take with them. This helped them, and at the same time relieved a portion of our storage problem. We gave away books to the McGill Library, and extra clothing to the Salvation Army. The ski club boys took turns moving our "lighter stuff" in their cars, and the movers came to transport the "heavy stuff," including the grand-father clock and the piano. At last the family was established in smaller, less expensive, but comfortable quarters, and Mother breathed a well-earned sigh of relief.

On July 1, 1930, with appropriate fanfare (and right on schedule) the Seigniory Club at Montebello opened its doors. Nothing had been spared to make the event an outstanding success.

The building itself was a modern miracle. Built in the time-honoured style of a log cabin, but vast in scope and equipped with all modern conveniences, the log chateau superbly fitted the Cana-dian landscape, incorporating the very best craftsmanship of Scan-dinavian log-builders. Its architect, Harold Lawson, and its Finnish master log-builder, Victor Nymark, had managed to capture the warmth and intimacy of a country dwelling, and to combine these into a magnificent building on the plan of a six-pointed star, the rays of which fanned out from an immense central stone chimney, with massive stone fireplaces facing outward, one to each of the rays of the star. The construction was accomplished by the CPR in an "associated arrangement" with a private club known as Lucerne-in-Quebec Community Association Limited. The entire job was carried out in a record time of only four and a half months, largely by hand labour, without fancy mechanical aids, employing an army of 3,500 men drawn from depressed areas across the continent. Three hundred of these were carpenters, whom Nymark personally instructed in the art of dressing and fitting the logs. Coming as this work did at the beginning of the Great Depression, the little village of Montebello was temporarily transformed into one of the few bright spots in the bleak unemployment picture of Canada, and the labourers were glad of the fifty cents an hour. Today, sixty-three years later, the Chateau Montebello is still the world's largest structure built entirely of logs.

The activities of the Seigniory Club were modelled after our previous home, the Lake Placid Club. It was a private undertaking, centred on recreational sports and catering to a special clientèle. Within its membership were to be found some outstanding names in Canadian financial circles, as well as many Americans, and it soon became a choice rendezvous for wealthy winter sports enthusiasts.

Now that the club was well launched it obviously needed operating staff. In this my brother Bob saw a chance for himself: he had heard that they were hiring bellboys. This was a job that required no previous experience, just lots of muscle and goodwill, and paid no salary – just bed and board. It was up to the bellboys to earn whatever they could in tips, and so they seized every opportunity to make themselves useful. Bob applied and was accepted. As for Dad, he explored the club territory looking for a suitable site for his championship ski jump.

He selected a hill with a northeast-facing slope, in rugged terrain some three miles from the Seigniory Club. This hill, however, was only high enough to serve as the *landing* for a championship jump, so he proposed a steel tower, which would provide the necessary approach and take-off. This was a sports mega-project of proportions that appealed to the owners. Dad submitted his plan, which was approved, and that fall he proudly watched his steel tower rise among the birch trees on the hilltop. At that time, it was the tallest ski chute anywhere.

Some thirty-four thousand cubic yards of rock and earth had to be rearranged on the hillside to provide the necessary grading of the slope. The landing hill, with a flanking judges' ramp and spectator bleachers, was set among standing pines. Seen from below, the top of the tower rose 301 feet above the level of the final outrun, and its starting platform, soaring above the treetops, could be seen from far across the Ottawa River. All in all, the jump was a tremendous satisfaction to Jackrabbit, for he knew that not only would it play an important role in developing winter sports at Montebello, but it would also be a fine advertisement for his services.

Back in Montreal, in the midst of all the hubbub of our spring move, I had written my matriculation exams. Then it was off to Camp Ouareau again; this year I *was* engaged as the new nature counsellor, and Peggy was happy to come with me as a helping camper. So all three of us children were independent that summer.

Ski jump at Montebello.

In the fall, Bob returned from "bell-hopping" at Montebello to enter Westmount High. Peggy moved up to grade six in King's School, and I proudly paid my fifty-dollar fee for the first term and entered McGill.

❧

That Christmas, when Bob was due to go back to work at the Seigniory Club during the holidays, Dad proposed that "for fun" they ski down the forty cross-country miles to Montebello from near the end of the CNR Laurentian line. He was anxious to see his new ski jump in action. The route they chose went through the bush. "But we don't really need a trail," said Dad. "We'll follow lumber roads where they happen to be, and we'll cut across country by map whenever that seems a better way. When we come to a lake, we'll take advantage of it and simply follow through."

Bob Cundill, one of their ski friends, happened to hear them plotting, and rashly asked if he could come along. "Sure," said Dad. "Glad to have you. But we leave tomorrow morning. We'll take the CNR up to Lac Remi, and leave from there about midafternoon. We'll have to ski all night, because Bob has to be on the job the next day."

The three of them were in high spirits as they left the train the next afternoon, with maps and food and extra clothing in their knapsacks. Snow conditions were excellent, the lakes were frozen, and although darkness falls early at Christmas, they had a full moon to guide them. They took turns breaking trail through light powder snow, up the hills, through the forest, and over the lakes, until after a number of hours of energetic exercise they came at last to the upper end of Lac Commandant. Speeding out onto its frozen surface, they headed for the ranger's cabin, midway down, where Dad proposed they should rest and have a bite to eat. But suddenly the lake gave out a mighty BOOM! as the ice expanded and cracked in reaction to the bitter cold. The sound, like a cannon shot echoing down to the farthest shore, was disconcerting (to say the least), for in spots the lake was windswept nearly clear of snow and gave the impression they were actually facing open water, although they well knew the ice must have been almost a foot thick. However, they reached the cabin at last, after a few more "sonic booms," and gained entrance through an unlocked window. There they made a roaring fire in the old iron stove, and were glad to warm up for a while and rest their weary bones.

After food and a rest, they packed up again and, leaving every-thing exactly as they had found it, they climbed out through the window, shut it securely, and continued on their way. They were rewarded by a glorious sunrise over the eastern hills as the kilometres sped by.

When they finally reached Montebello in the early morning and proudly skied across the CPR tracks to the Seigniory Club, they were hailed in great surprise. "How on earth did you get here at this hour?" they were asked, for motorcar travel was very limited in the winter.

"We came by train," said Dad.

"But the CPR doesn't get here until noon."

"I know," said Dad. "But we came by CNR to Lac Remi up in the Laurentians, and then skied across. We had a wonderful trip!"

And while he was in Montebello, the Seigniory Club asked Dad to lay out an Olympic cross-country training run, on which potential team members could test their skill during the coming winter and work up their speed in preparation for the following year's Olympics. This was the first of a whole network of ski trails that was to grow with the years.

By February 1931, the Red Birds had to make good their promise to the Ski Club of Great Britain to run off a preliminary Canadian Kandahar Downhill Race as a "bushwhack." Despite strong disapproval from both the Canadian Amateur Ski Association and the Montreal Ski Club, each of which felt that the whole idea of a bushwhack was ridiculous, the Red Birds were determined to make the event a success. They were young and eager, and after all, four Red Birds had indeed already proved that it could be done.

The competitors – all twenty-two of them – set out that morning on skis from Gray Rocks Inn on Lac Ouimet, skied to the foot of Mont Tremblant, and climbed it by way of the fire ranger's trail. From the top, no special course was set. It was simply a matter of every man for himself, to find the shortest and/or the fastest route to the finish line. Two stop watches were synchronized at the fire tower, and Jackrabbit set off with one of these watches, bushwhacking his way down, to await the competitors on the lake. The second stop watch was left in the hands of Bill Drysdale, who was to run last. At a given moment, Bill was to begin sending out single skiers at one-minute intervals, and finally to follow through himself, carrying with him the second stop watch and the list of competitors in their order of starting.

For the better part of an hour the mountain resounded to shouts and yells, as bodies crashed through the forest and competitors grasped at trees, rode their poles, or jumped down minor precipices. No holds were barred. No penalties were noted. It was simply a matter of courage, endurance, and skill. Harry Pangman covered the 2,045-foot drop in a breath-taking fifteen minutes and two seconds, with George Jost not far behind. And all the rest followed as best they could, leaving a swath of ski tracks, punctuated by falls and sitzmarks, a hat or two, and assorted fragments of poles, but all finally reassembled, panting, on the lake beside Jackrabbit, where some twenty spectators from Gray Rocks Inn had already stationed themselves to see the fun. The competitors were, needless to say, in various stages of disarray, but no one suffered any lasting damage in that massive scramble, and all were convinced that they had lived through a truly historic event.

Then everyone skied back to an open hill near Pinoteau's, to take part in a slalom race. This was handily won by George Jost, who was declared the combined winner. The fact that years later the race, by then one of the most important in Canada, was won in under three minutes, this time over a 1.87-mile, perfectly groomed trail, in no way detracts from the feat of these hardy pioneers, who defied all obstacles (and lived to tell the tale!). But as time went on, changes in the rules and greater caution on the part of the promoters led to the official withdrawal of the cup, and the Canadian Kandahar Race receded quietly into history (though efforts are still being made to revive it).

Meanwhile, in Shawbridge, something new had been added to the Big Hill by Alex Foster, an enterprising young ski jumper from Montreal. Realizing that people (even skiers!) were essentially lazy, he thought up a brilliant labour-saving scheme for those who wanted to pack as many downhill runs as possible into a single day. At the same time, he hoped it would put money into his own pocket.

At the foot of the Big Hill he and a friend installed the local taxi, which because of difficult road conditions had been taken out of service for the winter. This they fixed on permanent blocks. They removed the rear tires, and around the rim of one of these rear wheels they passed an endless rope, which they ran up the hill, around a pulley set high in a tree at the end of the track,

First ski tow in Canada, built by Alex Foster. Shawbridge Hill,
1932. Photos courtesy of Canadian Pacific.

View of Shawbridge from Big Hill.

then back down to the starting point. When the motor was revved up and the engine put in gear, the cable would wind slowly up the hill, bearing with it anyone who could hang on to the slippery rope. Users of the world's first ski tow paid five cents a ride. All they had to do was grasp the rope, clamp it against their side, and be hauled uphill at the astonishing speed of five miles per hour!

There were, of course, certain inconveniences, among them the fact that when there were insufficient riders the rope tended to drag in the snow, and become sopping wet. One's mittens then also became waterlogged and tended to freeze to the line on the next trip up. Damage to sweaters and mitts (added to the cost of transport!) had then to be weighed against the saving in energy, but these issues seemed worth it to some who were then able to zoom back downhill from top to bottom in a straight line before the astonished eyes of admiring spectators, amazed at such audacity. The hardy skiers would then pay another nickel, once more grab the rope, and be hauled to the top again and again and again. For twenty-five cents, they could have a day's pass.

Come spring, when the snow finally melted, the cable would be unslung, and the car, reconverted to a taxi, would go back to its normal summer job, none the worse for wear. "Foster's Folly" was the nickname given to this clever device, and before long Maurice Paquette, a mechanic in Ste-Agathe, had installed similar ski tows on various hills in that vicinity. It was the beginning of an irreversible trend.

Dad, of course, was interested in the mechanics of this project and encouraged the boys, but times being what they were, he certainly had no money to spend on having himself hauled up any hill. He could only echo the astonishment of other economy-minded skiers who simply exclaimed, "What! Pay to go skiing? When I can climb that hill on my own steam – for nothing? What an extraordinary idea!"

With the arrival of summer, all the Johannsens were busy on their own projects, Peg and I at Ouareau, Bob back in Montebello, Dad as a guide on occasional fishing trips, and Mother keeping the home fires burning. In the fall, Dad became president of the Montreal Ski Club, and he took his duties seriously, bringing in all the volunteer help he could muster. The Old Red House in Shawbridge was in constant use, and a natural ski jump with a small take-off of logs was constructed by the Viking Ski Club near the Big Hill. Here a number of successful meets were held, including several international intercollegiate ones, with many spectators, and with Dad among the officials.

But in November 1931 there came a final financial blow. It was not unexpected, but it was far more serious than the previous disaster, which had dislodged the family from Western Avenue. I will never forget the day the bailiff arrived, serving notice to Mother that the family would have to vacate the premises in three days. But where were we to go? How? And with what? It was a dreadful situation.

Dad and Mother had been considering for some time a move to the small village of Shawbridge, where living expenses would be very low, but they had delayed as long as they could, because of our schooling. Now, however, the time had really come. Dad got a lift with a friend who dropped him off at Shawbridge to investigate the possibilities there. Leigh Harding, at Laurentian Lodge, knew the town and might have some suggestions. And there was always the hope that Dad might find some sort of winter work in the mountains.

Now we discovered what truly wonderful friends we had. Margaret Dodds and her mother came to our rescue at once. Mother and I were invited to stay at their house "for a week or so, until things get sorted out." Bob was taken home by Doug Urquhart, one of the ski boys, and Peggy was temporarily "adopted" by her classroom teacher, Miss Crossley. Somehow we managed to pack up all our possessions in the required three days, and these took off, grandfather clock, grand piano and all, for "temporary" storage. It is amazing what can be done when it simply *has* to be done.

In Shawbridge, Dad discovered that Anna Harding's elderly Aunt Sue, an indomitable eighty-year-old lady of spartan tastes and strong opinions, needed someone to share her house. The Hardings thought it would be good for her if Mother were to "take over the housekeeping." So Dad, Mother, Bob, and Peg moved in to live with Aunt Sue. Peggy entered the final elementary year in the one-room Shawbridge schoolhouse, while Bob received his lessons from Westmount High and tried to keep up with his class, although he ultimately found the ski hills much more alluring. I had received a loan from McGill to cover my fees for the rest of the year and found someone who wanted a student to act as a housekeeper in return for board and lodging. Various professors offered me evening jobs of baby-sitting at twenty-five cents an hour, which allowed me time for studying and also brought in a little cash. So that took care of me. It was a major adjustment all around, most of all for seventeen-year-old Bob and eighty-year-old Aunt Sue, but things settled down at last, and life continued.

Meanwhile, Dad was in his element: out every day on his skis. "I really need the exercise," he insisted. "This way I can get out into the country and see what's going on in the woods, and clear my mind. What a relief not to have to go to the office every day, to struggle in that depressing atmosphere looking for business that no longer exists! Up here I can fill my lungs with good fresh air, and make a track in fresh snow over the hills. I can hunt, and I can fish in season, and I can always find some kind of work to keep bread in our mouths."

Mother, however, worried about his going off on those long stretches in the bush all alone. "You know you aren't as young as you used to be, Herman," she fretted anxiously. "After all, you're now fifty-five. By this time most people have already hung up their skis. Suppose something should happen to you when you're off by yourself in the woods. How would anyone ever know where to find you?"

But Dad was adamant. "You mustn't worry about me, Alice," he said comfortingly. "I'll be perfectly all right. I'll take other people with me. I'll be a kind of a guide. In fact," he added with a twinkle, "I'm beginning to feel as though I am really starting to live!"

It was, as it turned out, a turning point in Jackrabbit's life. The restrictions of business life lay behind him. He had literally gone back to basics, and he found a special satisfaction in pitting himself against the elements and in the feeling that he was earning his way with his axe. He would set out each day with a happy wave to Mother, and a cheery "Expect me when you see me!"

For Mother, however, things were not that easy, and she could not help worrying. Dad would be gone sometimes for a day, sometimes for two or three, and occasionally it would be as much as a week or more. He had an arrangement with some of the inns whereby he would get bed and board when he was working on their trails, and this he often found very convenient. He would telephone Mother at Aunt Sue's to let her know where he was, and then go happily about his work in the woods. He had a definite feeling of accomplishment with every blaze he cut.

In February 1932 the Third Winter Olympics were held at Lake Placid, a major milestone in the history of North American skiing. This was something Jackrabbit had looked forward to with great anticipation, not only for old times' sake (as a former resident of Lake Placid), but because the outstanding world skiers of the day would all gather there. As a respected authority on ski matters, Dad was one of the invited officials, and for him this was a memorable experience. He and Louis Grimes of Montreal were co-coaches of the Canadian team, and of course he was eager to revisit his old Intervale jump, now much enhanced, and the eighteen- and twenty-five-kilometre cross-country courses, over which he himself had run ten years before. But quite apart from the international excitement of mingling with the teams of many nations there was his pride in being asked to be one of the forerunners in the eighteen-kilometre race (to ski the course ahead of the racers to clear the track and ensure that everything was in order), quite a feat for a man at the "advanced age" of fifty-five!

The Norwegian and Japanese teams, among others, had arrived well ahead of time and were stationed at Mirror Lake Inn, where Dad immediately went to pay his respects. There was great rejoicing, and a fine flow of Norwegian talk, with much good-natured joshing in his mother tongue. And then there appeared Tozo Suzuki, captain of the Japanese team. To the astonishment of all the Lake Placid people present, Tozo and Dad immediately launched into an animated conversation in a foreign tongue, and the uninitiated were amazed to find that "Mr Johannsen also speaks Japanese!" It was some time before they realized that it was Tozo, who had spent some time in Norway, who was speaking Norwegian.

But Jackrabbit, as a coach of the Canadian team, had an important duty to perform. His "boys" needed exercise, and he was determined they should really get a feel for the Adirondacks as their initiation into the Olympics. "Besides," he said, "it will be good for their legs!" So he and Louis, two days before their scheduled race, took the Canadians on a full day's trip up Mount Marcy.

They skied cross-country from the village, out the ten miles past Abe Fuller's old farm in South Meadows, then up assorted brook beds to the summit, reaching the mountain top at dusk. They returned by the "summer" trail, dodging trees, clinging to branches, schussing the pitches. And when the trail became too steep for comfort they zigzagged through the woods. They reached the bottom in the pitch dark, and then made the ten-mile return journey back to the village, a total day's trip of some thirty-five miles in all, during which Jackrabbit had led, or had kept up with, the best ski-runners Canada could produce at that time. None of them ever forgot it.

Finally, however, the Olympics were over. The Canadian team set no records but they did very well, all things considered. Harry Pangman placed first among the Canadians in the cross-country, and Art Gravel did well in the jumping. Norway took top honours in the combined as Dad had expected, and he was happy about that.

Back in Shawbridge, that winter with Aunt Sue had been a difficult time for everyone, especially Aunt Sue herself, who was used to having her whole house to herself. She found that having the Johannsens "was a bit much." Bob's yodelling was getting on her nerves, and he, for his part, was glad to see the spring again, for during the cold winter months, sleeping as he did on the side porch in his sleeping bag, he had risked a frostbitten nose and ear. So it was with mutual satisfaction that the family left Aunt Sue's in June and moved temporarily into an unused but furnished house, owned by Colin Shaw, beside the CPR station.

By this time Bob had become very involved with the Oxford Group, a semi-religious body that had certain connections with the Boys' Farm. The farm was, in reality, a provincial reform school, operated at that time as a producing dairy farm, with the boys supplying much of the manpower. Bob, as an "Oxford Grouper" had a standing invitation to play baseball with the boys on their "off" days, and eventually he worked up courage to ask permission to invite two of them home for a Sunday meal at his house. This was an almost unheard-of request, and the boys had to "earn" the privilege in advance by two whole weeks of especially exemplary behaviour.

When that Sunday finally came, Mother, whose housekeeping budget was extremely tight, racked her brains to find a menu that would taste the best and go the farthest. Eventually she produced a great supply of corned beef and onions and potato hash, which filled three large frying pans to overflowing.

The boys came in, shy at first, but they soon loosened up when they caught a whiff of Mom's home cooking. We all sat down at the crowded table together, Dad and Mother, the boys, Bob, Peg, and I – and everyone attacked that succulent hash with fervour. To Mother's complete amazement, everything disappeared. Not so much as one crumb was left, and she was devastated to think that, in spite of having used up all the available food, there still did not seem to have been enough! But one of the boys soon put her at her ease.

"Don't you worry, Mrs Jo," he said as he patted his bulging stomach with satisfaction. "I ain't never before ben ast to nobody's house to eat, never in my whole life! That was the most wonderful dinner I've ever ate. I won't *never* forget it!" And then we all sat around, comfortably full, and talked of many things, while the quiet summer evening cast long shadows across the grass.

Suddenly Bob looked at the clock – and pandemonium broke loose. The boys and Bob fled from the house, to run back along the CPR tracks to the farm, which they reached just as the nine o'clock curfew sounded. What luck! No excuses had to be given, no explanations made.

Having delivered his charges, Bob returned soberly along the railway track, and what he had to say to Mother brought tears to her eyes. "I never realized before just what it means to have a *real* family," he said thoughtfully. "That's something I guess those boys have never had. They sure appreciated everything you did for them, Mom. Thanks!"

CHAPTER FIFTEEN

The Maple Leaf Trail: 1932–1939

With summer close at hand, Dad and Bob found time to get to know each other. They would go off fishing together, for Dad felt that quite apart from being fun for both of them it was a sure-fire way of bringing home something to eat. He had an uncanny way with a hook. The creeks were full of fish, and the two would take their rods, casting into pools as they made their way upstream, and very seldom did they come home empty-handed. Mother was always delighted with these exploits and, after leaving the choicest morsels with her, Dad and Bob would often go over to the neighbours with a gleaming pair of trout. "These aren't much," they would say, diffidently, "but we had a good catch this afternoon, and we thought these might taste good for your supper."

On such trips, the two of them would have long talks. "If we could just get the government interested in financing a main trunk trail," said Dad, "a route that would run right down through the Laurentians from inn to inn, serviceable both in summer and in winter, it would be a real drawing card for visitors. It would bring business to the Laurentians, and the railways would certainly be keen. We would call it 'The Maple Leaf Trail,' and people would come from all over, just to use it. They would walk or ski over the hills from town to town, then board the train again at some other point." The "Maple Leaf" grew in their minds to be a special kind of mission – an undertaking about which they would talk enthusiastically to anyone and everyone who would listen. And in the end, their idea became a reality – the flowering of a long-cherished dream.

Much manoeuvring had to be done to convince the necessary authorities that the project was both practical and worthwhile. Dad saw it as a broad scheme that would bring much-needed work to a number of people throughout the Laurentians, for the trail would have to be scrupulously brushed out and maintained from year to year. He saw himself as the overall organizer, the trail-maker, who would plot its initial course, taking advantage of the major scenic spots in the area. He would have a gang of efficient woodsmen who would fell trees, work out the stumps, and bridge small ravines so that the trail could run through rough country, giving travellers a real taste of the Laurentians. It would not be a racing trail, but rather a comfortable touring route to be travelled by families and friends of varying ages. It would start at Labelle, the town named for Curé Labelle, original colonizer of the Laurentians, and it would run for eighty miles – 128 kilometres – all the way down to Shawbridge, the gateway to the mountains.

But quite apart from labour costs and the need for a uniform system of marking, there was also the necessity of establishing a right of way. For many years it had been customary for skiers to fan out from the railway stations in all directions, picking their way through the snow-covered fields, with no particular regard for private property. Many of these skiers never gave a second thought to the long-term damage they might cause when they opened a convenient hole in a farm fence to assure themselves of a good downhill run. They were unconcerned with next summer's straying cattle. Consequently, many Laurentian farmers considered skiers to be a real menace. It was obvious that it would require both skill and diplomacy to convince the landowners that they *could* co-exist peacefully with skiers – if only both parties would agree to co-operate.

Dad always enjoyed talking to the farmers and getting to know them. He invariably spoke French, and although his accent may have been a bit strange and his grammar original, he would happily persist, and to the farmers his colourful conversation was evidence of his goodwill.

"These skiers," Jackrabbit would tell them, "don't want to make life difficult for you. They just want a right of passage." Then, waving his pole as a pointer, he would add, "If you would let me cut a trail from the other side of that mountain, down through your sugar bush, across your field and on over towards that next farm over there, you would find that people would follow the trail, and they wouldn't bother you around your house. If you agree you and I together could open up your fence in one specific spot. The trail would then lead people through your property, and skiers wouldn't be tempted to cut fences in other places, because this would be the easiest route. In spring, you would have only one or two places to repair. Besides, the procession of skiers through the winter would add a bit of 'spice' to your landscape!"

The next important step, Dad felt, was to communicate with the local politicians, and after much thought and several drafts he sent off the following letter to Herman Barrett, member of Parliament for the County of Terrebonne.

I am delighted to learn of the interest you are taking in the development of the Laurentian Mountains as a Tourist Centre for Skiing, Fishing and Hunting. I am especially glad that you recognize the Ski Sport as a potential revenue producer. There is no part of the Province of Quebec which has the same possibilities in this regard as the County of Terrebonne, where we have the best Ski Country east of the Rockies.

I have realized this during the years I have had the good fortune to make my home here, and am convinced that there is no more certain way of bringing prosperity to Quebec than to spend money on the development of skiing.

Thanks to the generosity of some of my friends, including Sidney Dawes of Atlas Construction Company and John Molson of the Molson Brewery, we have during the past few years succeeded in building a number of Downhill Ski Runs and Jumping Hills between Shawbridge and St-Jovite. This has been carried out based on the enthusiasm of these men for the sport, and I am glad to note that, despite inadequate overall funding, this has led to greater traffic for the Railways and Hotels, and a nice profit for the farmers whose land is constantly increasing in value. Were we to have sufficient money with which to build Cross-Country Ski Trails, the Laurentian Mountains would soon experience a remarkable prosperity.

I have for many years advocated that Cross-Country Trails be laid out, properly cut, and marked in such a manner that a stranger can find his way without danger of getting lost. Unfortunately, while some of these trails are shown on the maps, they cannot be found in the field. I would suggest as an initial step, that a definite trunk trail be laid out, with branch trails connecting the individual Centres.

If the necessary funds can be found, work should be started immediately, as this is the right time of year. I am in a position to undertake this work, and would be happy to receive your instructions.

Very truly yours,

H. Smith Johannsen

Other people also approached the government, and at last there came a glimmer of hope when the sum of $2,000 was finally awarded, through the member of Parliament, "for ski development." To Jackrabbit's intense disappointment, however, this money was used to send a dog-team to Madison Square Garden in New York to advertise existing Laurentian resorts, in the hope of luring Americans to come up and to see for themselves "the quaint way of life in rural Quebec." Only a few hundred dollars were set aside for markers for the Maple Leaf Trail, and there was no money at all for labour.

Needless to say, Jackrabbit found this a totally frustrating, "cart before the horse" idea. His main objective, the Maple Leaf Trail, which was to have been the "bait" to attract the tourists, was entirely submerged in this fancy dog-team display which, entertaining as it may have been to New Yorkers, certainly contributed no direct relief to the work-hungry people in the Laurentians. In the end, it was left to Jackrabbit to install the new trail markers by himself, or with the aid of volunteers.

One of his enthusiastic aides was young Stan Ferguson, then a bellboy at Laurentide Inn, who cheerfully set out with Jackrabbit on his days off to help clear the trail both north and south from Ste-Agathe. Stan was proud of this personal effort of his, and spoke of it often in later years, when he became a man of influence in the Laurentian hotel business.

Dad continued as best he could to lay out the trail of his dreams, trying as always to foster good will among the landowners, with sporadic help from skiers, who volunteered to help him, usually for a day or two at a time. The CPR continued to provide him with a railway pass, and the numerous inns would give him a meal and a bed now and then; though he often preferred to sleep out on the

The family, Easter 1934, Val Morin, Quebec.

trail, in his sleeping bag, under the stars, so that he could carry on next day from where he had left off the night before, without having to backtrack merely for the sake of sleeping indoors. Gradually, in its more accessible parts, the trail was begining to be known and he lost no opportunity to direct skiers over these better-known stretches so that the trail would look "used." The section north of Ste-Agathe, however, remained somewhat harder to deal with.

During the fall of 1933, the house beside the Shawbridge station was leased to others, and the Johannsens had to move once more, this time to a small cottage in Val Morin, from which Dad continued to work on his own on his trunk trail. This did not prevent him, however, from taking a certain amount of time off to do a little "necessary" hunting.

I remember one cold November Sunday when Mother and I stood at the kitchen window listening to the southbound CPR as it whistled into Val Morin Station. Dad would soon be home. It was just dusk when we saw him, a small dark figure at the far end of the lane leading up from Pinehurst Inn. Soft snow was falling as he skied slowly up the hill, pulling his laden dogsled behind

Sun Valley Farm, Val Morin, c. 1942.

him. On it was a fine young buck! We ran out joyfully to welcome the successful hunter and to exclaim over his handsome trophy. He had been up at La Macaza with friends from the Balsam Lake Hunt Club, and each of the men had shot a deer. The others were justly proud of their prowess, of course, but to Dad, his share represented an important portion of our winter's food supply. Mother and I helped him hang the frozen deer in the frosty basement under the house. Bit by bit, the deer was cut up into roasts and steaks and chops. Nothing was wasted. The deerskin served for many years as a cosy underpad in Dad's sleeping bag, and the antlers hung outside the house as a decoration long after the last succulent morsel of meat had been consumed.

Jackrabbit with son-in-law Peter Austin
at Sun Valley Farm, 1944.

That deerskin was properly inaugurated later in the winter on a special expedition that followed the lively weekend at the Second Kandahar Race. When all the other competitors had finally embarked on the return train to Montreal, Dad and four of the hardier ones – George Jost, George Sumner, Bob Cundill, and my brother, Bob – set out on a memorable excursion "over the frozen lakes and untracked snows of Mont Tremblant Park," as Jost later reported in the 1975 book by Brian Powell, *Jackrabbit: His First Hundred Years.*

There was no wind, and the temperature read five degrees above zero as we headed north from Lac Tremblant and into the chain of rivers,

Habitant Farm on the road to Sun Valley, c. 1946.

lakes, and woodlands towards Five Finger Lake, forty miles to the north, the start of a hundred-mile trek.

Herman's dog was harnessed to a sled made from an old pair of skis, on which we piled our sleeping bags. Provisions and personal gear we stowed in our packs. The food had been organized by Jackrabbit, who was lean and wiry because he never overate, and we suddenly guessed that he expected us to travel on the stamina of our ski legs rather than the sustenance in our stomachs.

Later in the week, with depleted provisions, our Friday evening meal consisted of fresh bread we had picked up at a lumber camp the previous day, and two partridges which a trapper had given us in exchange for two of the loaves. We roasted the birds on a spit in the trapper's open fireplace and bunked that night in his primitive log cabin.

We learned a lot that week in the bush with Herman, sleeping out under the stars, watching the few birds that inhabit the quiet woods in winter, learning the snow tracks of partridge, rabbit, squirrel, wolf and deer. Above all, however, we learned from our respected elder of the beauty and serenity of the deep woods, the sleeping frozen landscape, and the real brotherhood of friendship.

During the winter of 1934, there was a great stirring of anticipation among the school children throughout the Laurentians. Père

Deslauriers, the kindly, down-to-earth young curé of Lac Mercier Village, was looking for something to occupy the time and energy of many of his young parishioners, for whom these winter months were particularly difficult. Times were hard and jobs were scarce. The Canadian International Paper Company had laid off many men, the sawmills were closing, and many of the small industries that had grown up around the chemical by-products of the lumber industry – acetate, charcoal, and wood alcohol – had also been shut down. The whole country appeared to stagnate.

As Père Deslauriers travelled by horse and sleigh around his parish, he would often come upon a group of children playing on a hill on homemade skis fashioned from barrel staves, or out of old boards which they had carefully whittled, trying to copy the skis of the city skiers who would from time to time appear over the hills, skim down through their fields, then vanish over the horizon.

Jackrabbit, on his travels, too, would stop to chat with these children, encouraging them to "ride the bumps." He would sometimes ski for a while with them, showing them how to herringbone their way back up, or how to slap their skis down hard on the snow to get a better grip, then zigzag their way to the top. The children were delighted to copy this amusing old fellow, following in his footsteps as they discovered how to manoeuvre their boards under varying conditions.

Père Deslauriers was convinced that these youngsters deserved to be encouraged, and it was he who was really behind the first inter-village ski meet, held that year in Ste-Agathe. To it came schoolboys from all over the Laurentians. Jackrabbit was invited, together with a number of other men to act as officials. There were Fred Lapointe from St-Jerome, Christiansen from Shawbridge, Victor Nymark from St-Sauveur, Emile Maupas from Val Morin, Ken Harrison from Ste-Agathe, and Tom Wheeler from Lac Ouimet. They brought with them children from their home towns, and the interest and enthusiasm of these men did much to establish this meet as a truly important event. The second inter-village meet was hosted by the Boys' Farm in Shawbridge, with three exciting events, the downhill, the cross-country and the jump. Enthusiasm ran high, and the meet was repeated year after year. More and more, Jackrabbit recognized the active spirit behind competitive skiing.

That same winter of 1934, the Laurentian Ski Association sponsored the sixth annual Ste-Agathe to Val Morin Cross-Country Race which began and ended at Pinehurst Inn near Dad's house. On the day of the event, as the competitors were assembling, there appeared among them a completely unknown nineteen-year-old youngster, Gault Gillespie, from a farm near Ste-Agathe, who had left home that morning and skied the fifteen kilometres down to Pinehurst Inn. He arrived well ahead of starting time, but was all hot and sweaty despite the sub-zero weather. The officials were surprised at the obvious exertion he had already expended, and advised him to "go in and take a quick hot shower and rest up a bit" before the race was called. They looked him over, shook their heads, and pointed out that several other competitors had actually taken part in the Lake Placid Olympics two years before. The competition, they suggested, would be "rather keen."

Gillespie took his quick shower, and as he had no alternative clothing with him, got back into his damp and sweaty ski suit and lined up for the start. He had drawn starting number 8 out of fifteen entrants, and he watched as the first seven racers set off. Then it was his turn. He really had to move fast in order to keep warm, but he soon hit his stride and the kilometres sped by. Gradually he overtook all of the first seven racers, and skied to the finish line – the first to arrive. The officials were astonished, and convinced there must be a mistake. "You probably missed out on one of the posts and took a short cut," they told him. "Anyway, we'll just have to wait until everyone else is in and the posts have all reported." But Gillespie didn't wait to hear the results. He was somewhat tired, and as he still had fifteen kilometres to cover to reach home, he set off immediately.

Next morning the Gillespie family was amazed to receive a surprise visit from the mayor of Ste-Agathe, in person, who drove up to the farm excitedly waving a copy of the Montreal *Gazette*. "Local Boy Wins Laurentian Meet," read the headline. "Gault Gillespie Wins 15-kilometre Ste-Agathe–Val Morin Ski Race."

While the Gillespies were still digesting this fascinating news, a lean old man in a Norwegian sweater was seen poling his way up to the farmhouse door. "Is this were Gault Gillespie lives?" he asked. It was Jackrabbit. "I came to deliver to him the prize he won yesterday. He got away too soon!" And with that he handed over a copy of the latest map of all the Laurentian ski trails. "Your cup will come later, after it has been engraved," he said. "Then all you have to do is win it two more times, and it will be yours to keep!"

And that was just what Gault did. In 1936 and in 1937, he won the cup again, and fifty years later it is still proudly displayed in the family living-room.

❦

At the end of the 1934 ski season, Jackrabbit was restless again. By May he was itching to explore a canoe route through Mont Tremblant Park. "It's important that we travel over the same portages both in summer and winter," he explained. "Then we can get to know the real life in the woods." And he organized a group which included Alma Howard, a McGill classmate of mine, two of the ski boys, Douglas Urquhart and George Sumner, my brother, Bob, and me.

We entered the Park at St-Donat, and paddled and portaged our way over the height of land between the Ouareau and the Devil's Rivers where we found snow still lingering beneath some of the winter windfalls. The water in the lakes had just been freed of ice, and was bitterly cold to our hands as we plied our paddles over the choppy waves. It was an exciting two weeks. We surprised a bull moose foraging among the lily roots on a quiet stream, and listened to the distant howling of wolves as we lay comfortably in our sleeping bags beside the embers of our fire. The fishing in Five Finger Lake was wonderful and supplied a welcome addition to our dwindling food supply, for our return journey was delayed by a whole twenty-four hours when we had to hack our way over a long-unused and completely overgrown portage.

When we finally returned to St-Donat, we immediately raided the local bakery, emerging in triumph with two fragrant loaves of bread from which we each wrenched delicious handfuls, without benefit of a knife. We then retired to Hotel Thibodeau to quell our pangs of hunger with a hearty steak. It had been a fantastic expedition, and our temporary privation made each of us appreciate the basic joys of civilization all the more. To this very day the tingling aroma of fresh-baked bread and the mouth-watering sight of a tender steak never fail to call the haunting memories to my mind.

Family finances meanwhile continued very shaky, but people were by this time beginning to avail themselves of Dad's accumulated knowledge of ski matters, sometimes actually paying for his expert advice at ten dollars a day. Although their appreciation was more often expressed in less remunerative terms, Jackrabbit was always generous with his time, and would spend days on end preparing the way for ski-resort business hopefuls involved with various aspects of skiing or real estate, who sought his help to gain favour with certain landowners. Occasionally this would materialize into a "business" deal, but more often than not, these same speculators would come back to Dad, bringing perhaps a box of chocolates for Mother as their way of saying "Thank you" for his part in the transaction. Mother, though always grateful for the chocolates, could not help but murmur, after such visitors had left, "Wouldn't you think they would have realized that a good piece of red meat would have done us more good?"

During these winters the Johannsen children had been solving their own problems as best they could. After emerging from the little Shawbridge school in 1933, Peggy had returned to the city. There she lived for two winters with Emma Lawlor, secretary of Westmount High School, in a friendly and very compatible arrangement. Bob meanwhile struggled to continue to study at home, and would go to town periodically to try exams, while he stayed with the Urquharts, or with the Oliver family, our former minister at St. Matthias Church, or with the choirmaster, Mr Hislop. I spent my third college year with friends, the Perceys, with whom I had a "cooperative understanding" in exchange for minimal duties as household help, and I spent my final year alternately with the families of two of my close classmates, Alma Howard and Ragn Tait. It was a time of general adaptation for all of us, but we were warmly welcomed into each of these households, and to each of them we will be forever grateful.

It was in the spring of 1935 that both Bob and Peggy wrote their matriculation examinations, Bob having lost out completely on two years of schooling during the family's Shawbridge sojourn. In the end, however, he made up for lost time, living alternately with the Olivers, the Urquharts, and the Hislops while he finished at Westmount High. Bob and Peggy finally graduated from high school together. By working summers, Bob had managed to lay aside his university fees and was able to enter McGill that fall, while Peggy continued in senior matric at Westmount High.

This seemed a propitious time for Dad and Mother to move back temporarily to Montreal, to reunite the family during their college years, so in 1937 they rented an apartment on Crescent Street and Mother took in as boarders a series of McGill students, and others who were looking for a "home away from home." These young people brought with them an array of outside interests, to say nothing of problems of their own, but Mother took everything in her stride and fully enjoyed her extended family. "I feel almost as though I were going to college myself," she said. "There's certainly never a dull moment around this house!"

I went off for five post-graduate winters in New Jersey, Ottawa, and Manitoba, but I returned to Montreal every summer. Although we were all working towards our separate goals, we were at the same time striving for the collective good of the family. These efforts took many forms. For Bob it meant summers as a timekeeper on construction jobs, as a surveyor on the Senneterre highway in La Vérendrye Park, as a chemist at a paint company in Montreal, and as a guide at a fishing camp at La Barrière, north of Joliette.

At La Barrière, which was frequented by many Americans, he served as camp guide to a number of interesting guests, among them Dr Irving Langmuir who had received the 1932 Nobel Prize in chemistry. By coincidence, Dr Langmuir was also an enthusiastic skier. To Bob as an aspiring chemist, this meeting was an event of enormous importance, and he lost no opportunity to discuss the various chemical properties of ski wax and ski lacquer. Dr Langmuir was interested and impressed, and the two became fast friends.

Meanwhile, Peggy and I had been hired as summer naturalists at the Ausable Club in the Adirondacks, and Peggy had also had the good luck to earn a year of her McGill fees by winning the Major Hiram Mills Scholarship in Biology. This involved making and annotating a scientific collection of "150 flowering plants and ferns, forty invertebrates, and ten vertebrates," a time-consuming and exacting job. Of necessity it also involved the cooperation of many helpful individuals and caused numerous hilarious incidents in the course of our Adirondack naturalist activities.

Throughout this period, Dad was frequently up north on various missions, among them the first Veterans' Race at Shawbridge in 1936, which he, at the age of sixty-one, won "hands down!" That winter, too, he spent considerable time working on behalf of Fred Pabst, Jr, an entrepreneur from Milwaukee who was hoping to corner the "lazy skier" market by installing fifteen ski tows in the eastern United States and Canada, an enterprise that showed some promise. Three of these ski tows were destined for Shawbridge, St-Sauveur, and Ste-Marguerite. The future began to look more encouraging, and Dad hoped to get a commission on the sale of this machinery, even though he himself still preferred to climb on foot. "I've spent enough of my life feeling cold skiing downhill," he said. "Darned if I want to freeze going uphill, too!"

In 1937 two of Jackrabbit's old friends, Gerald and Nobel Birks, came to him with a request for his help, on behalf of some American friends of theirs, who were seeking the hunting and fishing rights to approximately 150 square miles of forest in the vicinity of Antostagnan Lake in La Vérendrye Park. It was near the area where Bob had been working, on the Senneterre highway, and the exploration project appealed very much to Jackrabbit. He was delighted to arrange a preliminary visit for the Birks brothers and himself, in early February.

Their expedition set out from Maniwaki by truck, following the preliminary construction on the Senneterre Road for fifty miles, then continuing twenty miles further, by bush road, to the "jumping-off place" at Government camp No. 1. From that point on, they were on their own. Jackrabbit was in his element. He had two dogs with him – huskies, borrowed from Harry Wheeler's dogsled team at Gray Rocks Inn – and his own two dogsleds. They stowed their sleeping gear and some of their provisions on the sleds, and set off, with Dad in the lead carrying his own loaded knapsack, followed closely by the dogs, each with his sled, then by the two men with their own packs and the remainder of the food.

They made a comfortable base camp on Antostagnan Lake, from which they fanned out for eight days, exploring the shores of numerous bodies of water and much of the intervening forest. The weather was very disappointing. There were two separate days of blizzard, followed by a night of minus thirty degrees Fahrenheit, then a night of rain before the temperature once more dipped below freezing. This made a particularly noisy crust and prevented the game from travelling. The country itself, however, was beautiful, with rolling hills covered with hardwood, interspersed with balsam, pine, and cedar, and with black spruce in the moist hollows in between.

They learned, from an Indian trapper, that moose and deer were plentiful, and that there were grey trout and doré in the larger lakes, and speckled trout in the smaller ones. Much of the area had been logged some thirty years before, but the remaining area appeared to be in virgin timber. All in all, they had no difficulty in recommending that the hunting and fishing rights be leased from the government for $550 for three years, following which the sponsors would be free to terminate the lease, should they so desire.

The party returned exuberantly to Montreal, highly pleased with their wilderness excursion. Their report went forward, and Dad was happy to receive not only his fee of $10 per day but also a splendid set of nesting aluminum cooking utensils, together with a very practical little primus stove "for future trips." The name of Antostagnan Lake and the date of their visit were engraved on the outermost pot, and the set, now comfortably battered and worn, is still a treasured reminder of that wonderful experience.

The following winter, another opportunity came Dad's way when his old friend Erling Ström, from Lake Placid days, invited him to join a special excursion to Mount Assiniboine Lodge in the Rockies. The CPR provided them with passes, and the CPR photographer Nicolas Morant made a splendid pictorial record of their activities, with Dad, Erling, and various other visitors trekking through powder snow amid spectacular scenery. Some of these pictures were later reproduced on English Wedgwood plates, a set of which was later presented to Dad. The family took special joy in watching the expressions on the faces of dinner guests when they discovered Dad skiing out from under their mashed potatoes!

In the fall of 1938 Arthur Terroux, one of Jackrabbit's good friends from Laurentian Lodge, who always referred to Dad as the "Chief," approached him to sit for a portrait by Edwin Holgate, an artist friend of his. "I can't imagine why anyone wants to paint a portrait of *me*," said Dad, whose outdoor life definitely overshadowed his interest in art. He reluctantly submitted, not when he learned that Holgate was a celebrated portraitist, but when he was told that the artist owned a camp on Lac Tremblant. That effectively broke the ice, and Dad and Holgate soon became fast friends. Holgate's *The Skier* now graces the walls of the Montreal Museum of Fine Arts, to which it came as a bequest, after Arthur Terroux's death. There stands The Jackrabbit, ski poles in hand, his blue eyes steadfastly surveying the throng of gallery-goers. In the background rises Mont Tremblant, with White Peak looking as it used to look, shortly after its green forest was stripped from it by clear cutting.

Peggy and Bob were increasingly busy at McGill: along with their major involvements with, respectively, botany and chemistry, and with various predictable (and unpredictable) affairs of the heart, both of them became deeply involved with the McGill ski teams. They took part in many intercollegiate meets, and in 1937 Peggy won, against stiff competition, the Holt Wilson Trophy, awarded in alternate years in the east and in the west to the best woman skier in Canada. Bob, for his part, became the 1939 Dominion combined champion in the four disciplines of jumping, cross-country, downhill and slalom. These were feats that gladdened the heart of the old Jackrabbit, who as a long-time member of the technical board of the Canadian Amateur Ski Association, could now bask in the reflected glory of two of his offspring who were doing their part to bring new glory to the Johannsen family name.

Bob, however, did more than win titles. In his senior year he went into production with his Jack Rabbit Ski Lacquer, a concoction that he was convinced would revolutionize the art of skiing. He set up a factory on the back veranda of the apartment house; and there, after mixing up his brew, he would commandeer Mother, the boarders, and the entire ski team, together with any unsuspecting visitors, to form a production line extending from the veranda into the house and down the hall. It was no mean task to fill a thousand little bottles with this waterproof lacquer, screw on the caps, wipe the bottles clean and paste on the labels, each of which bore instructions and a sketch of a cotton-tailed rabbit surging confidently downhill on his well-lacquered skis. Pat Paré, one of the avid skiers taking part in all this, created the design.

Dad, of course, was the official salesman, and he did a constant round of sporting-goods stores and ski clubs. The ski team members were happy to endorse the product, which they believed had contributed to their success in the intercollegiate races, and they were delighted to demonstrate Bob's contention that "With *Jack Rabbit* you are always one jump ahead."

It became a routine for them, when they journeyed to out-of-town meets, to bring along a suitcase full of Jack Rabbit Lacquer, which they would peddle to anyone willing to buy. This not only provided cheap word-of-mouth advertising for Bob, it also made the team members new friends and helped defray their expenses.

Needless to say, there were complications with regard to permission to manufacture, as well as problems of marketing and administration, but little by little these problems were (at least temporarily) overcome, and Jack Rabbit Lacquer became established as Bob's first business venture. It was hampered from the start, however, by having no "seed money" as capital investment, and the embryo business was no great financial success. Nonetheless, it did establish the name of "The Jackrabbit" unforgettably on the market, although it would be twenty more years before the product took its own strong position in the face of growing competition.

With increasing use of the Laurentians as a skier's paradise, a number of large companies suddenly discovered that by encouraging general interest in this great sport, they could comfortably keep their own product very much in the public eye. And that was how the *Sweet Caporal Skier's Book* was born.

The story was this: the Imperial Tobacco Sales Company approached Jackrabbit through the Montreal *Gazette* Printing Company to produce, on contract, a skier's guide to the Laurentians, including notes on equipment and ski technique, and to supervise creation of an accompanying map. He accepted with delight. A relief model of the area was constructed by Charles Furst, based on topographic maps. This was photographed, lit from the side to emphasize the relief, and on this Dad laid out the CN and the CPR railway lines, the communities they linked, all the main and secondary roads, and many of the farm and bush roads. To these he then added, in red, his accumulated knowledge of the main network of trails over which he had skied for many years, including his cherished Maple Leaf Trail, running all the way from Labelle to Shawbridge. Secondary ski trails were also included, as were dotted lines indicating desirable but as yet unmarked routes. Also prominently shown were the locations of all the existing ski tows, downhill runs, and first-aid posts.

The text was translated into French by the *Gazette*, and the whole came out as a bilingual booklet, complete with Dad's impressive signature, and he was launched as the author in 1939. In the back was a fifteen-by-eighteen-inch fold-out master map, and a number of smaller five-by-nine-inch sectional maps, drawn on a larger scale, which made it easy to follow a specific route on a day's trip. It was a handy little compendium that fitted neatly into one's shirt pocket, and I was proud to cooperate as "ghost writer," typist, and proof-reader. Imperial Tobacco issued these guidebooks as free advertising, and eager skiers were quick to snap them up.

It was around this time that ski developers in other regions began to seek Dad's advice. He was invited to Collingwood, north of Toronto, to look over a long line of hills, and was happy to lay out the beginnings of a successful development there, and also at Rawdon, Quebec. In Quebec's Eastern Townships, enthusiastic interest at Magog was centred on Mount Orford, and he spent a good deal of time laying out, with the local people, a network of trails extending from the summit, and including development of the promising basin at Three Creeks. He also spent time at North Hatley and at Lac Beauport, north of Quebec City, where he engineered some impressive downhill runs, a jump, cross-country trails, and slalom hills – until local politics intervened, and in the end he found it difficult merely to collect his expenses.

It was always the same old story. Everyone was eager to capitalize on Jackrabbit's name, his enthusiasm, and his expertise to back up their own initiatives and their search for funds for further development, but in almost every case there were others who, once he had pointed the way, stepped in to reap the financial benefits. Welcome as he always was as a trail-blazer, he was forgotten when business really took off. But, as he himself often said, "I'm really a *coureur de bois*. I like the challenge when the job is new, but I tire of it when the in-fighting starts."

In May 1939 Bob and Peggy graduated together from McGill, each with a degree as bachelor of science, and each fully aware of all the collective sacrifices that had made it possible. It was amazing to them to realize that their primary personal objectives had actually been reached. Now was the time to set new goals, and they lost no time in doing so. Peggy enrolled in a graduate programme in botany at Macdonald College, while Bob was determined to follow up on his theories on snow crystals and various methods of insulation. Not surprisingly he chose to go to Norway, where he could study at the University of Oslo, meet other members of the family, and get to know the land of which the Jackrabbit still dreamed.

It was therefore with much joy and many good wishes that the family saw him off on his independent great adventure, aboard the *Iddefjord*. He had signed on to work his way across the Atlantic as an able seaman, and the last the family saw of him was as he stood, stripped to the waist, wielding a paint brush on the afterdeck.

CHAPTER SIXTEEN

The Hungry Years: 1940–1960

Once the great whirl of convocation was over, Bob and Peggy and the various graduates who had made their home with Dad and Mother for the past few years all went their separate ways, and the apartment on Crescent Street was suddenly much too large. Peggy would be working back in the Adirondacks all summer, and Bob would be away in Norway for at least a year.

So when I returned, jobless, to Montreal after my years in the west, Dad, Mother, and I made a quick move into smaller quarters on Mountain Street. This new apartment would be large enough for all of us next year, and meanwhile we would have room to take in two short-term boarders – Natalie Harding from Shawbridge, to finish her high school in Montreal, and Murray Outhet, son of one of Dad's old Tremblant friends, who was desperately seeking a job. I took on a demonstratorship in zoology, temporarily replacing Kathleen Terroux, who was on maternity leave. So Mother again had a family to care for, and Dad was free to continue with ski jobs whenever and wherever they might appear.

The Penguin Ski Club had been founded in 1932 and was the only exclusively ladies' ski club in existence at the time. Ever since Betty Sherrard and ten of her friends had formed the club, these women had been making an impression in skiing circles. They held their first club championship with fifteen members in Ivry in 1933, and Jackrabbit and Harry Pangman, one of the founding members of the Red Birds Ski Club, were invited to attend, with

Eddie Sherrard, as "officials," lending real clout to the enterprise. The men entered enthusiastically into the preparations, and laid out a cross-country, slalom, downhill and bushwhack, and even a jump, which was won with a leap of twenty-seven feet! As Jackrabbit casually remarked, "Any *real* competition should test all one's capabilities, and any Penguin who can successfully negotiate these five events will definitely have 'earned her spurs.'" Hélène McNichols was the combined winner, and the overall result was a very determined group of young women who set out to show the skiing world that one's sex has very little to do with one's performance. Determination, judgment, and control can carry one through unforeseen circumstances, as many other Penguins were to prove in the years to come.

Skiing was becoming more popular than ever. In 1935 the Canadian Ski Year Book recorded that the CPR had run thirty-one northbound ski trains to the Laurentians every weekend, transporting in all some 10,000 enthusiasts to various towns along its line.

For the first few years of their existence, the Penguins were in St-Sauveur, where some of them took ski lessons from Duke Dimitri of Leuchtenberg, with excellent results (the Duke was a White Russian emigré who came to St-Sauveur in the late 1920s). They arranged with Mme David for slightly more spacious surroundings above the Banque Nationale, where after a long day of wet spring skiing they would drape their sodden ski clothes to dry on chairs grouped around the vents from the hot air furnace and all up and down the stairway banisters. Madame would shake her head uncomprehendingly as she murmured, "Quelle misère, pour le sport!" but she put up good-naturedly with these goings-on as being inexplicably part of "les habitudes des Anglais." Meanwhile, both Peggy and I had been elected to honorary membership in the Penguins, which pleased us immensely as we could not possibly have afforded it otherwise.

Eventually, the Penguins migrated to a house near the Piedmont railway station, to which they would repair on Saturday evenings after an energetic day of skiing, to settle into their sleeping bags on somewhat less than comfortable beds, and blissfully fall asleep. On Sundays they would go farther up the line, often with some of the Red Birds, for a long cross-country tour, and return at last to Montreal on any one of the evening trains, tired but content.

It was in 1937 that two well-known landowners of St-Sauveur, the brothers Herbert and John Molson, who also had ties with the Red Birds as honorary members, decided that with their enthusiasm and spirit these young women were really worthy of sympathetic support. To the astonishment and delight of the Penguins, the Molson brothers donated an acre of land and had built a beautiful log chalet in French-Canadian habitant style, which they turned over, completely furnished, to the Penguin executive, a clubhouse that included lodging for up to twenty-four members, and a three-year supply of coal. This was a tremendous encouragement, and forthwith the Penguins emerged in full competitive form.

The Red Birds Ski Club had been founded in 1928, and from the very beginning its members had been interested in far more than just the fun of skiing together. After the boys had organized and run off the First Kandahar Race at Mont Tremblant in 1932, they were encouraged by Tom and Harry Wheeler of Gray Rocks Inn to supply much of the muscle and manpower needed to open up some of the first ski trails on that mountain. It was not long before other hotel owners took an active interest in further developing these facilities, and this led naturally to more enthusiastic use by the rest of the skiing public.

The first Red Birds clubhouse was opened at St-Sauveur in 1931 in an old farmhouse on the Lac Millette Road. From there it was only a short run across open fields to the foot of St-Sauveur Hill where the club championship was annually held. The bushwhack was one of five regular events in which all members participated, and at that time the Penguins also were permitted to compete. I have very strong recollections of one free-for-all bushwhack in which Harry Pangman, George Jost, and Sterling Maxwell came out as victors, leaving the wooded hill behind them littered with male and female skiers entwined among the saplings, extricating themselves from unexpected pitfalls, or salvaging glasses, hats, ski poles, and mittens from temporary resting places in the deep snow – I know, because I was one of them. And then we would all gather at the Red Birds House for sandwiches, a glass of beer, and a singsong. Jackrabbit was almost always present as he usually had more free time than the rest, and indeed had done much of the preparation for the meet.

In 1933 the Red Birds moved to a cosy little cabin at the foot of Mont St-Sauveur, where members and guests would congregate at the end of a long skiing day to relax by the open hearth. Here ukuleles and accordions would lead the singing for as long as was possible, before everyone joined in a mad dash for the last south-bound train, to continue their singsong all the way down to Montreal.

❦

In September 1939 the Second World War was declared, and our lives – and the lives of all around us – changed profoundly. Suddenly everyone was intimately involved with the war effort. There were rallies, and parades, and fund drives. Mother and I joined the Norwegian Red Cross, and frantically knitted, or rolled bandages, or packed parcels at the headquarters in the Dominion Square Building. The campus became a parade ground. I remember Donnie Cleghorn from the Redpath Museum drilling soldiers from the Black Watch, just before their unit left for overseas. And I remember when the newspapers carried a shocking report: "*Athenea* torpedoed while returning from England." Food rationing and restrictions on travel were introduced, and there were shortages of meat and butter.

Dad, at the age of sixty-four, offered his services as a trainer for ski troops, but to his surprise and dismay he was turned down flat, as being "much too old." The world had suddenly become a place where only young men were wanted, and men of Dad's age were *definitely* not needed.

The winter wore on. Norway, in early 1940, was not yet at war, and letters frequently passed to and from Bob and other members of the family. Dad was particularly upset by all the war propaganda, and wrote to Johannes, in Norwegian, that "The politicians and everyone else in authority over here are all just monkeys or parrots. Nobody thinks for himself any more. Everyone just follows the leader." And Dad, distraught as he was, felt better for having unburdened his mind.

Mother, however, urged him not to be so outspoken. "You know, Herman," she said cautiously, "there *is* censorship. You might easily be misunderstood by the authorities." But Dad refused to listen. "Anyhow," he insisted, "the Canadian censors don't understand Norwegian."

Then, one evening, there came a knock at the apartment door. There stood two stern-faced members of the Royal Canadian Mounted Police. They demanded to speak to Mr Johannsen. It seemed that the censors had intercepted several letters from Dad to his brother, Johannes, including the one in which Dad had referred to Canadian politicians and to citizens in general as *apicoter og papagoyer* – nothing but "apes and parrots." The censors obviously had had no trouble reading Norwegian. Now they wanted an explanation, and Dad spent an uncomfortable three hours trying to set the record straight. The officers had done their homework and were well aware of Dad's student days in Germany in the 1890s. They demanded to know just where he stood with respect to Germany now, in 1940. They questioned him on Bob's activities in Norway, and on his own contacts with "Canadian youth" – and he was cautioned to hold his tongue. They made it very clear that he was being "watched," and they left him with the strong warning that he was on their "list." Dad was devastated, but he muzzled his speech, and we all became very careful about what we said, and how we said it.

In April 1940 Germany invaded Norway, and all communication with that country abruptly ceased. Bob had been living in a small cabin on the mountain above Oslo, while he attended university. Now, although we did not know it, he had been captured and interned. Nor did we know that our young cousin Herman, the son of Johannes (and named for Dad), had been killed with his entire platoon while leading an early skirmish back of Nordmarka. A sudden, complete, and ominous silence fell. The radio and newspapers were our only sources of information, and these were filled with all sorts of unbelievable stories. The war now touched our own lives very personally, and we clung together with scarcely a word.

Throughout all this time there was at the university one group, the McGill Outing Club, the MOC, which served as a reliable outlet for all those energetic souls who were interested in escaping whenever possible from the grim realities of war. The MOC was composed mainly of medical students and nature buffs who, with the Jackrabbit, firmly believed that physical exercise, available to everyone at no cost, offered a major key to fitness and health. "Why is it," Jackrabbit wanted to know, "that it should take a *war* to make people realize that regular exercise is the natural way for all of us to keep alive? It only makes common sense!" And he plunged more eagerly than ever into his work in the woods. "I feel I am in a way coming to grips with some of these problems as I slash my way through the underbrush," he said, mopping his brow. And the students agreed with him.

The gang would gather on Sundays at Park Avenue Station in Montreal with knapsacks, food, and assorted tools. We got off the train at Shawbridge, and picked up our trail-clearing where we had left off the previous weekend. We were making a trail from Shaw-bridge to Ste-Marguerite on a twelve-kilometre route through forested country along a path previously blazed by the Jackrabbit, and he was happy to join us whenever he could "to make sure that the trail really goes where it ought to." Professor Wynne-Edwards of the Zoology Department and Mr "Van" Wagner of the Athletics Department were frequent participants, as were Grant Townsend from engineering; Reid Hyde, Joe Stratford, and Harold Asselstine from pre-medicine; Sylvia Grove, Joan Anderson, Margie Wil-liamson, and Ina and Diana Charlton, together with many others. Armed with axes, saws, and bush scythes, with branch clippers, grass cutters, and hunting knives, we were a formidable-looking crew as we hacked and chopped our way over the hills, across the streams, and through the gullies. There were frequent shouts of "*T-i-m-b-e-r!*" as a tree was felled. Its branches were trimmed, and its dismembered parts lugged by other members of the team into the bush beside the trail.

The path looped in long curves through the woods, avoiding large boulders, swooping and dipping and climbing again, for Jack-rabbit maintained that "speed is the thrill, but also the danger, of skiing." We would imagine ourselves there on the trail next winter after a heavy snowfall, facing down slope, edging our skis, turning guardedly around a big rock, then letting go as we twisted our way down a long incline, to disappear around the final bend.

One evening each week, the students and some of the younger staff would meet in the Zoology Department to fabricate markers destined to punctuate the finished trail. Three hundred four-inch squares of masonite were cut, painted with two coats of red, and stencilled in white with the shield of the University and with the letters MOC. Holes were drilled in the corners for easy attachment. After the first snowfall, we went out with hammers and nails to complete our work by installing these colourful markers at strategic points along the route.

With what pride we then followed where our new path led, up along the cliff face above Paradise Valley and on through the open beech forest where we always stopped to examine the "bear trees." Here, long ago, a pair of bear cubs had scrambled up and down the pale grey trunks of some of the younger beech trees, scarring the thin bark with their sharp claws. The wounds in the bark had long since healed, leaving deep black scars that reproduced exactly the clawmarks of the bears. In the course of time those tree trunks had grown in girth and with them the paw marks, which by then had reached prodigious size. These scars were always great fun to point out to new, uninitiated MOC'ers who were properly impressed, although the bears themselves were long vanished from the scene. Today, fifty years later, these same tracks can still be found up there on certain venerable beeches – if you know just where to look!

Peggy, after a year at Macdonald College as a graduate student, had married Peter Austin, a rising young man with Imperial Tobacco, and they were now happily established in their own apartment in Montreal. They inherited Mother's precious piano as a wedding gift. There was as yet no word from Norway where Bob had completely vanished from sight; all we could do was to pray for his safety and hope for the best. I, meanwhile, in the fall of 1940, had been promoted to secretary as well as demonstrator in zoology, and Dad and Mother felt that their presence in Montreal was no longer needed. "The two of us can live more cheaply up in Shawbridge," they said, so they rented a tiny summer cottage from Mrs Martin on the corner of Maple and North Streets, and there they made themselves as comfortable as was possible.

One entered the cottage through the kitchen where there was a monstrous woodstove that served for both cooking and heating. In the living-room was a small fireplace for auxiliary heat, and from this room there opened out a bathroom and two tiny bed-rooms – one for themselves, and the other for any members of the family who might venture by. Across the front was a glassed-in porch, which provided a windbreak from the chill north breeze. This also served as a cold room for food supplies, a convenient storage place for skis and camping gear, and a sleeping area for any hardy visitors who might come equipped with their own sleeping bags.

The wind whistled through cracks around the windows, and the first thing Dad did was tape up all possible places where cold air could creep in. There was no cellar under the house, so he banked up the outer walls with soil and hay, and waited for winter to deliver sufficient snow to seal up any further leaks along the edges. But when Mother's Chinese carpet had been laid down to further insulate the living-room floor, and when their lamps and personal possessions had been installed, the little house began to take on a real look of home. There was of course no telephone, as that was a completely unaffordable luxury. However, in case of emergency, I had an understanding with neighbouring Mrs Martin that I could call her line and she would dangle a noisy cowbell out of her window to announce to Mother that there was a call for her. We were careful not to abuse this privilege, but it was reassuring to have such an arrangement, should need arise.

I had brought a fine big bicycle back with me from Winnipeg – a heavy, one-speed freighter of a bicycle, but an absolutely dependable one, which had served me very well out west. I found that on Saturdays after work I could dash home to the apartment, eat my lunch, stow my knapsack on the bike and head for Shaw-bridge, which was only forty-five kilometres (or two and a half hours) away. I could make the return journey on Sunday evening in two hours, if the traffic was not too heavy, and so, at no expenditure other than muscle, I could be home with the folks each weekend, at least until the snow flew.

A number of the MOC'ers also took to their bikes, and the family headquarters at Shawbridge soon became a favourite rendez-vous. Dad and Mother thus became "den parents" to the MOC and many were the Sunday afternoons that the whole tribe would congregate at the Johannsens' after a day's outing. Mother would brew endless pots of tea, and how she did it we never knew, but she always managed to have a cake on hand. It would be cut into ever smaller and smaller portions; but no matter how many people showed up, there always seemed to be enough for everyone "to have a bite." When seats gave out, the overflow would sit on the floor as we hilariously reviewed the day's adventures. Somehow, Dad and Mother's hospitable door was always unlatched, ready to receive one or two more tired MOC'ers.

Next fall, in 1941, the Athletics Department decided that the MOC was important enough as a morale-booster to warrant the university's renting a house in Shawbridge for the club, where they could cook their own meals, sleep in their own sleeping bags, and generally be independent. With Dad's help a suitable location, the Boyer house, was found; and Mother, while she still loved to have club members drop in, felt she could now enjoy them more from a distance with no responsibility on her part. Perhaps now Dad could even get more than just a taste of her weekend cake for himself!

The whole MOC crowd gathered one memorable Sunday afternoon for a final celebration at the Johannsens' before taking over their own quarters. With them they brought a bulky bundle, which they carefully placed on the floor beside Mother. There was the usual scramble for chairs and floor space, and when all were settled, Reid insisted that Mother open the parcel at once. The brown paper was cautiously removed, and there stood a little gate-legged table, with two leaves that opened up when the legs were unfolded. Mother was still gasping her surprise when Ina appeared in the kitchen doorway, with her own teapot and a cake in her hand. "I just knew that this was going to come in handy someday," she beamed, as she set her burden down on the little table.

The whole crowd clapped and cheered as Mother brushed away a tear. That little MOC table continued to nestle snugly for many years beside Dad's big wing chair, unfolding its legs and spreading its "wings" whenever it was needed for countless other visitors, and for innumerable pots of tea. It came in handy, too, on various later occasions when Mother would entertain the Shawbridge Ladies' Aid for tea and cookies, at one of the social events of the Shawbridge "season."

Jackrabbit's contract was renewed and a second Sweet Caporal skier's book was produced for 1940–41. It included updated maps, new notes on the Laurentian landscape, and a detailed description of the Maple Leaf and other trails. The following year there was a special section headed "Exploring on Your Own," for Dad was determined to promote a spirit of adventure and independence. He felt that his Sweet Cap book would surely lure people out into the back country. The first year he listed thirty-two ski tows and twenty-three ski schools; the next year there were forty-four tows, and the number of ski schools had risen to thirty-three. "Big business" was nudging its way around the corner, so he made a pitch for ski holidays and ski lessons as a release from wartime tensions. He further revised the maps to include trails and towns still farther afield: Rawdon, St-Gabriel de Brandon, Mt Orford, Sherbrooke and North Hatley, and the Lac Beauport region of Quebec. To him all these towns offered excellent means of bringing people into contact with the "farther hills." He repeated his admonition, "Always check your equipment before setting out, ski under control, and avoid skiing alone." It never crossed his mind that people would become so bitten by the "tow-bug" that the majority would soon prefer to stick *only* to the tow hills, becoming more and more addicted to speed on the smoothly groomed slopes, and less and less inclined to seek out the "farther hills" that meant so much to him. This realization was a bitter pill.

In September 1942 Dad became "Bestefar" in his own right, with the birth of Peter John, his first grandchild. This was a tremendous family event, and the little cabin was once more strained to the utmost on winter weekends with Peggy, Peter, and baby Peter John with all his equipment added to the comings and goings of all our skiing friends, for Shawbridge was still a very popular anchor point. A number of popular cross-country trails began there, the ski tow on the Big Hill was a steady attraction, and of course Jackrabbit's house was the departure point where many of the families frequenting the lodge would assemble to follow him on one of his "adventures." For young Peter John, I fashioned a *tikanagan* or Indian papoose carrier, modelled after a real one in the McCord Museum; and with "PJ" carefully laced into it, Peggy would join in these forays with young Peter John rocking peacefully on her back to the rhythm of her stride. In time, that papoose carrier circulated among Peggy's friends, and over the years many of the MOC'ers whenever they hiked or skied in the Laurentians transported their children in this same native style.

It was a cold and gloomy morning in 1943 when a communication arrived in Shawbridge from the Norwegian Red Cross. Dad had gone to the post office to collect the mail, on his skis as usual,

Peggy carrying Peter John in a *tikanagan*
(papoose carrier).

and he stared for a moment uncomprehendingly at the unfamiliar
envelope. Then, with trembling hands, and with a mixture of hope
and fear, he tore the letter open.

On impersonal Red Cross stationery there were but three typed
lines:

Dear Dad,
    I am well and all right and so is the rest of the family.
                              Love, Bob.

That was all. No details. No explanations. No embellishment.
Just the bare facts. But what facts! It was as though the sun had
suddenly broken through the heavy clouds, illuminating the hills,
the fields, and all the houses in Shawbridge!

Dad sped home down the snowy street, his ski poles flying.

"Alice! Alice!" he shouted, bursting into the kitchen. "He's okay!
He's alive and well! Here's a letter from Bob! And the family is

well, too!" He grabbed Mother and they sank down beside the kitchen table, sobbing for joy together.

It had been three whole years since they had last had word from Bob. They had prayed for him every night. Every day as they went about their tasks they had thought about him, wondering how and where he was. They had worried, but they had concealed it well. After all, other people had their own problems to bear. But here, at last, was assurance that not only Bob, but all the Norwegian Johannsens were weathering the storm. And Dad and Mother were profoundly thankful. Because of censorship and other wartime restrictions, they knew they could expect no further information, but through the Canadian Red Cross they sent back a quick reply:

We, too, are well. Peggy is married and has a son.

Love, Dad, Mother and Jo.

Dad then threw himself more enthusiastically than ever into his work on the trails. He continued to brush out the lower reaches of the Maple Leaf Trail with help of the MOC. He kept track of his skiing mileage, accumulating 1,132 miles (1,811 km) in one winter. He would travel up the line on his CPR pass, and ski home by one or the other of the trails which he felt needed attention. He might stop at Laurentide Inn, or Chalet Cochand, or Alpine Inn, or Sun Valley Farm, picking up anyone interested in a trip on condition that they lend a hand, which might mean anything from helping to break trail to eliminating deadfalls or cutting new growth. And as time went on more and more people were happy to boast that "we helped Mr Johannsen clear the trail." Some would last a day or two on the job, some longer, but he was grateful for all the goodwill and help these companions provided. Moreover, the participants felt that they had each made a significant contri-bution. This gave a certain boost to the efforts of the Laurentian Tourist Association, which was eager to advertise the growing network of trails, but which gave little or no financial support for the work. It was simply assumed that "Mr Johannsen must be wealthy enough – and willing enough – to do all this for nothing." And he became, in a sense, the victim of his own good inten-tions.

Life in the Laurentians was challenging in other ways too. Dad had been particularly interested in a proposition put forward a number of years before by Frank Duxbury and T.J. Wood, two energetic young school-masters who had a novel outlook on education. Their dream had been to establish a boys' boarding school where students would learn to live with nature, as well as in it. The school would take advantage of all that each season had to offer in the way of outdoor sports and knowledge of the woods. At the same time, it would give a thorough academic grounding in all the subjects leading up to college entrance. The search led Duxbury and Wood to Montebello, and they hoped that, with his interest in young people and his knowledge of the out-of-doors, the "Chief," as they called the Jackrabbit, would have some interesting suggestions to offer.

The Chief was delighted to help. The three of them reconnoitred the countryside, looking over old farm properties, and eventually they found the ideal spot. Valley Farm, secluded in its own little glen, had just the right mixture of wooded hills, open fields, and enticing terrain to meet all their needs, and in 1939 Sedbergh School opened its doors, with a student body of eleven and a staff of two.

That was the beginning of a long and enduring relationship. The school enrolment grew quickly; by 1943 new facilities were added to accommodate the increasing student body. And every winter, in early February, Jackrabbit would receive an invitation "to spend a few days at Sedbergh to get to know the boys and to run off for them a real school ski competition."

Classes would be suspended for the duration of his visit, and the Chief would lay out a cross-country run, always over some new route which he would first mark with strips of coloured bunting. The entire school would participate, streaming up and down over the hills, climbing fences, dodging bushes, and finally arriving, red-cheeked and breathless, back where they had started. After this would come the downhill and then the slalom, for which young saplings would be cut and stuck in the snow to mark the "gates." Then there would be the jump, for which Jackrabbit would shovel up the snow to make a take-off, and the whole school would tramp the hill to put it into shape. Each boy would then come down from the summit, crouching low as he approached the lip and leaping forward with outstretched arms as he soared through space, to land (or fall) on the lower pitch. It was exciting, and a real challenge for everyone.

And finally there was the bushwhack, the *pièce de résistance*, always held at some new and unexpected spot. The Chief would lead the procession up the back of one of the neighbouring hills to a point from which everyone could clearly see "Woody" (T.J. Wood) standing way off at the finish line, at the farther end of a field. At a given signal, the whole horde would set off at once, battling their way down through the bush without a trail, colliding with trees and each other, losing their poles, falling and righting themselves, and finally reaching Woody and the finish line in a flurry of snow and excitement.

That evening there would be a special banquet, and the awarding of prizes. The Chief would give an inspiring speech about the joys of winter ... about training and always keeping in good condition ... and about sportsmanship. The entire affair was something the boys would never forget. Next day, the Chief would vanish as suddenly as he had come, and the school would be back to normal again, but with renewed energy.

For Jackrabbit, each year was divided into two seasons, one with snow and one without. How often he would say with anticipatory pleasure as the autumn leaves began to fall, "On or before the 15th of November I'll be out on my skis every day!" And that was no exaggeration, for skis were his only means of winter locomotion. He would don them to go for the mail, to meet the train, to do the shopping. He never walked. He skied. And he always wore a knapsack on his back to carry whatever might be necessary and to leave his hands free for his ski poles. Even in mid-April he would set off, leading anyone who wanted to go, on a search for the last snowdrift so that they could "stretch their legs."

And then, when the final snowflake had vanished, out would come his fishing gear, and he would sit outdoors in the sun assembling his delicate fly rod, oiling his reel, trying his leaders, examining his hooks and flies. To check and maintain his equipment gave him almost as much pleasure as to use it. Every year he would plan a brief trip to test the waters with Harry Lawton, who worked for Laurentian Lodge and had a car. Together they would drive to Fourteen Island Lake for an evening of hopeful casting in the clear cold waters of the bay.

Meanwhile, the war was drawing to a close. The Allies had crossed the Rhine, the Russians had withdrawn from Finland, the *Blitzkrieg* was failing in England, but hostilities were not yet over.

Then, suddenly, there came more news about Bob, this time from Sweden! It was two years since his last note, and he had finally escaped from Norway with the aid of the Underground. It was a long and complicated story, but the gist was that his old friend, Dr Irving Langmuir, the Nobel chemist for whom he had guided at La Barrière and who worked for General Electric Company in Schenectady, New York, had been influential in getting him out of Sweden, and had offered him a job at GE. So in due course Bob was flown to New York, and was then temporarily reunited with the family in Shawbridge.

What a reunion that was, and what tales he had to tell! At first he had been interned by the Germans in solitary confinement in Oslo, and later, he had been released to Onkel Christofer, an influential citizen in Oslo, on condition that he report twice daily to the authorities, with the family standing as collective "hostage" for him to assure that he complied. In other words, the Germans had used Bob as a means of effectively immobilizing a certain number of Norwegians.

This arrangement had continued for some time, but he was eventually issued a card that limited his movements to a slightly broader region and afforded him a little more freedom. Eventually, as the Germans found their hands full of other problems, Bob's whereabouts were more or less forgotten. In the end, with family consent, he had simply disappeared into the countryside, with his skis and his ukulele. There he had roamed in Rondane and in Jotunheimen, skiing, making friends with the country folk, and keeping as far as possible out of harm's way.

In 1945, with the help of the Underground, he escaped into neutral Sweden and made his way to Stockholm, where he immediately got in touch with Dr Langmuir. He then looked up a local Swedish ski wax company that he had known during his pre-war period in Norway, and found a temporary job with them. After a whirlwind courtship, he had married Gerd Bylund, one of the secretaries, and then, finally, he had flown back to America alone. Gerd was to follow him as soon as possible. Meanwhile, he would settle in Schenectady and work with Dr Langmuir on problems relating to the de-icing of aircraft, and on his own time he would continue experimenting with ski wax.

For Dad and Mother, life in Shawbridge resumed on a somewhat more even keel, interspersed with Dad's continuing explorations in the hinterland with various friends, his lengthy trail-marking for assorted ski meets, and his frequent visits to Montreal to check maps and texts for the rejuvenated Sweet Caporal skiers' books. This series, discontinued during the war years, was revived in 1946–47, and with Bob now available as a ghost writer the new booklet contained additional notes on touring equipment and competitive skiing, with a veritable treatise on waxing. To these Dad added his own well-worn, but heartfelt, theme:

Tow hills [he wrote] are but a training ground for the fun that is yours when you set out on your own. You must feel the tug of your muscles as you near the top of a long grade, and know the joy of making your own track down an unbroken expense of powder snow. With a lunch in your pack, Sweet Caps in your pocket, and a good companion, you can set off with a light heart to conquer the wide open spaces. *This* is skiing. *This* is adventure!

The Sweet Caporal booklets continued for two additional seasons, each time with revised maps, new text, and updated lists of ski tows – by 1947 there were eighty. But there the series ended.

Today, other maps and other texts have taken over where the Sweet Cap books left off. Sweet Caporal cigarettes have vanished completely from the scene. But cross-country skiers blithely carry on over hill and dale, and in all kinds of weather. And every once in a while, on some sunny ski trail, some old skier will pull from his pocket a battered copy of one of those old Sweet Cap books, and with a sigh for the "good old days" he and his cronies will pore over maps of the trails they once knew, remembering the pungent odour of wood smoke and the delightful aroma of their noontime coffee as they had paused beside some other sunny trail, so very long ago.

Mother through all the years had eagerly taken part in family skiing. She had, however, her own peculiar style in going down hill, using a tried and true technique, which she was reluctant to display in public, but which was nevertheless guaranteed to deliver her intact to the bottom of many an otherwise unnegotiable slope. She would simply straddle her poles, bend her knees and ride her poles as though they were a broomstick, resting her forearms crosswise on her thighs, and regulating her speed by pulling upward on her poles as though applying an emergency brake. In this way she could ride serenely down under complete control, and on reaching the bottom could rise, unlimber her poles, and continue with her normal stride. She took her own time, took no chances, and managed very well.

In general health, however, she was by no means as hardy as Dad. She had recurring bouts of liver and gall bladder trouble, and had to be careful of what she ate, but she did take great pleasure in going with him on various of his assignments. In July 1948 while he was gathering information for his latest Sweet Cap Book, they were able to rent a car on his expense account and travel for a week to Shawinigan, Quebec City, Lac Beauport, and up through Laurentide Park to Chicoutimi, then down the Saguenay and across the St Lawrence, returning by way of the Eastern Townships. This gave them a delightful holiday.

And again, in the spring of 1949 when he was supervising trail construction for the Whiteface Mountain Authority and the New York State Conservation Association, she was proud to be able to ride up with the work crew in a "snowcat" to the four-thousand-foot level, and to ski with Dad on one of his new cross-country ski trails near the timber line. She was then sixty-five. Needless to say, she returned down the mountain by "cat," and not by broomstick.. But when she and Dad returned to Wilmington for more trail work in November, she had another of her liver attacks. Dad would be out on the trails all day, and would come home to her at night, but it was far better for her, she said, to be there with him at the inn, than it would have been had she been sick all alone, all by herself, away back home!

The following year they went down to Schenectady to be with Bob and to participate in making the winter's supply of ski wax. Bob and his family were spending the summer on an old farm at Niskayuna, and Mother took an active part in the proceedings, sitting outdoors in the shade with the others and folding by hand several thousand little aluminum foil boxes, which were then laid out in trays, two hundred at a time. Bob, working in the barn, would then dribble just the right amount of hot "mix" from an overhead container, which he slowly manipulated from tray to tray, and box after box, pouring just the right amount into each. The whole operation was delightfully redolent of pine tar, which tickled the nostrils and conjured up happy images of snowy hills and breath-taking downward slopes, despite the insufferable summer heat. When the wax was cool, each box with its own little dark brown slab of wax was slipped into a pre-fabricated cover, bearing the label

Smith-Johannsen Wax Company
Niskayuna, N.Y.

And across the face of that cover, Pat Paré's energetic little Jack-rabbit could be seen sliding deftly down on his perfectly waxed skis.

The wax was distributed by Bob in the United States, while Dad took charge of Canadian sales, travelling all over the Laurentians and always attempting to keep one jump ahead. For a family enterprise the project went reasonably well, but without professional financing and imaginative merchandising, the wax company was doomed never to rise beyond a certain point.

❦

It would be hard to say how many canoe trips Dad took, over the years, with McGill medical students or chosen Red Birds. On such occasions, they would supply the food and transportation to the starting point, and Dad would supply the leadership and the know-how. He taught them how to light a fire without a match, how to fish in the misty dawn for a breakfast trout, how to repair a torn canoe with birch bark and spruce gum, and how to tell the time by the stars. Many were the nights they would propel themselves silently, Indian fashion, without lifting their paddles from the water, as they cruised expectantly along the shore of a lake, watching for a deer to come down to drink. Or they would lie blissfully on fragrant balsam boughs and listen to the haunting call of the loons down by the bay. These were experiences etched deep in their memories, to be remembered and to be re-lived, over and over again as the years went by.

For many years Dad kept a diary, which is fascinating to read, but which adds little colour or sparkle to the daily events, for he recorded only the bare facts. "I'm no poet," he would say. "I can't put in all the flourishes you would put. I'm interested in who went, when and where we went, how cold it was, and how many fish we caught. Important things like that. But my impression of the count-less sunrises I have seen, the colour of the hills, and the sounds of nature, these are things I have always absorbed through all my own senses. They are part of the symphony of living, and they are so all-pervading that I felt I did not need write about them!"

Here are some extracts from those yearly journals:

1949	May 6	Went fishing with Peter John. He is 7, I am 74. We make a good team!
1951	Sept. 28	Fished Beausejour Creek. 15 trout.
1952	June 6	Went fishing with 3 small boys. Michel, Steven and Billy. 8 nice trout in Dagenais Creek.
	Aug. 1	Mother to Royal Victoria Hospital for X-ray. Negative!
	Aug. 26–28	Fishing with Dr Henry and John in La Vérendrye Park. Jimmie Brascoupé was guide.
1954	Apr. 28–30	Moved to Curtis's house, after 17 years with Mrs Martin.
	Sept. 13–16	Fishing at Mont Laurier with Raymond Paquette and Filion til 11 pm. Good catch. Moonlight. Went to get water next morning with first ice on lake. Path slippery. Fell on pail with axe in my right hand. *Broke left arm.* Driven down to St Jerome to have it set.
	Oct. 10	Moose hunting weather – but not for *me*!
	Oct. 21	Cast off. Exercising arm.
1955	May 5–19	Anson McKim came for us in his jeep. Drove to Lac Pelletier for two weeks of intensive trail clearing. $15/day with all expenses for Alice and me. Wonderful!
	June 8	My 80th birthday party given by Red Birds at the Yacht Club, with spinning reel and rod from all the gang. Biggest birthday cake ever seen! Home by 2:30 am with Hector Sutherland and Alex Rolland.

Alice and Jackrabbit greet visitors at their door
in Shawbridge, 1957.

June 11–14	Otto, Walborg and Peter Hunt, Ralph's son, for fishing at La Barrière. Up early. Fishing poor.
June 14	Sedbergh Old Boys gave me a surprise party at Laurentian Lodge. Another highlight – Sedbergh blazer with school crest.
Sept. 27	With Ralph Neill, Bill and Waldy Crites to Island Lake by plane. Put up emergency 2-way radio antenna. We have one whole month in which to hunt, fish, and explore the property, and to work around the camp, laying in a supply of wood, building railings, etc. 1,000 geese flew by overhead on way south. Shot many partridges. One day caught five 6-pound trout below the Crooked Lake Dam. Successfully called moose, but did not shoot, as it will be too costly to ship out the meat.
Oct. 24	Food getting low. Radio doesn't work. Called Maniwaki, Ottawa, and SOS, no luck. Put up signal flag.
Oct. 25	Plane passed, wagged wings, but did not stop.
Oct. 25	Quick jump in lake felt good. Very little food left.
Oct. 27	Food all gone. Nothing but partridges left! Pilot *happened* to pass and saw signal flag. Came down, and took us all to Maniwaki. Spent 3 hours with an Indian Family waiting for a lift out, and talking about life in the bush.
1957 Jan. 12	With 7 school children to St-Sauveur over schoolboy's race course, to pack trail before the meet.
Feb. 2	22 children to Paradise Valley for picnic with trailside fire.
Mar. 17	Wonderful trip with Bob and young Bobby, here on holiday, 1½ hours on solid granular snow.

	July 2	Surprise Party at Laurentian Lodge when Sedbergh Old Boys set up the Johannsen Trophy for school competitions.
	Aug. 19	Bill Wadsworth, with 9 American Boy Scouts and 4 canoes, dropped in on way to La Vérendrye Park.
	Nov. 11–15	Mother in hospital for gall bladder operation. Then home. Now I am both nurse and cook!
1958	July 22–24	Canoe trip with Alex Rolland, Dick Meyer and Tim Rath. Picked up canoe at Nominingue. Terrific storm on way home. Wonderful trip.
	Oct. 18	With bus to Piedmont. Walked over Windy Hill. Heard René Beaulne has a house to rent. Had a look. Alice and Jo went to inspect. Perfect! With a fireplace.
	Oct. 20	René Beaulne phoned – 'The house is yours from Nov. 1st!' And Peggy's son, Erik, was born today! A new grandchild!"

So they moved, lock, stock, and barrel, to Piedmont, and settled happily into their new little cabin as though they had always lived there.

Then, in 1960, when Dad was eighty-five, there came exciting news from Norway. Erling Ström, on his way out west, had brought an invitation from the 100th Anniversary Committee of the First Huseby-Holmenkollen Ski Meet and from Foreningen til Skiidrettens Fremme (Association for the Advancement of Ski Sport). They were seeking a skier, someone whose roots extended way back to the early days, to be their guest of honour at Holmenkollen. Would Herman Smith Johannsen, accompanied by his wife, accept their invitation? What a question! Was there any doubt? He accepted with speed, and with the greatest of pleasure! And that is how Dad and Mother came to take off on March 3 by SAS for Oslo, where it was arranged that they would spend several weeks with his sister, Helga, before the actual meet would begin.

It was most unfortunate that the Asiatic 'flu was rampant in Norway that winter, and that Helga, one of the early victims, was still sick when they arrived. After a hearty round of family parties, many other members of the family also contracted the 'flu, among them Tante Elisabeth and both Dad and Mother. They were all confined to bed, though Dad resisted as strenuously as he could.

On the 15th of March the guests of honour, both still suffering from the 'flu, were scheduled to transfer to the Holmenkollen Hotel, and Dad insisted on packing to go, but the family was horrified, and the doctor was adamant: "You go today, and I predict instant pneumonia!" he said, and Dad was forced to capitulate. "They have all combined to put me in the doghouse," he mourned in his journal. "I tried again today, without success. When the doctor, your sisters, and your wife all gang up against you, it's a tough life! I have never been such a good boy." On the 19th, however, both Dad and Mother were sufficiently recovered to be able to drive to the hotel by taxi, where Mother immediately went back to bed. The situation looked grim.

But the great day, the 20th, the Holmenkollen Day itself, dawned bright and clear, and Dad, although wobbly, was much better. They breakfasted in their room, and Dad took it easy all morning. Mother, however, agreed reluctantly that she would be far better off to stay quietly in the hotel. She would see the proceedings on television rather than tempt fate.

By noon, Dad was ready to go. His old friend Örnulf Poulsen, from Lake Placid days, came to escort him, and together with a number of other officials they walked the short distance to the jump, joining with thousands of others who were congregating for the festivities. Jackrabbit was amazed to see the reserved and dignified enthusiasm of the crowd and at the same time, to feel the intense holiday atmosphere. Flags were everywhere. The band of the King's Guard was playing. And bright costumes bloomed like flowers in the massive grandstands.

Herman was led immediately to the high tribune, where the Norwegian and Swedish royal families were assembled, and there, just before the program commenced, he was presented to King Olav, attended by one of Dad's old friends, Hoffsjef Smith-Kjelland, the chief adjutant. Both cordially shook his hand and bade him welcome, acknowledging his greetings from America.

The band played the national anthem, and as the last notes faded a hush fell upon the crowd. The loudspeaker introduced the guest

Jackrabbit with King Olav V and Jacob Vaage
at the One Hundredth Anniversary of the Ull Ski Club, 29 January 1983.

of honour to the assembled throng, recalling his prowess as a boy
in Nordmarken and his many years in America, where he had
helped to introduce "the ski sport," first in Lake Placid, then in the
Canadian Laurentians. Now he had come home to Norway, a
veritable ambassador of the ski sport in America, to share in this
100th anniversary celebration.

"Ladies and gentlemen! We ask you now to raise your programs
and wave them to greet our guest of honour, who is wearing his
Red Birds ski jacket, and is standing directly below the King!"

All eyes were riveted upon the high tribune. Then there burst
forth what seemed like a gigantic snowstorm, as 120,000 programs
were raised high in the air and jubilantly waved. For an instant,
the sea of spectators turned white! Then the trumpets sounded,
the first competitor soared from the takeoff, and the meet was on.

CHAPTER SEVENTEEN

The Tide Begins to Turn: 1960–1967

Jackrabbit and Alice returned, somewhat exhausted after their travels in Norway, but well content with what they had experienced, despite the 'flu. It had been good to be with the family again, and to relive the old days. For Dad, after thirty-four years of absence, it had been a special joy to see again the Norwegian hills he loved, to feel the pulse of national pride in skiing, and to renew old friendships with many who were still active in outdoor life, and whose children and grandchildren were following keenly in their footsteps.

And so they came back once more to normal life in Piedmont, where Dad continued his activities in laying out cross-country competitions and leading friends and other enthusiasts on weekend trips. Mother took an active, though cautious, part in these events. She was often with him at the distribution of prizes, and she still took short trips on Dad's special ski trail behind the house, but she felt that her most important role was to keep the home fires burning. She was always there to welcome him back with numerous friends at the end of a long day's foray, when they would all relax beside the blazing hearth with tea and her delectable cookies. To her, that was fulfilment in itself.

In May of 1962 Mother herself was invited back to Cleveland as guest of honour, with her class, to celebrate the sixtieth anniversary of their graduation from kindergarten training school. This was to be another super-gala event – Dad had had his day in

Norway, now it was her turn. Unfortunately, Monte Dodds, of the class ahead of Mother's, had died several years previously. Mother was one of only three survivors in her own class, but the entire association had tea parties, sherry parties, much sight-seeing, and much sharing of stories of all the years that had slipped by since Mother "had gone off and married that Norwegian nobleman." They had many a good laugh, and she had a marvellous time. When we met her at the airport on her return, she came down the passage wearing a corsage, and looking like a movie queen.

But it was just a year later, when early one morning in Piedmont, as she was preparing for the day, Mother suffered a sudden stroke. She fell, striking her head, and there she lay, unconscious, on the hard cold floor. Dad, who had been rummaging in the kitchen, heard her fall and ran to her side, but saw at once that this was something quite beyond his own power to help. He rushed to the telephone and called the doctor, who came immediately.

"Complete rest," the doctor said. "She must remain absolutely quiet, and let's hope the paralysis in her arm will gradually go away, and that her speech will return. Meanwhile, you, too, must take it easy. Neither of you are quite as young as you used to be! I'll look in and see you every day for a while."

Then there followed six weeks of gradual improvement. Mother was up and around again, although moving slowly, but when she looked out the window and saw the young buds on the trees and the regenerating earth, she said hesitantly, with a wan smile, "Well, I guess I've had my last trip on skis." She was just eighty-one.

In June, we finally laid her to rest in the little cemetery beside the church in Morin Heights. It was a tumultuous day for Dad, who could still barely believe what had happened. Alice had been beside him through thick and thin for fifty-six years, and now, suddenly, he was almost alone. Things would be very different now.

Dad felt that he had never before truly realized what it had meant to have her always there to wave him off in the morning, and to welcome him home at night. Now there was no longer a light in the window when he returned, no cheerful voice to hail him, no delightful aroma of supper under preparation. He began to wonder how he could possibly carry on without her. True, the neighbours were wonderful, and his children were within reach by telephone, but her sparkle, her light, her touch were no longer there.

Peggy and I rallied as best we could. We had many conversations, both with and without Dad, in which we searched for a solution to his loneliness. Perhaps he could establish himself as a "permanent guest" in one of the inns that he had helped and advised while he was building his Maple Leaf Trail. He could be available to take other guests on trips and could regale them in the evening with his tales beside the fire. Meanwhile, he was invited to spend several days at a time with family members or with old friends, but he was always drawn back to Piedmont, in spite of his loneliness.

On a raw, chill September evening, he came home to the darkened house, and instinctively turned to the empty hearth in the living-room. A good fire, he told himself, would probably cheer things up. He crumpled some old newspapers together, took his axe from the chopping block, and split a few sticks of kindling. It was good to be busy. From his pocket he took out his little *sac-à-feu*, and from it he drew his trusty strike-a-light, the one that had always fascinated the children whenever he showed them how to light a fire without a match. He struck the spark, and watched the tiny flame begin to grow. It caught in the tinder, spread to the paper, and took hold in the wood. He felt the welcome warmth spread slowly through him. Then he rose ... and there across the room, reflected in the picture window, he could see the fire burning brightly behind him, its reflection and his own framed against the distant shadows of the well-loved hills beyond. A sense of tranquil peace came over him. It was as though Mother herself were standing there beside him. He found himself thinking how profoundly thankful he was – thankful for all she had meant to him over the years, and for all that they had shared.

He drew his old wing chair closer to the fire and quietly lit his pipe, watching the smoke curl gently upward as he settled comfortably back into its depths. "Here is where I belong," he said to himself. "I cannot give up this place, with all its associations, with all its memories. I cannot go to live with strangers, however kind or congenial they may be. Nothing can ever take the place of home. I am far from being helpless. I am used to looking after myself. And Alice's memory will keep me going. The good Lord will continue to help me, I am sure."

His mind was finally made up. Piedmont would continue to be his chosen place of residence; here he would continue to welcome his children, and all his host of friends.

"This fire in the hearth is like a presence in the house," he reflected. "It's a mood-setter. I can feel its friendly warmth, and hear its crackle. I can smell the pungent smoke, and can watch the embers glow. Here is where I love to sit, in my own chair, beside my own hearth – where I can puff on my pipe and dream of days gone by. And I can cast my thoughts happily ahead to the many good days which I am sure are yet to come."

That winter Dad made real progress in the art of living alone. Unless he was off on some special project – cutting a trail or laying a race course somewhere in the Laurentians – he followed a rigid system for his daily routine. Having been an early riser all his life, he was usually up and dressed by six in the morning and through with his porridge by seven, after which he would set the house to rights and lie down for a short cat-nap. By eight o'clock, when most people were just beginning their day's activities, he would be out at his woodpile, chopping, bringing in the logs, and shovelling the path.

"By 8:30 I strap on my skis and go for the mail," he would tell people. "Usually I take the long way, which can be up to two miles, depending on whose backyards I go through. Or it can be reduced to half a mile, if the weather is bad and I take the direct route. In any case, it's important to keep my trail open by laying a fresh track after every snowstorm, so that any skiers who pass this way can see that it looks 'used.'" After various brief stops to pass the time of day with neighbours, he would be back to stoke up his fireplace and settle down to his correspondence, which was extensive. All kinds of letters drifted in, from around the globe, from Inuvik to Australia, and Dad kept very busy writing replies.

"By eleven, I start to cook my lunch – usually potatoes and onions and carrots, cooked in one pot. By noon, when the rest of the town is sitting down to eat, I'm through and I lie down for half an hour. By one, I'm up again, and out for a run on my skis, but by four I'm home for the day, to read by the fire, to eat my supper of soup and bread and cheese, and to listen to the news. I'm in bed by nine o'clock. And I sleep well – if I don't have cramps in my legs."

Whenever people asked if they might drop in to visit him, he had a standard reply. "Phone me anytime after five," he would say, "five in the morning, that is, and we can arrange a time – just so long as it's before eight in the evening. After that I'm no good! I'm in bed. I'm asleep." But he did love to receive visitors of all ages during the day. "They keep me young," he claimed. "We can talk of skiing in the old days. I can tell them of my experiences with the Indians, and with the Grand Trunk, and of how everyone used to be able to break trail – before ski tows made people lazy, and before equipment became so specialized that skiers found themselves the victims, rather than the users, of all that fancy gear!"

Each Saturday morning after my own week's work at Mont St-Hilaire, I would drive up to Piedmont early, and after setting the laundry to soak in the kitchen sink, we would do the rounds: the baker, for Dad's loaf of rye bread, the newsstand for his weekend paper, the cleaner, the drugstore or the hardware, then the grocer for the week's supply of food. This would include a chicken, a ham, or a steak for our evening meal, the remains of which would eke out his rations for the week. And always there were meetings and conversations with friends performing similar tasks, with visitors who were "just up for the weekend," or with old-timers who would pause to reminisce. After which we would drive back home in time to finish the laundry and cook our lunch. Dad relied on these weekend visits for variations in his diet, and for some inevitable little "surprises." "It's almost like having Mother here again," he would say. And I was happy for that.

And in the evening we would lay plans for the next summer.

A letter from Erling Ström helped. "Why don't you two come out here to Assiniboine for a few weeks next August," he wrote. "You could climb back into the saddle, and we could ride over some of the trails we skied on twenty-five years ago. It's good to turn back the clock once in a while, and I can't think of a better place in which to do that than right here!" Dad's eyes lit up with the fire of memory. "Why not?" he said with enthusiasm. And so, after a due period of practising on local Piedmont horses, we entrained for the West.

That was a wonderful experience for both of us. Dad was absolutely in his element. Erling met us and the other guests in Banff, and we drove out excitedly with all our duffle the ten miles to the corral on Brewster Creek. The panorama of Rocky Mountains, the feel of the summer sun on his face, the memory-tingling smell of the horses – all this stirred visions of long ago. Suddenly, it seemed he was back at Krigsskolen again, all set to curry Sleipner in preparation for the day.

We munched our sandwiches and watched attentively as Erling and Erik, his Norwegian "cowboy" helper, assembled our paraphernalia, carefully loading the packhorses one by one, and securing each with an expert diamond hitch. Then each of us was assigned a mount, and after much tightening of girth straps and adjusting of stirrups, we were at last ready to depart. Dad had just turned eighty-nine, and the other guests eyed him somewhat apprehensively. How would the old man handle the thirty-two-mile ride into camp? But Erling simply said in his Norwegian-accented English, "Yust you vait and see." Together, he and Erik gave Dad a leg up into the saddle, but once mounted he sat straight as a ramrod, and every inch a cavalry officer. There was no need to worry about *him*!

We rode the first ten winding miles that afternoon, climbing steadily, enjoying the squeak of the saddles and the ever changing scenery as the Bourgeau Range passed in review. We arrived at Halfway House in time for supper. This was a solid, two-storey Norwegian log cabin, the only human habitation in the whole valley. It was flanked by high peaks whose forested lower reaches were scarred by the avalanches that in winters past had roared down the steep slopes, piling trees and rocks and other debris as the gradient diminished near the valley floor. Low vegetation had in time overgrown these scars, which now, from a distance, looked like great green claw marks on the dark mountainsides. Blocking the head of the valley was a massive cliff, and Erling said, looking nonchalantly at it, "That's Windy Ridge. Next week we'll go up there on our horses. It's a wonderful view!"

I had no doubt about the view, but I wasn't too sure it would be best seen from the back of a horse!

We passed a comfortable night in Halfway House, and then, fortified with a hearty breakfast, we saddled up again. We climbed steep switchbacks through a flower-strewn forest, crossed over desolate, stony Allenby Pass, then skirted another apparently endless valley and climbed over yet another divide. There, suddenly before us, was majestic Mount Assiniboine, the Matterhorn of the Rockies, rearing his lofty head 11,315 feet above sea level. At his feet lay little Lake Magog and Assiniboine Lodge, our home for the next ten days.

There is something about riding a horse, especially when one is not used to it, that makes it difficult to stand, once one dismounts. We all appeared to suffer from the same affliction, and were having a certain preoccupation with our legs. Then, out of the corner of my eye, I caught a glimpse of Dad. He had slipped comfortably from his saddle and was helping several of the ladies to straighten out their wobbly knees!

Last of all, the horses, once their packs and saddles had been removed, were turned loose to run free. They thundered past us to roll ecstatically in the grass, joyfully kicking their heels in the air, as happy to be rid of their heavy load as we were to unburden them.

The lodge and its surrounding cabins occupied a delightful spot. Jackrabbit and I were assigned our own small sanctum facing Mount Assiniboine, and every morning watched the early light as it crept slowly down that rugged, massive mountainside to usher in another glorious day.

We rode on one occasion to the summit of Mount Cautley, climbing along a comfortable trail to a precipitous cliff-edge from which we could see peak after jagged peak of the Rockies as they marched southward towards the American border. Another day we rode up the back of Windy Ridge, and there, true to his word, Erling led us to the brink where we could look way down on tiny little Halfway House, deep in its avalanche-scarred valley. When we were not out on horseback Dad fished in Cerulean Lake, where the trout rose hungrily in the blue, blue waters. Finally, we returned once more over Allenby Pass in a blinding snowstorm, which gave us a striking preview of the winter that was soon to come. It was a glorious holiday, and we came back to Piedmont stronger and infinitely richer for this excursion into the past.

The following winter Bob, Peggy, and I had an inspiration. We would write to as many of Dad's surviving old friends and relatives as possible, harking back to his very earliest days, asking for a picture or some brief anecdote that we could incorporate into an album to be presented to him on his approaching ninetieth birthday. The letters went out, a hundred or so, and we settled back to await results. They were not long in coming. Peggy, then, was confronted with the formidable task of compiling all this into a vast commemorative tome, which would be pored over and enjoyed for many years to come, not only by Dad and the contributors themselves, but by hundreds of others who liked to feel that they had been "contemporaries" at some point along the line, or who ardently wished they could have been. This album promised to be a smash hit and we were more than content with the outcome.

One special gift, however, could not be incorporated into the album. It arrived in a large container, just as we were enjoying a visit from an old ski friend of Dad's who had arrived accompanied by his elderly small spaniel. The dog lay snoozing peacefully under the table, and opened one curious eye as Dad carefully removed layer after layer of wrapping to reveal a splendid life-size bust of himself by the sculptress Marjorie Winslow.

Suddenly, the dog leapt to his feet in astonishment to see this apparition emerge from the box, and went into a paroxysm of barking while the head was gently set upon the table. It was some time before the dog could be convinced that it was not "for real." It was, in fact an excellent likeness of Dad, and it has ever since proudly graced the bookcase where it continues to be admired by all beholders, both human and canine.

❦

One evening that spring I said to Dad, "Why don't we go back to Norway next summer? We could cover some of the same ground we went over way back in 1926, and we could explore some new places. I could rent a car, and we could be really independent. It would be such fun!" So both of us began at once to dream ...

Without telling Dad, I wrote my cousin Kirsten a joyful letter saying, "Guess what! Dad and I are coming to Norway this summer. We want to drive down to Horten and Larvik and see the places where he and your father were little boys. Can you come with us on that trip and show us around?" Her answer came almost immediately: she certainly could.

Meanwhile, the Red Birds had been cooking up their own little scheme, which was duly revealed. They had a bang-up ninetieth pre-birthday celebration for Dad at the Yacht Club, in the course of which they presented him with his ticket to Norway, so now Dad knew his dream was actually coming true. To celebrate, and to show his appreciation, he stood on his head, as was his custom, on the banquet table! I paid for my own ticket, and in due course we packed all our camping gear and suitable paraphernalia, and we took off.

It was a lovely summer day when we sat at last on the plane, straining our eyes to catch that first glimpse of Norway as it rose magically out of the void. I experienced the same thrill that many of my seagoing ancestors must have felt as they sailed home over the rolling waves to rediscover that rocky shoreline with its pine-clad hills. Tears welled in my eyes as we watched the rocky headlands and the tiny islets slipping by.

"There's Larvik!" Dad suddenly exclaimed, as he looked to the west. "And the long stretch where I was so seasick! And here beneath us is Horten, and the harbour, and the naval station! It's like a dream!" There were red-roofed houses, and cosy bays, and tiny sailboats in the water. Then, abruptly, there we were, rolling down the tarmac, actually in Oslo.

It was another wonderful reunion. The family was out in full force, and we were driven up to Kirsten's house, where she and Ditlef and young Gunnar and Ellen lived on the mountain over-looking the city. There was the usual scramble of aunts and uncles and cousins, and when all had been sorted out, and our itinerary established, the crew from the television station suddenly arrived for an interview! This had been organized by Jacob Vaage, an old friend of Dad's who, as director of the Norwegian Ski Museum, was eager to make the most of Jackrabbit's return to Oslo, five years after his appearance as guest of honour at the hundredth anniversary of the first Huseby-Holmenkollen Meet. So a tempo-rary "TV studio" was set up on the veranda, and the interviewer posed all sorts of questions, ending of course with the usual request for his recipe for a long and eventful life.

"That's easy," said Dad. "Just take things as they come. Don't overdo. Don't overeat. Get plenty of exercise, and plenty of sleep. Moderation in everything is what we need. I believe in smoking my pipe – but only one pipeful a day. And having a small drink, and enjoying it – but only one a day. You see, knowing when to stop – that's the secret. And if you follow these rules, anyone can live to be a hundred. I'm only ninety years old this year. I'm still a young fellow!"

It was wonderful to see Kirsten again. We set out several days later to drive to Horten, through country that had been settled by the old Vikings, and lived in for much more than a thousand years. Dad was excited, remembering every bump in the landscape. We visited Ekeli, which was now owned by a private company and used as a retreat by the employees. It had deteriorated considerably since the days of Dad's old Bestefar Smith, and the grounds were reduced in size, but we sat on the dining-room steps overlooking the harbour, and tried to imagine everything as it used to be when the orchards and gardens were in their prime.

We visited the schoolhouse, now tripled in size, where Dad had been sent home from the first grade with cramps in his legs, and had taken the opportunity to go skiing, on school time, to "loosen things up." And we saw the cemetery where the older boys had played "ghost" to frighten the old ladies.

Then we drove on down to Larvik, and found a large office building now occupying the site of Bestefar Johannsen's little white cottage, which had stood beneath the wonderful walnut tree. We ate our lunch in the restaurant that today overlooks the market-place, and were happy to see that Christiansen's brewery still stood where the boys had fought their battle with the firehose. And we went to the churchyard to visit the graves of Bestefar and Bestemor Johannsen, and of dear old Tante Anna.

It was there that we encountered two elderly women whose duty it was to tend the flowers and keep order on the premises. When we explained that we had come from Canada to visit the family plot, they proudly led the way. Then one of them, who had been looking closely at Dad, suddenly exclaimed, "I know you! You're the ninety-year-old gentleman from America we saw on television the other night. Wait till I tell my old man who it was who came to see us here today!" And with that she threw her arms around Dad's neck, gave him a warm hug, and said, "God bless you!"

Dad was completely taken by surprise, and he was also touched by her greeting, for it seemed to him that hers was a voice right out of the past. It was as though Tante Anna and his grandparents had spoken to him as he stood there, looking at the flowers that bloomed at the graveside. What an unexpected benediction, spontaneous and heartfelt!

Then, quietly, we left, warmed by the glow of the old woman's greeting, and bearing a lasting memory of dark red begonias beside the weathered tombstones. We were very happy indeed that we had come.

But that was just the beginning. Having paid tribute to Dad's earliest years, we returned to Oslo to leave Kirsten with her family, and then the two of us continued northward to follow the boyhood trail of Dad and Johannes as they had explored the Rondane.

We drove up along the western side of Lake Mjösen, drinking in the summer scenery and admiring the rich old farmlands, the copious red barns, and the big white timbered farmhouses. As we turned in at a roadside stand to replenish our gas, the young man who came to serve us looked curiously at Dad. "Say!" he finally blurted out, "Aren't you the old man from America who was on television last week?" And Dad, surprised, agreed that he guessed he was.

"Hei! Far! Hei! Mor!" shouted the boy, so excited that he almost dropped the hose. "Come quick! Here's the man from America who was on television last week. He's come to see the Rondane again, and he's buying gas from us!"

"Far" popped out from the barn and clumped across the field in his rubber boots. "Well, well!" he exclaimed. "You look just as good as you did on television! So you've come back to Norway! When my boy's filled up your tank, please come in and meet my missus." And he clumped quickly over to the house to warn his wife.

We really had no intention of lingering, but thought we might just stretch our legs and say hello. After paying for our gas, we were ushered to the kitchen door by the excited boy. And there stood "Mor" with a big smile of welcome, and before we knew what had happened some of the neighbours had dropped in, the coffee pot began to simmer on the stove, the cups and saucers came out of hiding, a cake appeared from somewhere, and we all sat down to a real *kaffeeklatsch*. They were eager to hear about Canada, and Canadian skiing, and life in the Laurentians. Eventually, after a very pleasant visit, we left, carrying with us their hearty wishes for an eventful holiday.

Jackrabbit shows a young admirer
how to light a fire without a match.

We stopped a little farther on at Skumsrud, the farm at Biri on
Lake Mjösen where Mother and I had passed the summer of 1913
with all of Dad's family. And wherever we went, Dad was welcomed
like some kind of a folk hero. He would recount tales of that teen-
age trip with Johannes seventy-three years before, and he would
top it all off by lighting a fire with his trusty strike-a-light. It was
in a sense a triumphal visit, for just about everywhere we went
there always seemed to be someone who had seen the television
show, or who had known Dad in the past, or who wanted to see
his famous "fire-lighter." By the time we reached Jotunheimen we
felt that we had made many, many special friends in Norway.

Jotunheimen was to be the centre of this Norwegian holiday
and we had made careful advance plans for a six-day hiking trip
in the high mountains, to cover the latter part of that same teen-
age tour, only this time we were to be accompanied by Ellen and
Ragnhild, the granddaughters of Johannes and Elisabeth. For Father,
at ninety, this would be a real reliving of the past. For me, at fifty-

Jackrabbit with his niece Kirsten, in Norway for his ninetieth birthday.

four, it would be a reconstruction of bygone days. But for Ellen at nineteen, and for Ragnhild at twenty-one, it would be an entirely new experience to follow in the footsteps of the old patriarch, their great-uncle, and to see the world through his eyes.

The Norwegian Tourist Association, being the long-established sporting organization that it is, has a fine network of trails throughout Norway, with overnight stopping places where meals are served. This makes it possible for hikers to explore on foot and at minimal expense many of the outstanding scenic spots in the country. The association has been in existence since 1868, and Herman, Johannes, and Karl had been among the early users of several of these *hytter* on their famous trip. Today, however, thousands of hikers annually follow these same paths, and accommodations are frequently strained to the utmost.

Dad and I had arrived at Leirvassbu the previous evening, having driven in our little rented car to this comfortable guest house at the very end of the road, which could accommodate up to one hundred hikers. Ellen and Ragnhild were waiting for us, along with Ellen's parents, who were eager to see us off on this nostalgic odyssey. We were to travel light, as there was no need to carry food or sleeping bags, so our packs contained only the essentials: raingear, a windbreaker and a heavy sweater, a complete change of dry clothing, plus first aid equipment, a map, a compass, and a knife. To this, each day, we would add our lunch. Thus each of us would be, in a way, self-sufficient.

It was beautiful rugged country, with towering mountains, hanging glaciers, and rushing streams. We walked comfortably, taking pictures, observing everything closely, and pausing now and then simply to enjoy the view. Other hikers would occasionally overtake us, pausing to chat for a moment, expressing curiosity about Dad's age, then wishing us well as they moved along. Among the first to pass had been two young boys, who kindly volunteered to reserve beds for us, for, so they assured us, they intended to arrive early. So we continued to take our time.

When we finally arrived, it was to find that isolated Spiterstulen was literally seething with people who had converged from many different directions, every single one of them intent on finding a place to spend the night. Thanks to our young friends, who had heralded the approach of our ninety-year-old prodigy, Dad and I were among the lucky fifty who rated beds. Eiliv and Charlotte Sulheim, the genial hosts, saw to that. But 150 hungry people sat down to supper in three separate shifts. And what a scuffle there was, later on, to occupy every available bed and chair and sofa! When these gave out, the remaining hikers made themselves as comfortable as possible on the floor, which soon became literally carpeted from wall to wall with sleeping human bodies. Every blanket that the establishment owned was in use. Most remarkable of all was the stoical way in which everyone accepted the prevailing difficulties, making the best they could of an uncomfortable situation. However, by early morning everyone was up and active, anxious to get a good start on the day, and even more anxious to beat the rush for accommodation at the next port of all.

Jackrabbit had a phenomenal memory for landmarks, and on our walk the day before he had remarked that "although the mountains look almost the same, the ice looks different." He remembered how, seventy-three years before, a certain glacier had extended much deeper into the valley; in the intervening years the body of ice had withdrawn into the heights due to the warming climate. "These mountains seem powerful and enduring," he observed, "but time changes everything. What's here today, may be gone tomorrow ... or even before." For as we climbed the first steep slopes next morning, suddenly a thick fog closed in, and nearby landmarks vanished. "This begins to look interesting," said Dad. "We'll have to move cautiously so as not to miss the fork in the trail."

We grouped at one of the piles of stones that served as a trail marker. Dad would then go forward, groping his way through the mist until he found the next cairn. He would then call, the girls would proceed to him, and I would follow when they called. Then Dad would go forward again. And so we advanced in inch-worm fashion, always establishing one "pair of legs" in the new position before bringing up the remaining "pair." It was cold and chilly, and we were thankful we had our heavy sweaters, our windbreakers, and our rain gear.

Eventually, after several hours of struggle over that rock-strewn mountainside, we felt the trail begin to drop again, and finally we emerged once more into the clear. The valley opened below us. The sun was beginning to disperse the cloud, and the sudden opening out of sky and valley affected us as almost a religious experience. During most of that day we had been floundering, but now at last we could see clearly what lay ahead. "And this is the way things go in life," said Dad. "Sometimes you have to feel your way among unfamiliar landmarks, but sooner or later the way opens up, and you can carry on." I knew that in the back of his mind he was thinking of our early days in the Laurentians, when he had had such a hard time making ends meet, and I sensed how thankful he now was for the wonderful way in which our lives were continually opening out.

We spent that night at Glitterheim, another of the Tourist Association's *hytter*, which (fortunately) was less crowded than Spiterstulen had been, but even so a good sixty hikers had managed to come in from different directions, all of them hungry and tired. But that evening will be forever engraved on my memory because of a spontaneous event that took place out in the open air in the *tun*, or courtyard. After supper had been cleared away, and Father had retired for the night "to escape from all this noisy nonsense!" an ancient hand-cranked gramophone was fixed astride the kitchen windowsill to spill its lively fiddle music out into the evening air. And there, on that uneven ground, the rest of us gathered, now fully recovered after our hearty evening meal, to dance exuberantly through the long evening twilight to polkas and schottisches and well-loved folk tunes. We were a motley crew of students, teachers, doctors, lawyers, housewives and shopkeepers, most of whom before this day had been entirely unknown to each other, but who, touched by the ambience, were irresistibly swept back in time to the "good old days," and had now become fast friends. To each of us it was the very best of entertainment – hearty, self-generated, and altogether memorable.

The next day, under faultless skies, we skirted Russvann as it lay in ultramarine splendour, crossed a rushing torrent on a spindly swinging bridge, and climbed over the far rise to look a thousand metres down into the turquoise waters of Lake Gjendin. And after we had jogged down the steep trail we boarded the little motor launch that took us down the lake to Gjendebu. There we looked up at the frowning cliff where poor old Karl had been assailed by mountain sickness those many years ago. And finally, on the last day, we followed the long tortuous valley back to our starting point at Leirvassbu.

It was hard to believe that we had been gone only six days, for somehow the total experience had seemed much longer. We returned to civilization with the sensation of having visited another world, and so indeed we had, for Jotunheimen, the mythical "Home of the Giants," had cast its spell on each of us.

Each year our holidays offered more and more of a challenge as we strove to re-experience some significant happening of long ago. That was one of the exciting things about life with Father. No sooner would one event be carefully stored in memory than he would say, "Well now, I wonder what new adventure is waiting just around the corner?" It was this constant looking forward to something unexpected and exciting that gave him such a zest for living. Action was what he wanted, and action was what he got when in

1966 we tied my aluminum canoe atop my car and drove out, this time following the path of the old Canadian fur traders.

We did feel a bit self-conscious crossing Beartooth Pass in Montana with the inverted canoe outlined against those craggy peaks ten thousand feet above sea level. But, to balance this, we had a delightful short trip on one of the tributaries of the Snake River, where we launched the canoe and paddled down through sparkling ripples and twisting reaches that gave us a small taste of this western stream. In the end, however, we succumbed to local tradition and took a five-day pack trip from Heart-Six Ranch up to the headwaters of the Yellowstone River. Dad, then ninety-one, had little difficulty in getting into the saddle again, and he revelled in his rôle as "guest."

❦

Another challenging experience came in 1967, when Canadians were seeking a project with mass appeal for all ages, a project that would combine an interest in the out-of-doors with the relish of adventure, and which at the same time would satisfy a desire for healthy recreation – in short, a suitable project to commemorate Canada's one hundredth year of Confederation. And thus was born the Canadian Ski Marathon, devised by Don MacLeod and twelve other determined skiers.

This scheme lay close to Jackrabbit's heart, and he eagerly supported it, although he had nothing to do with its management. He was attracted to it because it was "adaptable" to many ages and interests. One could enter as a competitor, and be timed over the whole course, or simply as a tourer, to enjoy a day's outing with no restrictions as to time or distance. The trail was "broken," beginning at Pointe Claire near Montreal and ending in Ottawa, a distance of roughly 190 kilometres, with three days and two nights to be spent en route. Each day's quota was divided into four "legs," and people could make up their own teams, to ski as a group or as a family, or to ski individually over one or more segments. It called for only whatever personal strength or ingenuity one wanted to dispense. A total of 375 people took part in 1967, a number which at the time we thought was fantastic. The youngest were two little girls of five years old. Dad was the oldest, at ninety-two.

I remember the mass start at eight in the morning at Check-point A in Pointe Claire for all who were registered for the first leg. A small gale was blowing, the temperature was minus fifteen (centigrade), and everyone's breath streamed like smoke in the wind. The sound of the starting gun was almost drowned out by the noise of people hopping on skis from one foot to the other to keep warm, but as soon as the few who did hear it started, the rest were off like a flash, and they spread out over an open field, gradually narrowing down to a single track as they began to hit their stride.

The rest of us, who were to ski the remaining laps, then piled into our cars and drove to Checkpoints B, C, or D, leaving the cars there to be picked up by teammates who were carrying extra keys, and who would move the cars to the next appointed stopping place, while we others would ski on over our own assigned part of the course. Remarkably, all the cars made it eventually to the indicated spots in Lachute, and the skiers soon found their way into every available bed in town. Our own team of five – including Jackrabbit, Pat Baird, my brother Bob, his son Bobby, and myself – shared one double motel room, and we drew lots to see who would get the beds, while the "leftovers" slept in their sleeping bags on the floor.

Day two was a repetition of the first, with much juggling of cars and people, and that night we gathered in Plantagenet, where we literally doubled the population. We were billeted in every spare bed that could be found, in houses and on farms, by members of a tremendously cooperative community who were proud to welcome us and to share in all this exciting activity. The super bean-feed that night in the church basement was something none of us will ever forget. On the final day we skied on into Ottawa itself, the nation's capital, and wound up the marathon with a banquet in the concourse of the old Union Station, later destined to become Ottawa's Centennial Centre.

The whole operation had been an excellent exercise in logistics, but as far as ski country was concerned, Jackrabbit was visibly disappointed. Although he was loath to discourage the organizing committee, he had a few opinions, which he voiced in his banquet speech. "All this wonderful work that committee members have done to prepare our trail should really have been done up in the

Laurentians, where the real ski country begins, not down here on the flats! Up there we have splendid forested ski terrain, with hills and lakes and cosy valleys. That's where the marathon should be run, not here beside the railway tracks! Next year the trail should go through rough country, with real ups and downs, so that every-one gets a feel for the wilderness, where you can see plenty of animal tracks, and can get to know what the real Canada is all about!"

Coming from anyone else, such a comment might have been taken amiss, but coming from Jackrabbit, it gave people food for thought. And next year, indeed, and for each year ever since, the trail has led through the Laurentians. There, despite annual changes due to unforeseen logging operations and the building of cottages, the tradition, twenty-five years later, is still going strong. The trail now runs for 160 kilometres (one hundred miles), all in the Prov-ince of Quebec, from Lachute to Hull, and is compressed into two days instead of three. Participation has grown from 375 in 1967 to a high of 4,500 in 1988, with entrants from every province in Canada and many parts of the United States. Over the years there have been participants from Norway, Finland, Italy, France, Swit-zerland, Hong Kong, and Argentina.

That first year, three men managed to cover the entire distance, which we all felt was a remarkable achievement. But in 1974, as the trail became progressively better maintained, Jackrabbit was again heard to mutter, "Now the marathon is getting too easy! We should have a system of *coureur de bois* awards: a bronze medal for those who do the full one hundred miles for the first time; a silver medal the next year for those who can re-run the entire course and carry a pack weighing twelve pounds; and a gold medal for those who can do it a third year, carrying their sleeping gear and their food, and sleeping out in a hole in the snow!"

"Is Mr Johannsen crazy? Is he trying to kill us?" people asked. Who could have guessed that, in 1989, 104 people would ski fifty miles, actually camp for the night near Montebello, cook and eat their own supper around a dozen camp fires, then crawl into their sleeping bags in some hole they had dug in the snow? Or that many of these would qualify for a gold medal after they had completed the second day's journey? More astonishing still, as time went by, a number of them would win a small gold bar to attach to the gold medal they had already won, and one man, Dr van Rhyn, a second-generation Dutch Canadian, would win nine gold bars, making him the all-time champion, having completed the entire hundred-mile trek twelve separate times! Obviously, the old spirit still lives on.

❧

It was in the summer of that centennial year that I had planned to earn my way to Norway by leading a McGill tour. Dad was coming as "co-guide." Montreal would be crowded with visitors, and it seemed like a good time for us to get away. Shortly before our departure, I received a letter from Margaret Peterson, an old McGill friend then living in Michigan. She was looking for an inexpensive place where a group of her friends could stay, in rotation, while they explored Expo '67, and a great idea flashed through my mind. Why shouldn't Dad and I turn over my apartment in Montreal and his house in Piedmont to Margie's friends for the summer? Their rent would pay Dad's air fare. My own fare was already included in the trip as guide. It was no sooner proposed than arranged.

Our own trip that year was a special one arranged for old friends who were interested in natural history, in hiking in the ever-changing Norwegian scenery, and in seeing some of the ancient customs. It included, among others, my old geometry teacher from Lake Placid and several McGill professors. The route reprised some of our itinerary of two years before, which had been in a way a "dress rehearsal" for this year's five-day walking tour in Jotunheimen. It was every bit as exciting as our first trip had been, and Dad proved to be even more of a phenomenon than before.

When we came home, we found at Dad's house a notebook recording the thanks of various of the families who had used our houses during our absence – 130 people in all, or 499 bed-nights. Some were families with as many as four children, and one family had this to say:

You can never completely imagine how much we all enjoyed your lovely cottage. I could never have hoped to bring the whole family to Expo without some fairly permanent arrangement such as this. There were 10 of us – with 3 airedales and a pet flying squirrel (in his own cage). With

220 rue Beaulne,
Piedmont, Québec

Jackrabbit's house in Piedmont,
now the Jackrabbit Laurentian Ski Museum.

our 17-foot cabin-boat-and-trailer parked in the yard, we were able to sleep the three boys there, and we used the sofa cushions for one small girl on the floor, and your two easy chairs together face-to-face for the 8-year old. The rest of us used the four beds. We were all most comfortable, and able to enjoy Expo and everything else to its fullest. Three of the children are diabetics, so it was imperative to be able to feed them properly to hope to keep them "balanced," with all the extra excitement, not to mention the odd hours kept.

Another note read:

Our fingerprints are on your trophies and our footprints are on your Windy Hill ... We'll always remember your view and your hospitality, and have left a bit of our hearts for a cheery greeting on your return.

Our own holiday in Norway had been wonderful in itself, but the delight we found recorded back in Piedmont was an extra-special bonus.

CHAPTER EIGHTEEN

Reaping the Benefits: 1968–1975

In January 1968 Jackrabbit's old friend Carl Gray invited him to attend the annual reunion of the Sun Valley Ski Club, which was to be held in Idaho in the United States. Sun Valley is a rendez-vous for financial wizards and ski enthusiasts who have congregated there every year since the resort's founding in 1936, to ski and to reminisce about old times. The Sun Valley Ski Club had been founded in 1958, and this tenth-year celebration promised to be something very special. Dad and I thought this invitation over carefully, and on the whole it seemed too wonderful an opportunity for him to miss. Carl had said, "We'll take complete charge of him, don't you worry about a thing. You have only to put him on the plane, and the airlines will see to the rest. We'll meet him at the airport, and he'll have the best of care, with a room of his own where he can get away from everything, if he wants to. We'll all be so happy to see him out here. He'll be the highlight of our reunion!"

It did seem a bit risky to send Dad off all by himself (after all, he was now ninety-three), but he saw it as another "adventure," and there was no holding him. I had my own job to do at work and as there was no question of my accompanying him this time, I saw him off on the plane. He took his full ski gear with him, smiling his winsome smile in farewell.

And, true to his word, Carl had everything organized. There were receptions, cocktail parties, and luncheons galore. Dad was fêted, lionized, and given the complete VIP treatment. And then he was asked to lay out a cross-country track for the first ski race of this kind ever to be held in Sun Valley. That was something Jackrabbit really wanted to do, and he did his best.

But his usual routine of "up at seven, with a short cat-nap every few hours," was thrown completely out the window. "These people never go to bed," he wrote me. "They stay up most of the night. They drink, and they talk, and they never sit down. At cocktail parties no one ever sits. They all stand up, close together, like sardines, and they all *breathe* on you. And all the women want to kiss me! What a life! They don't know how to live. And I don't know how I'll ever find time to lay out that cross-country track!"

However, he persevered. The race, scheduled for the afternoon, was to be on the golf course, and that morning, as he was putting in a few "surprises," people kept interrupting him and trying to talk. He wrote to me about it.

"First of all there was a television crew, and a big fat man who kept trying to carry on a conversation with me. But I just said to him, 'Listen! I'm sorry, but can't you see I'm busy? I have to get this trail ready for this afternoon!' The man looked a bit surprised.

"Then one of the television men came over and said, 'Please, Mr Johannsen. Just for a moment, come over here. We want to get a shot of you two talking together.' I thought that by humouring him, I'd get it over with, so I stood where he asked me to, and the cameras started to roll. I really didn't know what to talk about, but I turned and asked the man, 'Have you been skiing for a long time?'

"He shook his head. 'No,' he said. 'That's one of the reasons I came here.'

"'Oh,' I replied, poking a finger in the direction of his fat stomach. 'You should come more often. It will help you to get rid of *that*!' And everybody roared with laughter. The cameras stopped abruptly, and I felt that somehow I had said the wrong thing. But anyhow, he *did* look as though he needed exercise. The cameramen went away, and I continued with my trail.

"After the race I asked Carl, 'Who was that man this morning who kept wanting to talk to me? Everybody seemed to know him.' Carl looked dumbfounded. 'Don't tell me you didn't recognize him! That's John Wayne, the movie star!' And even then, for me, the name rang no bell. So Carl filled me in, and I tried to be impressed.

Obviously, my education has been very incomplete, and suddenly I could see the ghost of that other movie skier, Tom Mix, coming back to haunt me from those old Lake Placid days. Somehow, I guess, I'm not cut out for the movie world!"

There was, however, one person whom Dad was very anxious to see, and that was his grandson, Peter John Austin, Peggy's oldest boy, who was working at Sun Valley Lodge, in much the same way as his Uncle Bob had worked as a bellboy in his early days at Montebello. PJ at eighteen had wangled a job that year in room service. In his free time he managed to do a good deal of skiing, but as part of his job he was proud to bring Dad's breakfast to him in his room each day. This gave Dad a welcome respite from all his other excitement, and at the same time it gave them both a chance for brief visits. The two were duly photographed together by the *Valley Sun*, and PJ's stock rose high among his peers when it was discovered that his grandfather was among the VIPs!

Eventually, after seven days of competitions and various other extraordinary events, the reunion finally ended. There was a splendid banquet at which Jackrabbit made an unforgettable speech and was presented with a handsome trophy: a pen set mounted on a marble base, with a fine statuette of a skier proudly holding his skis, and a plaque that read:

Herman Smith Johannsen
Skier since 1875
An inspiration to the skiing world
Sun Valley Ski Club Reunion
1968

That prize still occupies a place of honour on his writing desk, a permanent reminder of that great adventure into sophisticated skiing circles.

They saw him off on the plane for the long trip back to Piedmont. There were two changes of aircraft, and a very long day of travel. I met him at the airport, and even from a distance I could see the bright flush on his face. His eyes were burning, he had a high fever, and his knees were very wobbly. "I'm sure glad to get home," he croaked, his voice almost completely gone, as I rushed him back to my apartment and into bed. "Reunions are all right –

in their place," he muttered, "but those people don't know how to *live*! No wonder I caught the 'flu! The hours they keep! And the hot air! And the close quarters! That's enough 'high living' for me for a while. From now on I'll stick to the simple life! And, *please* — don't send me any more movie stars!"

It was several weeks before Dad was well enough to return to his normal routine, but once again his marvellous health and physical conditioning allowed him to shake off his illness completely.

Later, in November of that same year (1968) Sir George Williams University bestowed on Jackrabbit the honorary degree of Doctor of Laws, *honoris causa*.

"In offering you this honour," said the university spokesman, "we wish to pay tribute to all you have done in opening up skiing as a source of delight, exercise and the development of skill, for thousands and thousands of Canadians."

A reporter who interviewed him also summed things up very well. "Johannsen," he said, "has found the secret that makes the 'generation gap' a worthless phrase. He has discovered the living spark of adventure and purpose and friendship that many start out with, but later lose somewhere along the road of life."

The following summer in 1969 it was my own good fortune to be sent to France in connection with my museum work, and I remarked to Dad, "After my conference is over, I think I'll go on up to Norway for a few weeks. You'll be all right here in Piedmont for a little while on your own, won't you? When I come back we'll take a trip together, somewhere here in Quebec."

"I'll be okay," said Dad reassuringly. "You can count on that!" Little did I suspect that after I returned to my job in town he would take a bus into the city, and go to the docks in Montreal to meet the freighter *Topdalsfjord*, just coming into port. He had been a passenger on this ship several years before, and knew the captain. He went aboard, and asked the Captain, "Have you any use for an extra hand on the ship on your voyage back? I need to get to Norway, and there must be something I can do to earn my way."

Captain Haaland looked him over in surprise. "You say you'll be ninety-four this summer," he observed. "What do you think you can do?"

"I don't know," said Dad, "but I'll try anything you say."

"Go see the bo'sun," said Captain Haaland. So Dad went.

"I duno," said the bo'sun, looking him over thoughtfully. "Can you splice wire rope?"

"I've never done it," Dad replied, "but I can learn."

"It'll take two of us," said the bo'sun. "It's not hard, just boring. You'll wear heavy leather gloves, an' you'll hang on tight. I'll do the rest." So it was a deal.

The following weekend, when I came up to Piedmont, Dad remarked casually, "I think we'd better take that trip this summer over in Norway, rather than here in Quebec. I've found a job on *Topdalsfjord*, and I've written to Helga to tell her I'm coming."

You could have knocked me down with a feather! And the same went for Helga, who had not been very well. But I packed him up and, together with Peggy and her family and two Red Birds, we went down to the boat to see him off on this ten-day sea voyage, the Red Birds bearing two bottles of champagne.

Then, on the day before my own scheduled departure by plane, my cousin Einar, Helga's son, cabled urgently, "Hold him there!" Don't let him come! It will be too much for mother. He wears the family out."

But it was too late. Dad was already on the high seas. So I cabled back, "Don't worry! I'll get there ahead of him, and I'll take care of him when I come. We won't bother you."

And so it was that I arrived in Kristiansand after my conference in France was over. I immediately cabled Dad, whose ship was by that time crossing the North Sea. "Happy birthday!" I said, for it was June 15th. "Take the train from Stavanger to Kristiansand. I'll meet you at the railway station."

That was how the radio operator learned of Dad's birthday. He alerted the captain, who invited the Jackrabbit, "their oldest seaman," to join the passengers at dinner that evening. Dad arrived, over the heaving deck, bearing his two birthday bottles of champagne, and a lively time was had by all. Then he returned, this time escorted by one of the guests, both of them holding fast to the rope that led back to the crew's quarters!

Next morning the boat docked in Stavanger, and after a six-hour train journey Dad arrived in Kristiansand. He was wearing his knapsack, and jauntily waving his cowboy hat. True to form, he had during that long ride made friends with the whole trainload of passengers, who gave him a rousing send-off!

From Kristiansand we proceeded on our own in a rented car, with first a stop in Oslo to check briefly with the family, and to assure Tante Helga that she could recuperate in peace. I really think she somehow had a vision of Dad as still the same old teasing big brother who, long ago, as she recalled, "ruined our 'farm' by dumping fresh cow manure on it to make it look more realistic!" In any case, I could see it would be best to keep them separated until she was feeling better.

While we were in Oslo, we visited again the Viking Ship Museum with its proud thousand-year-old vessels. There was the beautiful Oseberg ship, which still looks seaworthy, and which had been exhumed from a mound not far from Dad's old home in Horten, together with all the trappings of a Viking queen. And there was the Gokstad ship, a longboat, or cargo vessel, clinker-built of oak, seventy-seven feet long, seventeen feet wide, with a height of over six feet from keel to gunwale. It had been capable of carrying thirty men, their equipment, and some livestock on long sea voyages. We marvelled at the skill and determination of those old Vikings, as they had set resolutely out on their long seafaring expeditions so very long ago.

And then we moved on, back up to Brekkesaeter in the Rondane. There we made daily walking trips into the countryside, sometimes taking with us other hikers who were eager to see the things that interested us.

High on a treeless mountainside there was an X-shaped system of stone walls stretching across a narrow pass between two hills. This was part of an ancient *dyre-grav*, or animal deadfall, located on an old migration route of reindeer. The four stone fences converged on what had once been a deep pit, which the old hunters had cleverly camouflaged with branches. Then at migration time they would conceal themselves on the hills immediately above, and lie in wait.

When at last the reindeer came, travelling in fairly close formation, the lead animals, unaware of the hidden trap, would stumble into the pit, there to be trampled to death by the oncoming herd, which then broke ranks and scattered in wild confusion. The hunters would leap from their hiding places, shouting and shooting with crossbows at the bewildered beasts. In this way, one small team of well-organized men could secure a large supply of meat, bones, and fur to meet their families' needs for the coming winter. To me, a twentieth-century onlooker, the dyre-grav was a hypnotic thing, and the little valley became filled in my imagination with snorting, frantic animals, and with bounding, bloodstained hunters. It was a gripping experience.

Later that summer, as we followed the coastline in our little rented car, we pictured those majestic fjords as they must have looked in the days when sleek Viking ships, like the Gokstad ship, sailed out to the open sea to raid, or to settle in the Orkneys, the Shetlands, or the Faroe Islands. "Wouldn't it be interesting," I said to Dad one day, "to follow each year another section of this 'Viking trail' travelling a bit farther each time, to see where those old sea-rovers actually went – to Iceland, to Greenland, and finally to Newfoundland?"

Jackrabbit was thrilled at the idea. He had met Helge Ingstad in Montreal, and that same year the Norwegian archaeologist had sailed down the St. Lawrence River to begin his excavations at the site he had previously located on Newfoundland's northern tip. Dad had been fired by his account of all they hoped to find.

It became our dream to follow the path of the Viking explorers, and so, the following summer, together with Valma Gurr, an Australian friend of ours, we flew first to Iceland, and from there with a small group of other tourists to Narsarssuak in Southern Greenland. This had been the site of Bluie II, the old American air force base in the Second World War. By 1969 only the airport was still in (reduced) operation, as were a few of the buildings in the otherwise almost completely demolished base. The Danish government had, however, retained enough facilities to provide acceptable accommodation for the occasional adventurous tourists who came looking for a different type of holiday.

By coincidence, Bluie II was situated on Eiriksfjord, which a thousand years before had been the home of that old sea-rover, Eirik-the-Red.

In a small motorboat, dodging the floating icebergs in the fjord, we were able to visit the ruins of Eirik's own old farm, Brattalid, and we could picture how from this very spot Eirik's son, Leif the

Lucky had set out on the expedition on which he was to discover the New World. For us at that moment, history was truly reincarnated.

Dad was completely "tuned in" to all of this, but for him perhaps the most important event of all was our long hike up the river floodplain to the foot of one of the glaciers that spilled down from the inland ice. Here we actually set foot on a portion of the ice cap over which Nansen and Sverdrup had made their historic six-week crossing of Greenland on skis in 1888. Although their trek had been much farther north, this was almost "holy ground" for Dad. We listened spellbound as the guide recounted vivid details of that remarkable expedition, and as we stood there on the ice, Nansen's whole trip seemed to pass before our eyes, as in a motion picture. Dad relived the whole journey, almost as though he, himself, had been there. It also brought back a strong recollection of the meeting he had had with Otto Sverdrup in Spitsbergen some fifty years before, and it was with almost a physical wrench that the Jackrabbit came back from these memories to find himself standing once more in the present. Those who were with us also felt a personal link with those former days, glimpsing them as we did through Father's eyes.

We turned then, our minds still filled with visions of Nansen and his men, to wend our way homeward over the terminal moraine, down onto the stony floodplain, and along the trail back to Eiriksfjord.

I lingered behind to snap a few pictures, and so was surprised to see the group suddenly cluster excitedly ahead of me at one of the shallow stream crossings. "Someone must be in trouble!" I thought, hurrying to catch up. When I reached them, imagine my surprise to find that Father, in making the crossing, had somehow missed his footing and fallen in! The group had immediately splashed across the ford to help him out onto the farther bank, where he was regaining his breath as they stripped away his sodden shirt. He was already struggling into someone else's dry sweater, while the water still dripped from his trousers and oozed from his socks and boots.

I splashed anxiously across, just in time to hear him splutter through chattering teeth, "Th-th-that s-s-sure is c-c-cold w-w-water! It only j-j-just m-m-melted after th-th-thousands of years of being ice!" Then, grabbing my arm, he commanded, "Come on! I have to r-r-run before I f-f-freeze up myself!"

So we jogged on together at a fast clip, followed by the guide. There were several kilometres to cover before we reached the boat, which had been moored beside a deeper crossing of the main stream. There the guide rowed us quickly across, and Dad and I continued to jog ahead while the guide went back to fetch the others.

"Th-th-this is one time when I s-sure can use a sh-sh-shot of wh-wh-whisky!" Dad panted. And when we got back to head-quarters, that's exactly what he got.

Those at the home base were amazed and shocked. "Imagine!" they repeated to each other in astonishment. "He's ninety-five and he fell into that ice water! And then he *ran* back here! He'll probably catch his death of cold!" But Dad did not stop to hear what they had to say. He was already soaking in a hot shower – and the whisky definitely helped. Then, having donned a complete set of dry clothing, he lay down to rest.

When he reappeared for supper, he was in fine form. "It really wasn't so bad," he said, "it was just like a snowbath after a ski run. The hardest part was getting back here, still wearing most of my old wet things." The event, however, certainly did shake up the conversation. And it supplied Dad with a fine addition to his repertoire of stories.

"I remember one time when I was in Greenland," I heard him expounding to an old lady some time later. "We were coming back from a trip to the edge of the inland ice. I missed my footing and fell into one of those glacial streams."

"Good heavens!" exclaimed the lady. "You fell in!"

"Yes," Dad recalled. "I got wet up to my neck, but I managed to get out."

"But you might have drowned!" gasped the lady, picturing a swirling torrent.

"Well, fortunately, I didn't," Dad continued. "The water wasn't deep – but it was very, *very* cold!"

I didn't think it would be cricket to point out to her that you can "get wet up to your neck" in water barely a foot deep, if you lie down in it – even for the briefest of moments. But the fact remained that he *had* survived, and that, after all, was what really mattered. However, hearing him tell the story, I felt that under the circumstances even old Eirik-the-Red would have been proud of him.

It was several years later that we finally put a cap on this whole Viking story. We were visiting Newfoundland, and had driven up along the western coast to Anse-aux-Meadows, and there we saw the old Norse settlement, just as it had been excavated by Helge Ingstad and his wife, Anne Stine, during six summers in the 1960s. The site lay in a sheltered valley at the end of Epaves Bay, where Black Duck Brook winds its way down to the sea beside the barely visible vestiges of those ancient turf-built houses.

That settlement, called Leifsbudir, had lasted (according to the sagas) for a number of years, long enough for a total of some 160 Greenlanders to have arrived, in a series of longboats, bringing sheep and cattle and probably hoping to live here permanently. They had hunted and fished and grazed their livestock, but strife with the natives and disagreements among themselves had ultimately led to failure of the enterprise. The survivors had returned to Greenland, where they recounted their adventures in sagas that have been repeated from generation to generation down through the centuries. We could imagine their longboats, similar to the Gokstad ship, pulled up on shore beside the boat sheds, and I could almost smell the smoke from the charcoal kiln beside the little smithy. (Since our visit, the National Parks Service has reconstructed some of the complex, so that now a visitor can enter a turf-built structure and sense the actual conditions under which those early people lived.)

I thought as I stood there side by side with my own old viking, that it would have taken only *ten* men of his age – ten sturdy men, no more, really, than could comfortably have sat together all at once in his own little living-room in Piedmont – to span the gap in time back to those old Viking days. And suddenly, the living past seemed very close indeed.

❦

Back in Piedmont, Jackrabbit would occasionally fix his eye on his upcoming hundredth year as a more and more attainable goal. "I'm still a young fellow," he would say. "There's no need for me to pack up yet. I still have many more miles to cover!" And he continued to do his two to five miles daily on his trusty skis, enjoying to the full the clear winter air and the whisper of his boards on the fresh new snow.

Then, in 1972, two important events combined to make a fitting prelude for his approaching centennial. First of all, at a reception in Montreal at the home of the Norwegian consul, Olav Solli, Jackrabbit was presented with the Medal of St. Olav on behalf of His Majesty, King Olav V of Norway. This was the first time this medal had ever been bestowed on a Canadian. In making the presentation the Consul had said:

This is given in recognition of Smith Johannsen's great contribution to the advancement of ski-touring in Canada – something which has long been the most important winter sport in Norway. You are a monumental example of a life-style based on enjoyment of the environment and of nature.

It is of great satisfaction for Norway to see one of her own sons so ably and graciously assisting his adopted country, Canada, to explore and to enjoy more fully two of her great riches, her wilderness and her nature. More than fifty years of activity on your part in the ski touring and ski trail business are thus crowned with enormous success.

And Herman Smith Johannsen took home with him this cherished medal, which he continued to regard with the utmost pride and joy.

Several months later, Jackrabbit returned from the post office one morning bearing an embossed envelope from Government House in Ottawa. He opened it carefully, and read:

Dear Mr. Johannsen,

His Excellency the Chancellor of the Order of Canada has asked me to inform you that the Advisory Committee of the Order has recommended your name to him for appointment as Member.

I am writing, therefore to ask whether you would be prepared to accept the appointment if it were offered to you.

Yours sincerely,
Carl Lochner
Director, Honours Secretariat

Needless to say, Jackrabbit was delighted, though somewhat overwhelmed at the thought. "I must say," he commented, "it always seemed to me that this sort of thing was only reserved for diplomats, artists and intellectuals, not skiers and sportsmen." He seemed unaware that he, himself, might truly qualify on each of these counts, but after some hesitation he accepted, and conveyed to the Chancellor his "heartfelt gratitude for one of the greatest distinctions of his life."

In due course an invitation was received, together with one for me as a guest, to attend the Investiture the following April. For this, Jackrabbit rented white tie and tails and shiny black shoes, maintaining gruffly that "it's a lot easier to get into my ski clothes than it is to put on all this fancy harness." We took the train to Ottawa, where we stayed with all the other appointees and their guests at the Skyline Hotel; then we were driven collectively to Rideau Hall for the ceremony itself. Dad, proudly wearing his Order of St Olav, cut an impressive figure.

It was a resplendent evening. Flowers banked the ballroom, and the crystal chandeliers sparkled over the assembled guests, who wore either civilian evening dress or military mess garb, with decorations. The band of the Royal Canadian Mounted Police played, and Their Excellencies entered in procession. After the vice-regal salute, and the invocation by the Chancellor, the recipients were presented, one by one, to receive their insignia, while the citations were read. For Jackrabbit, it was particularly significant that he should receive this honour from Governor General Roland Michener, an ardent skier.

Following the ceremony, each guest in turn was presented to Their Excellencies. And finally, everyone sat down to a gala repast under silken banners in the banquet hall. It was altogether a most impressive evening.

Throughout 1974, events continued to build towards Dad's centennial. Among the major happenings were two documentary films, which, to be available on the appropriate date, had to be prepared a year ahead of the birthday. The Jackrabbit was to play the leading role in both of these, and the family teased him mercilessly, saying, "Now then, Tom Mix and John Wayne, move over!" but Dad took it very seriously and retorted, "This is *really* important! Both of these companies want to take us to Norway, so I'd better be good!"

Order of Canada, December 1972.

The arrangements did cause us some concern, however, for each film crew required independent footage, with no interference from the other. Both would use the Canadian Ski Marathon as part of the background. It was agreed that Bill Brind of the National Film Board, with his six-member team and a full ton of baggage, would tell the story of Dad's life, dipping into the family background and the Norwegian years, then come back to Canada to record his part in the development of skiing in the Laurentians. They would emphasize his lifestyle, his philosophy, his contribution to the ski sport, and his example to Canadians, and this would occupy approximately three weeks of filming.

Doug Sinclair, on the other hand, had a team of two – his wife and himself – and considerably less baggage. He would concentrate on contemporary cross-country skiing in Norway, delving into some of the early ski equipment from the Folkmuseum in Lille-hammer and showing the importance of skiing in the everyday life of Norwegians. He would need about one week of our time.

Our job would be to cooperate with each team to the full, while keeping them entirely separate. Our expenses would be covered, and Dad would receive a moderate honorarium for his work on each film. Scandinavian Airlines would fly us all over and back, independently.

Needless to say there were many "spin-offs." There was the party for the NFB crew at Kirsten's house, when Dad appeared "from America," knocking on the door and calling out, "Is anybody home?" and the joyous welcome from Kirsten and Ditlef, and Dad's two "baby sisters," Helga and Elisabeth, both now in their nineties. There was the trip down to Horten to visit Bestefar Smith's old home, Ekeli, and another trip to Froland Verk, to Tippoldefar's beautiful big mansion and the church where many of Dad's ancestors lay buried. There was, of course, all the confusion of "takes" and "retakes," of waiting for the "right" light, and of "doing it all over one more time," through which Dad was wonderfully patient, despite such unpredictable moments as when his microphone tumbled unexpectedly into the toilet during a brief rest period. And there was much involvement of family and friends as we finally said goodbye to the National Film Board.

After the NFB film crew had gone home, we went up to Lille-hammer for a week's filming with the Sinclairs. Among the ancient timbered farmhouses in the Folkmuseum, Dad demonstrated the use of the old-time skis and explained the early equipment. There were wonderful shots of youngsters skiing two miles downhill to school, and of life at the timberline resort of Pellestova, with some memorable close-ups of Dad skiing determinedly over those glorious open slopes, paced by Doug (unseen of course by the audience) as he rode alongside on a snowmobile, confidently wielding his camera.

Both films were excellent in different ways, and the effort every-one put into them has been rewarded by the enjoyment of thousands of skiers, who as a result can thus enjoy "skiing with the Jackrabbit" down through the years.

And then the centennial year itself dawned – and everyone else wanted to get in on the act. On the average, there was one major episode every two weeks throughout the year, allowing just enough recovery time between them so that Dad could look refreshed and relaxed before the next event!

The year began with a birthday celebration at Laurentian Lodge Club at Shawbridge, staged by the New England Ski Touring Council whose members arrived thirty strong from the United States, led by Rudy Mattenich and Rolland Palmedo, to celebrate with Jackrabbit what he had done to encourage skiing and ski competitions in the eastern United States during the years he lived in Lake Placid. There was an enthusiastic round of speeches, and a huge birthday cake, followed by a mass visit by the entire troop to his home in Piedmont to see where, almost fifty years later, he had finally put down his roots.

Then there was a gala dinner in New York, to which Peggy escorted him as guide and chaperone, where he was pronounced the "Dubonnet Skier of the Year," and given a huge silver cup to commemorate the event; and another week-long visit to Sun Valley, Idaho, where he once more astonished those veteran skiers with his prowess "on the boards." And this time Bob and I were invited to be with him, to enjoy the skiing, the sunshine and the remi-niscing of that delightful place, while keeping an eagle eye on Father lest the cocktail parties and his enthusiastic female admirers should get completely out of control!

In Montebello, Quebec, there was an enormous birthday cake at the dinner, midway in the 1975 Marathon, when skiers gathered to toast his hundredth year. A fine bust of Jackrabbit by Harold Pfeifer, commissioned by Meg and Hans Webber, was unveiled during that marathon, and is now in the Canadian Ski Museum in Ottawa.

Back home, he was celebrated in poems and songs, of which he received framed copies, and in several cases a taped recording by the musicians themselves. There was one rollicking folksong, composed and sung by Prof Max Dunbar of McGill University, " 'e learned about skiin' from 'er!" humorously commemorating Dad's own mother, our Bestemor. And there was another lively piece, composed and sung by Stanley Triggs of the McCord Museum.

Then, on March 9 after due advertisement, the CPR staged "Le Jackrabbit Train de Ski," a revival of the old ski train of the thirties and forties. This was a one-day excursion to the Laurentians, for which one thousand of Dad's "faithful followers" paid ten dollars apiece to ride a six-car doubledecker diesel train to Val David, and while the ultra-modern aluminum commuter cars resembled very little the once-familiar old yellow cane-seated coaches of former days, the old-time spirit was very much in evidence. Skiers converged from all sides, bearing skis and poles and packsacks, and the station platform, with its standing forest of skis and skiers, looked much as it had in the good old days.

Jackrabbit was driven in state by the mayor of Shawbridge in a horse-drawn cutter to the Shawbridge Station, where he disembarked to hail the assembled throng. There were speeches, picture-taking, and a sea of happy faces. And finally the train, with a sudden "A-L-L A-B-O-A-R-D!" sucked into itself all this human baggage like some gigantic vacuum cleaner, and was off with a toot of its whistle and a long, but imaginary, trailing plume of steam. The skiers, meanwhile, in all their colourful garb, settled into the coaches with ukuleles and accordions, and before long each carriage was rocking up the old ski songs.

At Val David we were met by what appeared to be the entire population, headed by local dignitaries, while we ourselves were escorted in a special sleigh to La Sapinière for the start of a great cross-country ski trek. It was a clear, cold day, with excellent snow conditions. Everyone was equipped with knapsacks and lunches and extra clothing, and they clustered outside the hotel, hopping up and down on their skis to keep warm as they listened to long-winded speeches.

Finally, it was Jackrabbit's turn. He was short and sweet. "I guess by this time we've had enough hot air," he boomed into the loudspeaker. "Now let's all go SKIING!" And he led off down the hill on his trusty wooden skis, while the crowd followed joyfully behind. Participants could go as far as they wished, and could pick up the homebound train that evening at some station farther down

Jackrabbit greets his well-wishers at Val David
on the one-hundred-year ski-trip and train ride, March 1975.

the line. Meanwhile, all were strictly on their own for a glorious day in the sun. It was just like old times.

Dad and I, meanwhile, were whisked off by the local committee for a helicopter ride from which we could watch the skiers fan out through the trees on a network of routes which spread through the country from his old Maple Leaf Trail. It was a nostalgic excursion: we looked down on the Laurentians, remembering many a trip up and down hills that now looked so insignificant from above, but had represented many, many hours of toil and hard work as he had hacked out the original path.

The helicopter set us down at Alpine Inn at Ste-Marguerite Station, where a room had been reserved in which Dad could relax and talk quietly with numerous non-skiing visitors who also wished to share this special day. Peggy and Peter joined us there after their own day's ski trip, and after a gala dinner we were all driven up to the station to join once more the ski train with its now tired but still tuneful tourers, for the trip back home.

It had been a splendid day with many old friends, among them ninety-year-old Lindsay Hall, survivor of many good trips with the Chief and a friend from his earliest days in the Laurentians. We "took the salute" from the platform at Shawbridge, waving to many who felt that this time they too had indeed relived the past.

Then there was a brief interval of several weeks during which Dad could catch his breath.

The Sedbergh Old Boys' Association in May gave a Jackrabbit banquet at which were present many of the "youngsters" who had graduated during the thirty-six years since the founding of the school in 1939, all of them veterans of Dad's many visits and of his famous annual bushwhack race. And many of them had well-remembered bumps to prove it.

He was, himself, the guest speaker at the Selwyn House School Closing, where he explained to a whole new generation of young-sters the joys of wilderness living, and of "how skiing can help you as you face the realities of life."

As the actual birthday approached, the town of Piedmont took its place in the celebrations. Dad, the mayor, and the aldermen were driven in a big box sleigh (mounted on wheels for this June event) with a spanking team of horses, from the town hall to the place of festivities at the Piedmont Golf and Country Club. There the family and many friends and neighbours were assembled. Baskets of flowers were presented to Jackrabbit by a pair of pretty little girls. Then a silver medal was displayed, designed and made by a local jeweller, showing an energetic Jackrabbit striding across the countryside on skis with a big 100 emblazoned against the familiar hills. There was a festive dinner, another huge birthday cake, and more speeches.

At the annual meeting of the Red Birds Ski Club, Brian Powell's book was officially launched and a copy presented to "the Chief" with great fanfare. *Jackrabbit: His First Hundred Years* was a compilation of fifty-seven separate stories submitted by friends who had known him at various stages during his long life. There were commentaries by Governor General Jules Léger, by King Olav V of Norway, and by Pierre Elliott Trudeau, who was then prime minister. The book was published by Collier Macmillan, and went through two printings with a total of twenty thousand copies, but is now long out of print. In one of the stories, Jackrabbit was asked,

One hundredth birthday at St Francis Church, June 1975.
George Romer, Herman, and Alice.

"What would you consider the most thrilling moment of your life?"
To which he replied, without hesitation, "Well, I married the right
girl. Without my wife, I wouldn't have been where I am today. I
owe everything to her ... She was a wonderful woman!"

And the celebrations continued. On June 15, his actual birthday,
we held an open house at the Church Hall of St-Francis-of-the-
Birds, where Dad was honorary church warden. At this the entire
family was present, plus members of the church itself, many old
skiers, and representatives of the Norwegian Seaman's Church in
Montreal. The secretary of the Norwegian consulate, Gerd Halle,
her daughter Monique, and I, all of us in Norwegian *bunader*, led a
festive parade around the church grounds, in which we were happily joined by all the guests.

The very next day, Dad and I took off for Norway, where there
were copious family gatherings. We then left for Berlin to attend
the annual Stiftungsfest, held this year in celebration of Dad's one-
hundredth birthday by his old fraternity, Berolina. There was much
wining and dining and reminiscing by the sons and grandsons of
his old contemporaries, culminating in an urgent invitation for him

to return in 1986 for Berolina's *own* centennial. "I can't promise," said Dad with a wink, "but I'll do my best! You never know!"

And then, on June 28, we joined the *Royal Viking Star* in Copenhagen for a cruise to Spitsbergen. This was a trip in which the McGill Graduates' Society was one of the co-sponsors. I had arranged well in advance to be leader of the McGill contingent. It seemed most appropriate that Dad should accompany me on this trip as his birthday gift from me, and so we two were able to relive some other special moments as we sailed in this magnificent ship along the fjord-strewn coast of Norway. We visited King's Bay in Spitsbergen, where some of Dad's early machinery had been bought by the Norsk Kulkompani back in 1905 for the opening of the first coal mines there. We cruised the edge of the pack ice under the midnight sun as Dad called to mind the time he had been caught in the crush of that ice back in 1920. And we returned to Montreal, exhilarated and refreshed by a great experience.

In the fall he was taped for an appearance on "Front Page Challenge." For this exciting event we were flown to Toronto, put up at the Park Plaza Hotel, photographed and interviewed, and again given the complete VIP treatment. We enjoyed to the full all the behind-the-scenes manoeuvring, having many times watched the program in the privacy of our own living-room. On the program Gordon Sinclair asked Dad the usual questions about how he had managed to live so long, and what was the secret of his good health. To which Dad replied, "Why should I tell you, Gordon, any of my secrets? You would only make money out of them! These secrets are not for sale! Good health means moderation in all things, and above all, keeping yourself in good condition, and anyone can do this, if he uses good common sense!"

Later, on Lorraine Thompson's "VIP Television Show," when this shapely interviewer ran an admiring hand over his biceps and commented on his "extraordinary good condition," Dad, not to be outdone, leaned over and with an exploratory hand on her knee, said confidentially, "You're not in such bad condition yourself!" This frank interchange brought down the house.

But the most important event of all – the "icing on the cake" – was when he received his honorary degree as Doctor of Science from McGill University. It was a very special occasion on the stage of the Place des Arts in Montreal. In that august setting, before the assembled staff and student body, all in academic gowns, he

Jackrabbit receiving his Doctor of Science degree
from McGill University, November 1975.

stood erect at the podium, wearing his scarlet robe and the black velvet doctor's cap, while I had the honour of reading the citation. This was a very moving event for both of us, as Dad became the "oldest graduate" of the university from which all three of his own children had previously received their own degrees as Bachelors of Science.

All in all, it was an exciting but thoroughly exhausting centennial year – a combination of events that might easily have overwhelmed a less durable man than Jackrabbit, and many of those who shared in these celebrations well remember how tired *they* were when the events were over. "When you come to think of it," Dad remarked with his usual twinkle, "all my friends have done their very best to kill me off with kindness and good will, but I managed to fool them all. You can bet I'll still be around for another ten years yet!"

CHAPTER NINETEEN

Capping the Climax

If we had thought there would be a cessation of activities at the close of his centennial year, it was soon apparent that, while the tide of events might diminish somewhat, it would certainly not cease.

Early in 1976 Dad received an interesting call from Bill McNeill of CBC's "Fresh Air." This was one radio program to which we always listened, and it was like welcoming an old friend to have Bill come to see us in Piedmont, unfurl his tape recorder, and get Dad to talk. In all, he did an interview of more than an hour, and I often think of the day when the two of them sat together there on the sofa, reminiscing away. By the time Bill had edited his tape, it had turned into six separate episodes, which have been repeated on a number of occasions over the years. Listeners often recall how vividly the sound of Jackrabbit's voice brings back his lively image.

A letter received about this time from John Reeves, producer of CBC radio features, was another case in point. He invited Jackrabbit to take part in an international radio program called "Nineteen Hundred."

"This is a program which will be heard in sixteen different countries," Reeves explained. "It will consist chiefly of events recalled by people old enough to remember the turn of the century clearly. We feel that you could make a very good contribution to this program. If you were to record a short reminiscence in English and Norwegian and French and German, then no translation would be needed for listeners in countries where these languages are spoken or understood. Would you be willing to participate?"

Reeves's letter came to me at St-Hilaire, and I passed it on to Dad in Piedmont with a note. "This man would like to fly down from Toronto, rent a car and drive out here to interview you. We can give him lunch afterwards, and then he can go on his way. I said nothing to him about an honorarium, but I would think, if they are going to save translator's fees in three other languages, they might be able to pay you *something*!"

Dad replied directly to Reeves. "Your program '1900' sounds interesting, and I shall be pleased to see you on the 13th, in spite of the fact that I much prefer to spend my time skiing instead of being interviewed! Looking forward to seeing you, Chief Jackrabbit."

Needless to say, the program was a great success, and it was duly acknowledged by the CBC, with thanks. However, there was no honorarium.

In 1978, the Canadian Branch of the Society of American Travel Writers presented Dad with a plaque honouring him as "the individual responsible for more travel development in Canada than anybody else. To millions of Canadians," they said, "he is known as the 'father of cross-country skiing' in North America," a myth which Dad steadfastly denied. "In spite of his age," the story went on, "he skis every day during the winter months, smokes a pipe every now and then, and even accepts a schnapps of aquavit! In addition to which he hasn't forgotten how to pinch a pretty girl in the derrière!"

"Can you imagine that?" said Dad with a grin. "What they won't put in the papers!"

Despite all this "exaggerated talk," in 1979 Laurentian University in Sudbury sought out Jackrabbit to confer on him its honorary degree of Doctor of Laws. Jackrabbit responded with enthusiasm, realizing that this would require a brief trip back to the area where, in his early days, he had sold heavy machinery to the developing railroads. It would be good to see that part of the country again. He was also pleased to be asked to give a short blessing to the ceremony, and to the graduates and their families who would be gathered there.

This was just at the time when public feeling was running high with regard to the Quebec referendum on sovereignty, a situation which concerned Dad very much. In fact, he seldom lost an opportunity to make it clear that he, certainly, was "no separatist." However, as this convocation was to take place in Ontario, I felt there was no cause for undue alarm.

I proudly watched my one-hundred-and-four-year-old father march in with the academic procession, speech in hand, and take his place in the front row with the other dignitaries on the platform. And I thought with a smile of the contrast he made that day, in his dark suit and his blue-lined robe, to the way I was used to seeing him, in his more habitual dress of knickers and ski boots! I noticed his neighbour lean over to him. They exchanged a few whispered words, and I was surprised to see Dad hand over his speech to this man without hesitation. Then the ceremony got under way.

Some four hundred graduates received their degrees, with appropriate fanfare and speeches. Then it was Dad's turn. He rose when he was called, and walked sedately, cane in hand, to the podium – but he had left his speech with his neighbouring seatmate! I was dumbfounded, and not a little worried.

His citation was read. His resplendent hood was slipped over his shoulders. He heartily shook hands with the principal. And then he turned to the audience and, grasping the lectern firmly with both hands, began to speak.

Mr Principal, and fellow graduates. These are times which strain our endurance and our capacity to overcome obstacles, but we should accept these difficulties and hardships as blessings in disguise. We derive great benefit from hardships, because through them, we discover in ourselves talents we never thought possible. This is a time to make use of our own initiatives, instead of waiting for the government – or someone else – to help us out! We should appreciate all the blessings which we have.

We live in a country that has more to offer in physical and personal resources than any other country in the world. It is up to every individual to make use of these blessings, not only for his own sake, but for the sake of the country itself, which is made up of the collective strength of all its citizens.

Enjoy whatever you do, and do it to the best of your ability. And don't forget from time to time to turn back to the wilderness, and learn from Nature how to make use of her bounties – without straining or abusing them."

His voice was high, but his message was clear. Speaking in French, he continued earnestly,

"I am neither French nor English, but very much a Canadian. We must keep the French language and culture, *by remaining in Canada*. If we were ever to withdraw from Canada, French-Canadians would run the risk of being swallowed up by the United States. We must stick together!

Continuing in English, he went on:

May God grant that we be thankful for all our blessings, that we may share these blessings with others, and that we may be capable of using these blessings for the lasting good of the Canada we love and cherish.

He strode back to his seat, and sat down to thunderous applause. his neighbour leaned anxiously to him and said, "But your speech! You left it with me. I hadn't meant to take it from you at such a critical moment!"

To which Dad replied, "Never mind. I didn't really need it. It's only paper, anyway. You see, if you have the strength of your own convictions, you really need very little else!"

❦

In the fall of 1979 we received an urgent telephone call from Tony Wise in Telemark, Wisconsin. Tony was the proprietor of Telemark Lodge. The 1980 Winter Olympics were approaching, and the North American Cross-Country Ski Championships, which were to be held in Telemark that December, would see final selection of the American and Canadian cross-country ski teams. The sponsors wanted to dedicate this important pre-Olympic event to Jackrabbit. Would he do them the honour? All expenses would be paid for Jackrabbit and his daughter for four days at Telemark Lodge, with transportation to and from Montreal, by air! Also, this event was to be linked with the Fourth Annual Gitchi Gammi Games, associated with North America's Indian forefathers, represented by the Ojibway Indians of Wisconsin.

"It is especially fitting that you should be honoured at these Gitchi Gammi Games," said Tony. "After all, among your best friends are skiers and Indians, and there is no one more deserving of this honour than you!" What could we say but yes? Nearly two hundred competitors and more than one hundred Indians were to be on hand, and the whole undertaking promised to be an exciting reunion for all concerned.

But neither Dad nor I was really prepared for the magnitude of the event. To begin with, a private airplane was sent to fetch us — a jaunty, twin-engined six-passenger jet, which landed at Plattsburg Airport. The pilot and co-pilot then drove an additional seventy miles into Canada to pick us up in a rented car. The six-hour flight to Telemark took us at low altitudes over Lake Simcoe and Georgian Bay (where Dad could look down excitedly upon one of his early ski developments at Collingwood), then on over Lake Huron and across the state of Michigan, over Lake Michigan, and finally across the state of Wisconsin to land at the very doorstep of Telemark Lodge. There we were greeted by Tony himself, his staff, a jubilant throng of skiers, and Jimmy Running Elk, also called Chief O-ma-scuz, resplendent in a full-feathered war bonnet.

The Games were officially opened that evening with an Indian-style banquet for three hundred. As Jackrabbit and I arrived for dinner, wearing our ski clothes, we were welcomed by six Indian braves beating on a gigantic portable drum. They led us, between long lines of gaily dressed skiers, and Indians in full costume, to a high table set at the end of the room. There stood Tony Wise. Beside him was Chief White Eagle, wearing his war bonnet. There was the Chief's wife. And there was Jimmy O-ma-scuz, magnificently attired in full regalia, every feather of his headdress proudly erect.

At a given signal, the audience of Indians and skiers stepped carefully backward to reveal upon the floor behind them four long strips of paper tablecloths, extending the full width of the room. Along the sides of each tablecloth seventy-five paper plates were set, and the guests quickly sat down cross-legged on the floor, each at his own place setting. The whole process went like clock-work.

In the hush that followed, small baskets of cigarettes were passed down the lines of guests, and everyone was solemnly invited, in keeping with Indian custom, "to light up for a ceremonial smoke in peace and harmony." This induced the proper mood.

Then, in came a sumptuous feast of fried chicken, steamed corn-on-the-cob, tomatoes, and baked corn bread, all served by Indian maidens who filed past the seated guests, doling out individual portions from huge bowls.

When the meal was over, the paper tablecloths were rolled up from the far end, with all the paper plates inside, the chicken bones and corncobs and the remains of the banquet were whisked away in no time at all. Then, at last, the ritual began.

Chief White Eagle introduced Jackrabbit in Ojibway and in English, "an honorary visiting Chief from Canada, renowned for his ability on skis." Chief O-ma-scuz, standing beside Jackrabbit, then removed his magnificent feather war bonnet and placed it ceremoniously on Jackrabbit's head, its long red train, flanked by tufted eagle feathers, reaching to the floor. Father stood trans-formed. And the crowd applauded wildly.

This headdress was a marvellous work of art, consisting of a hundred white eagle feathers, the black tip of each one crowned with a tuft of red-dyed eagle down, and the whole intricately bound together on an inner cap, from the beaded headband of which there flowed two double strips of white rabbit (*wapoos*) fur to frame his face. It was a phenomenal production, and in all our museum collection at McGill I knew there was none to match it.

As we watched, another Indian strode forward bearing O-ma-scuz's own war bonnet. This was duly settled upon his head and the train adjusted, then, with a pounding of the drum, the cere-mony continued.

An armful of medals was placed on the table before Jackrabbit – each medal bearing a likeness of Jackrabbit on skis, and Jimmy O-ma-scuz on snowshoes. They were exchanging a pipe of peace, against the background of a map of North America. And each medal bore the inscription, "International Friendship through Cross-Country Skiing." To each was attached a long loop of red-white-and-blue ribbon.

Jackrabbit, escorted by Chief Running Elk (O-ma-scuz),
marches to the head table at the Gitchi Gammi Games, December 1979.

Chief White Eagle then called on all the Indians to form a line
down the centre of the room, and to advance slowly one by one,
so that each could receive his own commemorative medal from
the Jackrabbit's own hand. And this they did, each brave, each
matron, and every child looking Dad straight in the eye as he
slipped the colourful ribbon over each head, to let the medal fall,
shining, upon the recipient's breast. And every Indian, from the
oldest elder to the tiniest tot, when he received his own medal,
said, "*Megvitch!*" meaning "Thank you!" as he filed back to his
starting point.

Finally, it was the turn of each competing skier, and lastly, every
member of the press. Not a soul was left out. Everyone was a true
participant. And throughout the ceremony, there was the constant
beating of that six-man drum.

When everyone had been suitably decked with his own be-ribboned medal, the drum picked up a more insistent beat – and the dance was on! The Indians spread out in a great clockwise circle, each one dancing his own intricate steps, while the entire group moved slowly around the room. There were sedate matrons in deerskin dresses leading small children. There were handsome braves in fringed leggings and beaded jackets. And there were ardent teen-agers, each intent on his own steps, his feathers rising and dipping as his patterned moccasins kept the beat. It was a sight I will remember always. And finally, Dad and I and the others at the head table were drawn into that vibrating circle, feathers and medals flying, as we, too, joined in that many coloured round.

The festivities – and the ski competitions – lasted four days. The Olympic teams were finally chosen, and we were proud to see two of our own Indian girls, Shirley and Sharon Firth from Inuvik in the Northwest Territories, high among the list of finalists.

Then came our return flight, and we once more saluted Dad's old ski development at Collingwood on Georgian Bay. And at last we caught a sunset glimpse of our own old High Peaks in the Adirondacks, as we settled down at Plattsburg Airport for the homeward drive to Mont St-Hilaire.

What an experience! And what memories! Dad's marvellous headdress is now carefully rolled up in its own special container, which I fashioned for it after an original war bonnet case in McGill's own McCord Museum, and every time we open that case to show the headdress to visitors, that whole panorama of events unfolds before our eyes.

❦

Looking back over all these recent happenings, Dad had been particularly pleased to speak to the young university graduates who represented the future doctors, lawyers, teachers, engineers, and scientists who would in time be running the country. He was happy, too, to have participated so actively with the native people in that exciting international event in Wisconsin. But he was equally delighted to see the phenomenal growth of the Junior Jackrabbit League, a project begun in Manitoba in 1976 as a ski program designed for boys and girls from six to twelve years old, to develop their skiing skills in a competitive atmosphere of fun.

The league operated on a badge system, with points awarded for each of ten successive basic skiing skills. Each year everyone kept close track of his accumulated mileage. And each year they all took part in timed events to develop their speed. By 1981, the program had been taken over officially by Cross-Country Canada and there were soon some six thousand little jumping Jackrabbits spread across the country from St John's, Newfoundland, to Vancouver in British Columbia, and to Inuvik in the Arctic. Dad felt confident that the future of cross-country skiing in Canada would now be safe in the hands of these enthusiastic youngsters, and it was with great joy that he took part in the Shell Jackrabbit Day in Ottawa in 1982, when he was awarded his "Leader's Badge," with Governor General Edward Schreyer in attendance. Today there are thirteen thousand individual members, each one of whom feels he has a personal link with the old Jackrabbit.

However, by 1983, Bob, Peggy and I had begun to feel that it would be wise to start to "wind our father down" a bit. While Jackrabbit had been content to live for twenty-two years by himself in his little house in Piedmont, where he could relax between "gusts" of frantic activity with weekend supervision by me and occasional "cold weather" visits to St-Hilaire, we at last made a temporary arrangement with Madame Richer, proprietress of a near-by private old folks' home in Piedmont, to have two hot meals a day delivered to him. This provided daily routine "check-ups," but left him with the privacy of his own home, and personal responsibility only for his own breakfasts. I continued to come up to him each weekend to keep his spirits high.

But at last, after two years, Dad admitted that he was becoming "slightly more wobbly," and we decided reluctantly that the best thing for all concerned would be to transfer him to the Griffith-McConnell Residence in Montreal. There during each week he would be assured of much more regular care. I still had my own weekly work to do at St-Hilaire, but I would take him "home" to Piedmont on week-ends. By that time Jackrabbit was 109.

This was, however, a major change to which he found it particularly hard to adjust. To become suddenly one of three hundred and fifty elderly retired people living in a large city complex was very different indeed from being in his own little house in the country, where he could come and go as he pleased. True, there were some advantages, such as hand rails in the corridors, and lounges, kitchenettes, a library, and hobby rooms, but these were all geared to people who were used to life indoors. He needed to get outside, to breathe fresh air, to walk, or to sit with his pipe, or to do his exercises. "These people are all much too old for me!" he would say. "They have no spark, no sense of adventure. They are all content simply to sit in a row ... to stare into space ... and then doze off to sleep! I need action, and interaction! When you come to think of it, I'm chronologically thirty years older than most of them here, but I'm at least twenty years younger than they are in spirit! This whole place gets me down!"

He tried valiantly to jolly the old ladies along, but they were too timid. He tried to converse with the few men on politics or current events, but he found them strangely unresponsive. He rode his newfangled wheelchair up and down the corridors, but people complained he was "too restless." Finally, he prevailed upon the authorities in the winter months to clear a path in the snow behind the residence. This he called his "moose yard," and here he would spend two hours every morning, walking up and down in the sparkling sunshine, ski poles in hand, sniffing the "awful" city air.

He was grateful to family members, especially to his grand-daughter Karin and her two small children, as well as to a contingent of old friends who faithfully came to walk with him in his "moose yard," or to share a little snack with him in his room. "But this is not really living," he would say. "I'll sure be glad to see you, Jo, next weekend, when we can go home to Piedmont! Those weekend vacations are what I live for. They are my only safety valve. They do give me the strength, however, to come back here to town again the following week, where I can try to cheer up some of these stuffy old souls again!"

At one point the Provincial Association of Health Care Workers met at the Griffith-McConnell Home to discuss ways and means of making life more interesting for the elderly. Dad was asked to give a short talk on behalf of the residents, and he did his best to awaken these professionals to his prime concern that "everybody needs exercise and a chance to breathe fresh air." They found him "extraordinary," and his outlook "invigorating," but, sad to say, he found *them* "overcautious" and "without imagination." He concluded that:

The cards are all stacked against you, anyway, for whatever could anyone do with a population of old fogies who have never, since their earliest childhood, been really brought up in the out-of-doors? What's basically wrong, is that these old folks weren't properly brought up in the first place. By the time they're seventy years old, it's too late. There's no spunk left in them. No wonder they can't do anything more exciting than just plain sit!

Every two years on average since Mother's death in 1963, Dad and I had managed a brief trip overseas, driven by his unflagging wanderlust. This required some financial ingenuity, and was a challenge that we met in various ways. On four occasions I had led a travel group to Norway on behalf of the McGill Graduates' Society. This covered my own expenses. Dad had come along as "helper." One year he sailed across as a passenger on *M/S Topdals-fjord*, and another year he worked his way over as a bo'sun's mate. Scandinavian Airlines had flown us both over several times, and had subsequently flaunted their "oldest traveller" in their *SAS News*. KLM, the Royal Dutch Airlines, too, generously flew us on several occasions, also taking advantage of his presence for appropriate publicity. And every time, regardless of the airline, we were royally treated by all the staff, from passenger agents to stewardesses and pilots, who never failed to note that "despite his age – 103, or 105, or 107 – Jackrabbit still prefers to fly our airline."

In 1985 we flew over once more, this time to celebrate the centennial of the founding of Dad's own Skiklubben Ull (Ull Ski Club – "Ull" is the Norwegian god of skiing). This was a major event in the little cabin, Ydale, high on the mountain above Oslo. All the Ull members were present – all twenty of them – and that evening King Olav was their guest! This was a truly gala evening, with the King sitting in the high seat, flanked by Dad on the one hand and by Jacob Vaage on the other. There was much animated conversation, and many a skaal, and although the King and his aide-de-camp were scheduled "to withdraw" at nine-thirty, they stayed until eleven o'clock, as they were having such a good time.

In 1986 we went over again, this time for Dad's 111th birthday celebration, which was held at Bob's home near Tönsberg. The entire membership of Ull trooped down to mark the occasion with the family. There, on the icing of a huge birthday cake, was depicted a map of the North Atlantic – with Norway, Greenland, and Canada framing the area, Panama and Cuba clearly indicated in the south, and with three huge candles, representing 111 years, rocketing out of the Caribbean Sea! As Jacob Vaage remarked in his official speech, "In all his long and eventful career, Jackrabbit has seen the sun rise – and set – 40,000 times, and he has never tired of that glorious sight! He has been our most enthusiastic tour-skier through all those years. With axe, and saw, and Bowie knife, and with the aid of many friends, he cut the 128-kilometre Maple Leaf Trail in Quebec, and he is still going strong! What more can we say than, 'More power to him!'"

There was, in fact, one more important event to come, for the next week we flew down to West Germany to attend that long-anticipated centenary of his college fraternity, Berolina.

Following instructions received in advance, Dad had, before leaving the aircraft, donned his *Band und Mütze*, his fraternity cap and colours. We were officially conducted to the dignitaries' lounge, where the sons, grandsons, and successors of his ancient classmates awaited us, each wearing his own cap and colours. It was a convivial gathering, with hearty handshakes, happy greetings, and welcoming smiles.

The president of the University of Berlin in person presented to "our oldest living graduate" two massive tomes on the history of Berlin. Jackrabbit inscribed his impressive signature in the University's Golden Book, and he spoke animatedly to reporters of his early days in Berlin and of his joy in returning. Everyone marvelled at his command of language, as he slipped confidently from German, to Norwegian, to English, to French, with scarcely a trace of a foreign accent. "His grammar is excellent," they said in astonishment, "and his vocabulary unbelievable! For a man of 111 years, this is a real *tour de force.*"

We were then spirited away to a quiet little hotel on the Kurfürstendamm, which we used as a home base for the next seven days, and to which we could quietly retire whenever he needed solitude.

It was a wonderful surprise to meet his oldest grandson, Peter John, or "PJ" – who was now a successful businessman with Siemens, a German firm. Peter John "just happened" to be in Berlin at this

In Berlin in 1986 for the hundredth anniversary
of the "Berolinastudent" fraternity. At 111, he was the Technical University's
oldest living alumnus.

moment, and we were overjoyed that he could join us in some of
the fraternity festivities, and that we could take part together in a
special luncheon given for Dad by the officials at Siemens.

At the Corpshaus there was a wonderful welcoming picnic in
the garden with as many of the Old Boys as it was possible to
muster for the occasion, together with all of the active members
and all the young *Fuchsen* (new initiates). Jackrabbit was photographed with the young, and with the not-so-young, and was
interviewed at length as he recalled their invitation eleven years
before "to return for our Centennial." "I can't promise," he had then
said, "but I'll do my best!" And now here he was. It was another
dream come true.

There was a private rendezvous for coffee with Acting Mayor
Diepgen in the city hall, and a boat trip on the Wannsee. There
were special events "for the boys alone," and sightseeing tours for
the ladies, conducted by the fraternity sisters. There was a special
men's dinner held in the banquet hall of Logenhaus, a beautiful
seventeenth-century chateau, which had miraculously survived
destruction during the war years.

And finally there was a grand ball at Hotel Kempinski, with music and dancing and wine, and although Dad did not dance, he made a remarkable speech, extolling the virtues of fraternity life and the friendships that had survived "all the horrors of war." In token of our own friendship, he proudly presented to Corps Berolina a fine example of Indian craftsmanship in the form of a small replica of a West Coast Indian chief's ceremonial chest. This was something distinctively Canadian which he offered as a special gift from "their own old Chief Jackrabbit."

Throughout all these proceedings, Dad steadfastly withstood the strain like a staunch and weatherbeaten mast in a heavy storm. He slept well, ate sparingly, took short cat-naps between events, and always managed a quip or a jest at the right moment. When it was all over, he made his final farewell to the fraternity, with profound thanks for all their enduring friendship, and he bade them an exuberant *"Auf Wiedersehen!"* as we boarded the plane for our return trip to Norway.

"Well!" said Dad, with a great sigh of relief as we sank into our seats. "Now at last I am happy to return to being 'just me.' It was a terrible strain to have to be always on my best behaviour for such a long time. Now, I'll just put my feet up – and have a rest."

There was no denying it. He was dog-tired.

Bob met us at the airport in Oslo, and drove us quietly down to Tönsberg, Dad dozing most of the way. But there, we discovered to our dismay, that the whole family was battling the 'flu. This was one unexpected event too much. Dad was put to bed at Veierland, and carefully doctored, but to no avail. Despite all precautions, not surprisingly, he too fell an easy victim of "the bug."

He did, however, manage one final salvo. "At least," he said, "I've finally sailed back to my own home port. Now, I guess, it's time for me to admit that, all things considered, I've probably weathered my last 'full gale.'"

CHAPTER TWENTY

The Strength of the Hills: 1987

It had always been a "long, hard haul" to get over the 'flu. There had been the time when Dad was eighty-five, at the Huseby-Holmenkollan Meet, when both he and Mother had recovered ever so slowly after that great event. There had been the time when he was ninety-three at the Sun Valley Reunion, when he had nearly succumbed after his exposure to "high society." And now, in 1986, at the age of 111, when he had successfully survived the centenary of Berolina, he was faced with yet another challenge by influenza. "The struggle gets harder every time," he admitted, "and it always takes more out of me."

Many a man would have given up long ago, but not Dad. He knew it was almost time for our return flight to Canada, and he was determined I should not go back alone. "Remember," he said firmly but quietly, "I want to be buried beside Mother in the little cemetery of St-Francis-of-the Birds in St-Sauveur. There I can really rest in peace." And for the first time I realized he was actually thinking of the "end."

But the doctor, once more, was adamant. "There is absolutely no point in his undertaking another long journey in his condition," he said. "Just let him stay here in Norway to enjoy our beautiful autumn. Why don't you come back here yourself at Christmas? It would be better for all of you."

And so it was finally decided. Dad spent four happy months at Bob's home on the Island of Veierland, recuperating slowly. He would sit outdoors in the sun as he watched the seagulls swooping over the little sailboats in the fjord, "just as I used to watch them when I was a boy in Larvik," he said. Bob and Aase would take him for a short daily stroll, arm in arm, along the old farm road "to limber him up." And he would faithfully do his exercises, sitting in his chair, stretching his arms, one after the other, using his pulley, breathing deeply to expand his lungs. "I have to keep moving," he insisted. "That old motto of Berolina still holds true – *Nicht rasten und nicht rosten* – Never rest and never rust." He still, however, had a very persistent and deep-seated cough.

I came back to Veierland the week before Christmas to find the countryside blanketed in fresh new snow. The sun did not rise until nine in the morning, and it was down again by three o'clock, so that at both breakfast and dinner time there was darkness everywhere. But during the dim winter evenings all the little houses sparkled reassuringly with their Christmas lights, and the fir trees stood, heavy laden, against the starlit sky. It was the kind of winter Dad had always loved.

He was overjoyed to see me, and we had many a cosy chat, thinking back on "the good old days." On Christmas Eve, after he had been tucked up for the night, the rest of us, Bob, Aase, and I, with their children and their spouses, their grandchildren, and other assorted relatives, had a wonderful old-time family celebration, dancing around the Christmas tree in true Norwegian fashion, while Oldefar – Great-grandfather Herman – dozed quietly in his bedroom down the hall. He was with us in spirit, if not in person, and we all accepted it that way.

But several days later, when the doctor came again to see him, it was decided he should be taken over to the hospital in Tönsberg "for closer observation." I saw him there just before I flew home for the New Year. He was propped up on pillows, but in fair spirits, despite his cough. "I'm just tired, Jo," he said, "but I'll be all right. You go back to Piedmont and get the house ready there. It was great to have you here for Christmas. Bob and Aase are so good to me. So long, now, Jo, ... and *lykke til* (good luck to you)!"

But on January fifth there came a call from Norway. It was Bob. And his voice was sorrowful. "It's over at last," he said. "That cough finally turned into pneumonia. Dad died quietly this morning in my arms ... No one can last forever, but he certainly held out for a long, long time. In the end, though, he simply nestled down against me with his head on my shoulder, just like a little child. He went to sleep ... and just stopped breathing. He never could have found a smoother or more peaceful way of going. We can be thankful, now, that he at last has found it good to rest."

Peggy, Karin, and I flew back to Norway together. There we met Peter John, who had come up from Germany, and Bob's son, Bobby, from Texas. Two of Dad's staunch Canadian ski friends, Sandy Mills and Victor Emery, were there, and Brian Powell who had edited *Jackrabbit, His First Hundred Years*, and Canon Baugh, the former rector of our own St-Francis church in St-Sauveur. Each had made that special journey to be with him one more time.

There was a beautiful service in the three-century-old chapel outside Tönsberg, only twenty kilometres from his birthplace in Horten. Some two hundred people were with us in that flower-filled church. The afternoon sun streamed through the chancel windows, illuminating everything. And on the casket, with the flowers from the family, rested his little *Band und Mütze*, symbol of his college years.

We sat there together, Bob, Peggy, and I, the three children of Jackrabbit and Alice, surrounded by family and friends, remembering our own childhood. There in the congregation were Kirsten, daughter of his brother, Johannes; Beth and Leif, the children of his sister, Elisabeth; and Knut, the son of his sister Helga. There was no one left from his own generation, as they, one by one, had already slipped away, but there were seven cousins from our own generation, with wives, husbands, and children, and some of their grandchildren. And we thought how miraculously everything had come together, how Dad's years had finally completed a wide and sweeping circle. He had indeed returned to his starting point after a full and fascinating life, and every one of us was richer for his having lived so long and so well, and for his having shared so much with so many.

The Canadian ambassador, John Harrington, was present from the embassy in Oslo; Jacob Vaage and Dad's friends from Skiklubben Ull; Karl-Eduard Naumann from Corps Berolina in Germany; and Reidun Hongslo, who had helped us so often from Scandinavian Airlines. And there were many, many friends from Oslo, and Tönsberg and the surrounding district.

We thought, too, of the literally thousands of skiers and outdoor people whose lives had been touched, one way or another, by Jackrabbit during those 111 years – people on two continents, both young and old, who could rightfully claim a personal connection with him, and who could proudly say that they had actually "followed in his tracks." What more could anyone have asked, than to have had the comradeship of all these old friends, and to have savoured the joys they had shared together?

That evening when the formalities were over and the family had returned to Veierland, a clear, full moon rode in the sky. It was then that we went for a "memorial ski trip" – Jackrabbit's three children, Bob, Peggy, and I; three of his grandchildren, "PJ," Karin, and Bobby; and his old friends, Sandy, Brian, and Victor. We skied thoughtfully over the rocky hillocks and through the moonlit valleys, where the fir trees cast long shadows on the sparkling moonlit snow. And Bob yodelled, and we sang some of the old ski songs, and we felt that the spirit of Jackrabbit was really with us. It was a night to be remembered, always. And we were glad.

Back in Canada, two weeks later, another memorial service was held in the little Church of St-Francis where skiers of all ages came together with the family to share once more in memories of former days. Bishop Hollis led the service, with five other ministers taking part. There were the present rector, Archdeacon Bate; Canon Baugh, who had been with us in Norway; Father Adam of the Roman Catholic Church in St-Sauveur; Father Marcel de la Sablon-nière, the "skiing priest," and Annestein Lothe, Pastor of the Nor-wegian Seamen's Church in Montreal. Throughout it all, there was a wonderful sense of continuity, a feeling that we were all inheritors of a fine tradition, a heritage of clean, fresh air, which would go on from year to year as long as the snow should fly and the sun shine, bringing health and happiness to all participants.

When summer returned, we placed Father's ashes beside Mother's in the little cemetery at St-Sauveur, just as he had wished. It was a simple ceremony, for the family alone. And there the two of them rest together, beside the beautiful granite boulder that bears their dates and names.

This is a memorial stone like no other, with a history all its own. It had been transported by the continental ice many thousands of years ago from an unknown site in the Laurentian

Mountains, and was stranded on Mont St-Hilaire when that glacial ice melted. It was rounded and polished by the waves of the Champlain Sea, which had invaded the St. Lawrence Valley, making a temporary island of the mountain. For more thousands of years it had lain as part of an abandoned ocean beach. And it had been among the other glacial boulders that we, as nature interpreters, had used to explain the geological sequence to countless numbers of school children. This story was crystal clear to me as a geologist, and I could think of no more appropriate memorial to Father and Mother than this smoothly rounded fragment of our own Laurentian Hills.

Jackrabbit's little house still nestles against the evergreens on Windy Hill, like a cosy Norwegian *hytte*. With minimum alteration, it has become the Jackrabbit Museum, a place where people can drop in, much as they used to do when he himself was here. His old wing chair rests comfortably beside the fireplace, his axe is ready at the chopping block, his trophies line the walls. When the fire crackles in the hearth on a blustery winter day and the aroma of woodsmoke hangs in the air, it is as though Jackrabbit were really with us.

We can almost hear him say, "All my life I have been anxious to see what lies on the other side of the hill, and at the same time I have never failed to enjoy the scenery along the way. With all my senses 'tuned in' – sight and hearing, taste and smell and touch – I was able to reap full benefit from each experience. So, I say, set your goals high, and stick to them, but approach them step by step so that at any given time your expectations are not impossibly out of reach. Climb your mountain slowly, one step at a time, following a well planned route. And when at last you stand upon the summit, you can look beyond, to the farthest horizon!

"I certainly owe a great deal to my good wife, Alice," he would go on to say. "She was always ready to comfort me when I was tired, correct me when I was wrong. She stood beside me through thick and thin, always dependable, always courageous, always true to the things we both believed in. I can't thank her enough for all the comfort and support she gave me. She really made me what I am. All things considered, we are the result of all our life's experiences. We are richer, tougher, stronger because of them. They have been milestones along a rough road, adventures on our route.

Some of them we might dread to live over again, but others we would now be better able to meet, in the light of what we since have learned along the way."

Dad, throughout his life, had made no pretence of being any financial wizard. He had little patience with the pursuit of money for its own sake. However, energy, enthusiasm, and *joie de vivre* he had in abundance, and these were qualities he found sadly lacking in many people. "What good is all their money to them," he would say, "if they don't know how to enjoy it? What I have is something *beyond* price – good health, a cheerful outlook, an inquiring attitude, and a thirst for adventure. These are things I can share. They cost no money, but they cannot be bought – at any price. They must be earned. They must be nurtured. They must be safeguarded, as carefully as some people hoard their money. But, while money may be a means to an end, these things are the end in themselves."

Jackrabbit would sit beside his fireplace, dreaming of many things, watching the embers glow. It was a rare day when he did not recall a quotation from Henry Thoreau, the well-loved American philosopher and naturalist, whose words had so often been repeated at council fires at Camp Nominingue. "Rise before dawn," Thoreau had said, "free of care. And seek adventure. Let noon find you by some other lake. And evening overtake you, everywhere, at home."

That had been Dad's credo on many a camping trip. We would set out shortly after sunrise, to get the most out of every hour of daylight, making our camp early so that we could be "at home," wherever we were, well before dark. That was his way, always to be "at home" in the wilderness, always at ease.

And as the daylight slowly faded he would murmur quietly, with deep conviction, another verse, which also came from Nominingue.

There's a land beyond the ridges where the evening shadows fall,
There's a lake where trout are rising, underneath the mountain wall.
There I'll pitch my tent at sunset, and my evening smoke shall rise,
While on boughs of fragrant balsam sleep shall bless my weary eyes.

Jackrabbit